D1565608

A RETURN TO FREE MARKET ECONOMICS?

A RETURN TO FREE MARKET ECONOMICS?

Critical Essays on Government Intervention

JOHN JEWKES

Foreword by
SIR FRANK MCFADZEAN

First edition 1978
Reprinted 1979

Published by
THE MACMILLAN PRESS LTD
London and Basingstoke
Associated companies in Delhi
Dublin Hong Kong Johannesburg Lagos
Melbourne New York Singapore Tokyo

Printed in Great Britain
by Unwin Brothers Limited
The Gresham Press
Old Woking, Surrey

British Library Cataloguing in Publication Data

Jewkes, John
    A return to free market economics?
    1. Great Britain – Economic policy – 1945 –
    I. Title
    330.9'41'0857   HC256.6
    ISBN 0–333–23062–0

To S.J. who, as usual, has done most of the work

CONTENTS

FOREWORD

by Sir Frank McFadzean

For the few years following the war I worked in what is now Malaysia; it was necessary to visit Britain periodically. The contrast in atmosphere between the two countries was in some ways distressing. True, Malaysia had not suffered the same degree of physical destruction as the United Kingdom but the rubber plantations had been neglected, the tin dredges had been cannibalised and the country's infrastructure was generally run down. In spite of political tensions, however, the dynamics of rehabilitation were unmistakable.

Britain presented a different picture. Shortages of essential commodities – of food, clothing, furniture and many other items – contrasted sharply with the abundance of political rhetoric. Many politicians fanned the belief that no task was impossible provided it was handed over to governments. The exercise of state supervision and control throughout the economy had contributed to winning the war, ran the argument; their continuation would help to win the peace. It was an era of 'big thinking', embracing such widely varying activities as the nationalisation of coal, East African groundnut schemes and eggs from the Gambia. If the proponents of the various projects had been using their own money their critical faculties might not have been quite so deeply submerged as they were under the tide of emotional enthusiasm. It was also an era which saw the establishment of central economic planning as an instrument of peace-time policy and the introduction of an almost light-hearted approach to public expenditure which culminated some three decades later in the worst inflation that Britain has ever experienced. Government intervention plus money were paraded as the keys to success; in practice they proved a recipe for decline.

It was, in many ways, Lenin's technique all over again. People who complained about the shortages of everyday life were roundly denounced as not being the people of Britain at all. Apparently the people of Britain were those who stoically accepted their current lot and focused their attention on the far horizons beyond which the foundations of a New Jerusalem were supposedly being laid. It was all so unreal; and the fact that many of those engaged in 'planning' were both sincere and enthusiastic only served to heighten the tragedy without in any way easing the stultifying effects of the masses of forms and permits required for even relatively simple types of economic activity. Instead of vigour, large sections of industry had sunk into lassitude as they reeled under the deadweight of government intervention, while their entrepreneurial functions were being usurped by individuals and institutions ill-equipped to perform them.

Before embarking to return to the Far East after one of my visits – it was 1948 – I purchased a copy of John Jewkes' *Ordeal by Planning*. Reading it on the flight had a tonic effect on my depressed spirits. It was, and for me remains, the most lucid assault ever written on the trendy interventionist 'economics' which, in the forties, contributed in such large measure to the strangulation of initiative and enterprise in Britain. Many of us thought it was a passing phase; what we did not foresee was that over a quarter of a century later the arguments in the book would still be relevant to the problems confronting our country. We underestimated the culinary ability of the planners – their skill at dressing up yesterday's cold mutton to look like today's new spring lamb.

The essays in *A Return to Free Market Economics?* span a period of some three decades; they represent John Jewkes' vigorous and penetrating comments on some of the economic problems of the times in which they were written; but here again they are far from being of interest only to the economic historian. They cover topics that are still the subject of keen concern and debate – the role of the economist, the obsession with high technology, nationalisation, economic planning and the fact that almost everywhere business and businessmen are being thrown on the defensive. Although each essay is self-contained, a common theme runs through the book – leaving the bulk of economic decisions to the market place will not only preserve an essential ingredient of freedom but will also result in the requirements of the consumers being met in a more efficient manner than can be achieved in a centrally planned economy.

The basic thesis of this book has for long been under attack by what John Jewkes himself described as 'the scribblers of the left'. Fairly typical of the attitude is Lord Balogh's rather sad outburst against some of the recent recipients of the Nobel prize for economics. No doubt with such distinguished scholars as Friedrich von Hayek and Milton Friedman in mind, he denounced the whole proceedings not only as a 'sorry charade' but as 'insulting to people who, like myself, see in economic analysis a means of lessening the misery of the mass of grossly underprivileged peoples and bringing about greater equality and security'. Apart from its pathetic pomposity, a widespread reaction to this statement was that the grapes have turned sour; but, although his choice of words makes it seem so, it is doubtful if his attempt at self-canonisation really had its origins in envy; the motivation is more probably to be found in the false assumption, which he shares with so many interventionists, that only those who believe in economic planning are capable of compassion. The assumption is just as arrogant and offensive as it is incorrect. True, von Hayek, Friedman and Jewkes do not indulge in hymns of hate and bitterness; but they have every bit as much compassion as the Baloghs and Galbraiths of this world.

Claiming monopolies of compassion merely confuses the problems. In spite of the increases that have been achieved in national income over the years, there are still, in Britain and elsewhere, large pockets of poverty with all their consequences in bad housing, inadequate medical services and so forth. The real issue is the system of economic organisation which, while maintaining essential freedoms, will produce the best rate of economic growth, as this alone will provide the means of ameliorating, if not eliminating, the social problems which most of us – not just the interventionists – would like to see tackled from a stronger resource base.

One of the consequences of the undermining of the market economy has been that Great Britain has suffered grievously from panacea pedlars with their simple nostrums for complex problems and their constant search for new elixirs. Upon the body of our nation all manner of procrustean and silly experiments have been performed and 'cures' administered even before the disease has been properly diagnosed. Any benefit to their fellow men of the presence of the economic witchdoctors upon the earth has not been very visible. Indeed the main consequence of this ignorant tinkering has been to reduce the economic metabolism of the country to an extremely low ebb.

Mr Heath's stricture a few years ago about 'the ugly and unacceptable face of capitalism' was probably in its context justified; but since all organisations are staffed by human beings, with both the merits and demerits of the species, they are likely to produce an ugly and unacceptable face at some time in their histories. In spite of efforts to keep human frailties in bounds they are almost certain, sooner or later, to rise to the surface; and this is just as true of the church as the trade unions, of business as well as politics, of the BBC as well as the press. To me the unpleasant and distasteful face of politics is mainly to be found in the parade of false promises at election time. Strict standards are enforced concerning the contents of a business prospectus; this is all to the good; it is only a pity that the same standards of veracity cannot be enforced on some of the politicians themselves. And it is the issue of promises well beyond the capacity to deliver that has been at the root of some of Britain's economic troubles. The expectations of the electorate have repeatedly been raised to levels well beyond anything that could be justified by the underlying realities; in a misguided attempt to redeem some of the promises resort has been made to the printing press – and the disastrous results are all around us to see.

In his essay on 'The Nationalisation of Industry' John Jewkes disposes of this particular solution to our economic ills. Having recently moved from the chairmanship of a private sector corportion to one in the public sector I am intrigued by the many differences involved. However what has struck me most forcefully is the messianic innocence of the Webbs, the Fabians and some of the Bloomsbury set who produced what they regarded as the intellectual arguments for nationalisation. The wicked capitalist syphoning off profit lay at the root of industrial strife; eliminate this from the scene by nationalisation and all will be sweetness and light. In such circumstances it will be silly and futile for workers to strike as they will be striking against themselves. Wage differentials, job preservation by overmanning, demarcation disputes, the peculiar British institution of being 'agin the gaffer' and the effect of tightly knit groups of politically motivated individuals had no place in their scheme of things. Only people remote and cocooned from the realities of life could have been so naive; if the 'workers' ever heard of their faulty analysis, which is doubtful, they have long since forgotten it.

Although it is sometimes difficult to define precisely, there are limits to the diversity of tasks which any organisation can handle; and that includes governments as well as the many other groupings and associations that have either been created or sprung up spontaneously to meet society's requirements. The effective load that can be carried depends in large measure on the administration of the organisation concerned and how rapidly it can adjust itself to changes in its scale of operations or the complexities of the problems to be solved. There is also a wide area of judgement as to where the balance lies between delegation of authority and the maintenance of sufficient control to prevent the organisation losing purpose and degenerating into a collection of tribal chieftains. Personalities inevitably play a role but we should always remember that there are no supermen.

Now in spite of the undoubted ability of most of the senior civil servants no organisation could possibly have discharged efficiently the enormous and wide-ranging burdens that politicians thrust upon the government machine in the last decade. Moreover it is now painfully clear that politicians advocating, as they do, many policies, have little notion as to the final effects of the interaction of these with each other or the rest of the economy. It is futile for them to become testy when this observation is made; the alternative is to claim that at all times they are in control of the economic situation which produces as a corollary that they deliberately planned the chaos to which Britain has been reduced over the last few years.

By any performance standard government in Britain is grossly overloaded. Richard Crossman's *Diaries* only confirmed what was becoming obvious. The main requirement now is to contain the horizons of government and then push them back. Many of the decisions at present taken in government offices, often with inadequate knowledge, must once more be returned to the market place. The difficulties in this reversal should not be underrated but there are growing signs that the long swim against the tide by John Jewkes and some of his friends will probably not have been in vain.

ACKNOWLEDGEMENTS

I wish to acknowledge with thanks permission from the following to republish certain of my earlier writings:

Lloyds Bank Review
Brookings Institution, Washington, DC
The Three Banks Review
The Manchester School
The Economic Journal
The Wincott Foundation
The University of Chicago Law Review
Economica
Manchester Statistical Society

J.J.

1 GENERAL INTRODUCTION

These papers cover a longish period, although some are printed here for the first time, and comprehend a wide range of economic topics. There are, however, three reasons which I think justify publication in one volume. First, there is a common theme, a central proposition, running through them. Second, they are all concerned with economic issues which are surprisingly contemporary, immediately relevant to the controversies, confusions and indecisions of our day. Third, a rereading of them raises doubts about the value in recent years of the contributions to national economic policy made by academic economists and this, in turn, poses the question of what should be their proper role in the future.

The central proposition, some may describe it as a prejudice, which I claim can be found running through the papers is that any large community which sets out to maintain and enhance liberty for the individual and to combine this with material prosperity will, in the long run, only succeed in its double aim if it makes a full and constantly extending use of free markets. Of course, there have been, and perhaps there will again be, cases where a country has suddenly and dramatically become rich through the discovery of some natural resource, such as happened recently with the oil countries. There may be cases where, through some unexpected upheaval of our knowledge of nature, rendering free exchanges and markets irrelevant, the State is forced to accept responsibilities which, by general consent, cannot be carried out otherwise, as is true of nuclear energy which cannot be used freely without incurring unacceptable risks of pollution.

Such special cases do not, to my mind, dispose of the doctrine that, for the long haul, the manner in which a society organises itself, or allows for spontaneous organisation, critically determines whether or not there will be freedom and prosperity and that to this end, the free market, in all its endless forms and uses, is the key to success. Attempts to deny this and to find substitutes for free exchanges seem always to bring great suffering and humiliation for the victims of the experiments. For anyone who has eyes to see these things in simple terms, there is one decisive comparison. On the one hand lies the open society of the United States, admittedly making its social and economic mistakes but always in process of correcting them by freedom of speech and, at the same time, providing an unmatched standard of living and dominating in the arts and the sciences. On the other side is the slave society in Russia, with a savage ban on free comment and therefore on social change, scratching out an uncertain living, even as to food, in regions of potentially rich natural resources.

These papers, therefore, are an attempt to test out this central proposition at widespread points in the economic and social system: points where, for one reason or another, it has been easiest for me to make observations and to submit theories to the test of facts. I conclude that my probings have served to strengthen my prejudices.

Looking back over the last quarter of a century it is nothing short of amazing that, despite an enormous growth in the study of economics and in the number of professionals who have been trained in and have devoted their lives to the subject, we are still confronted with the *same* unsolved economic problems, the *same* conflicting arguments bandied about on the *same* subjects, the *same* confusions in the mind of the public on matters which most intimately affect their lives. Consult the economic columns of a newspaper today, especially a British newspaper, and in all vital respects one might be reading a newspaper of 25 years ago. How best can the national currency be given a stable value? What price might have to be paid for such stability in terms of unemployment or the restriction of individual liberty? What forces and factors determine the wealth of a nation? To what degree can Governments influence the level of prosperity by the management of the economy? What institutions and conditions are most favourable to scientific and technical progress? If free exchanges and competition are desirable institutions, how can it be guaranteed that freedom to compete will not degenerate into freedom to combine? Where are even broad rules to be found as to what proportion of the income of the individual should be disposed of at his will and what proportion dispensed by Government? Why should it be supposed that it makes for efficiency to nationalise industries, to organise them under State agencies with monopoly powers? And how can accountability to the public be guaranteed under these conditions? Even if intuition indicates that free markets and private enterprise seem to be the best bet for providing economic prosperity, who will be prepared, by word and deed, to defend such a system? Can we, for instance, have enterprise without entrepreneurs who deeply believe in it and accept what it implies?[1] He would indeed be a bold man who would dare to assert that there is now, on such matters, more systematic and persuasive knowledge than 20 or 30 years ago. If these papers were to do nothing more than drive home the need to make this humiliating confession some useful purpose might be served.

Should there seem to have been little or no progress in establishing an accepted corpus of knowledge as to the means of attaining agreed economic and social ends, must we resign ourselves to the conclusion that the so-called science of economics is largely spoof and that the world would have got on better without economists? Or is the fault to be found elsewhere? Is it that the subject, and those who profess it, could have been more useful if our rulers, the politicians, had taken more careful note of the findings and warnings? If economics is really humbug, is this inevitable in the sense that economic attitudes and activities are so lacking in regularities that nothing useful can ever be confidently said about them? Is it that, although economists could have given sound advice, they have not been clever enough to devise the economic and social institutions which would prevent politicians from compounding with error, knowingly or innocently? Has the economist failed in his task of bringing home to the entrepreneurs, without whom free markets and enterprise stand no chance of survival, the attitudes and actions essential if the businessman is not to destroy the system of which he is the main agent?

Anyone who reads these papers will discern the way in which my mind has been moving through the years. First, I recoil from the idea that the study of economics has contributed nothing to our knowledge of society and can, indeed, never do so. This would be a confession of despair. For more than 200 years, economics has been the most important of the studies of society. It has become the life work of many scholars recognised for their powers of thought and analysis. It has resulted in a flow of literature at times unsurpassed in fluency and lucidity. To imagine that all this has gone for nothing, that the understanding of society has in no way been advanced would be to assume a propensity for self-delusion, even a streak of chronic lunacy, in the minds of men regarding economic matters. Nevertheless it is undeniable that something has gone sadly wrong with the subject of economics in recent years. There is, for instance, the squabbling among economists to which there seems no end in scope or fury. Of course, intellectuals in every field, even among the natural scientists, disagree a lot. But whereas in the natural sciences the disputes go on between scholars who share a large central corpus of accepted knowledge and who, therefore, tend to differ about matters on the margin of new knowledge and to conduct their disputes quietly, as it were within the family, economists seem to have nothing in common, to be challenging each other about the very basis of their subject and to carry on their violent controversies in the full glare of publicity. And since the public realise that what is being talked about intimately affects their lives and since politicians are usually seeking desperately to redeem their promises, an ear is lent to this pandemonium. All this must threaten the credit of economists and their subject.

Add to this the odd swings of view, clearly apparent to any observer with a memory, among economists. Not so long ago it was widely held that the real danger to the western world was an imminent lack of

investment opportunities calling for very low rates of interest; that international trade would become a steadily decreasing element in the world
economy; that no poor country could become prosperous except
through hell-bent industrialisation; that increased industrial efficiency
must depend progressively if not wholly upon vast, multinational companies; that increases in investment in science would automatically
bring about national economic growth; that unemployment could be
virtually eliminated through Government expenditure; that the 'free'
British National Health Service could cater for all expressed medical
needs, make the people healthier in consequence and thereby become
the envy of the world; that the western world was threatened by underpopulation. In these days very opposite views seem to be as widely and
tenaciously held. And although many economists might properly
protest that the violence of these ebbs and flows of opinion has not been
their responsibility, that often their preliminary thinking aloud, what
they have merely hinted at or vaguely speculated upon, has been widely
taken up by the publicists as the product of immaculate analysis and
reliable prediction, yet there can be little doubt that economists have
played a major part in increasing the 'fluctuations of thought' which it
should have been their responsibility to impede and correct.

My diagnosis of the causes of the arid period through which
economics has been passing, expressed in various ways and in terms of
various specialised problems in these papers, is that too much has been
claimed for the subject and too much attempted in its name. The discouraging present situation is the resultant of a number of factors. On
the one side, academic economists have sought to rank themselves along
with the natural scientists. In the search for precision and elegance for
their findings and for the power to predict and reproduce experimental
results, which scientists insist upon if conclusions are to be generally
accepted, economists have increasingly turned to mathematical methods
and formulations which have forced upon them the need for such
simplifications in their basic assumptions that increased precision in
their findings has been achieved only at the expense of producing conclusions more and more remote from the realities of the economic
world.[2] This has gone along with, and has often been the cause of,
growing neglect of, or even contempt for, the study of economic history.
Thus many members of our profession have in practice cut themselves
off from the real world, partly because they have chosen to speak in
language and symbols incomprehensible even to the intelligent layman,
and partly because they have remained indifferent to what might have
been revealed by a close and direct study of the activities of man. A
further manifestation of ill-directed efforts to force economic thinking
into a mould which, as I submit, it will never fit, is the popularity of the
construction of economic 'models', where once again the simplifications
which have to be accepted result in a final product which bears about as

much relation to real life as do the grotesque movements of a mechanical man to the real working of the human body.

There is an even more disturbing drift. Many academic economists have turned into overanxious do-gooders or even into pseudo-politicians keen to exercise influence in public affairs. They have been only too ready to accept and cultivate the idea that economics *is* a science in the sense that it renders possible the forecasting of the future and the public management of an economy more prosperous, stable and just that is achievable in any other way. However numerous and gross have been the errors and disasters occasioned by the ridiculous view that their grasp of economic science has conferred upon them the power to regulate a highly complicated economic system with the confidence and knowledge with which an engineer might regulate a petrol engine, this has not deterred them from pushing on with their plans for regenerating the economic world. The grotesque results of their activities present a picture as fascinating and bizarre as the study of myths and men of magic in more primitive societies.

The politicians, also, must carry their perhaps greater, share of the responsibility for what has happened. Everywhere, but in Britain particularly, rulers have found that the easiest route to power is to promise to sweep away economic miseries and hasten prosperity. Once in power and confronted with the need to fulfil, appear to fulfil or, at least, find excuses for not fulfilling, their promises, and with few ideas of their own, it becomes only too seductive for them to concoct vague 'strategies' for planning, restructuring, regenerating, revivifying, reorganising, reorientating or otherwise gingering up the economic system and then to call upon those economists who share their views, or have a yen for power, to produce the methods and means for bringing about the promised results. So the subject of economics is caught in a vicious circle. The glittering prizes for economists become more readily available to those who already share the views of the politicians or are prepared to submit to them as a price to be paid for the glitter.

Anyone concerned with the future standing of economic studies cannot evade the question of how academic economists can best deploy their energies in order to extend the understanding of the economic system, and thus help to restore their faded public reputation as scholars of independence, and to discourage or frustrate politicians in their scheming to seduce the electorate by irresponsible promises. Here it is easier to suggest what economists should *not* try to do than to define what they should do in a more positive way.

Nothing will avail unless it is recognised that economics is not, and never will be, a science in the same sense as the natural sciences. There are far too many variables, too few opportunities for testing hypotheses under precisely controlled conditions to make this possible. Hence the absurdity of predicting with confidence what will happen or what would happen if this or that form of Government intervention were attempted. The modesty and caution shown by the natural scientist in his speculations contrast sharply with the pretensions of the economist and lead the former frequently to look contemptuously upon the latter. This is not to say that what may, in short, be termed the negative functions of the economist are not important. He can usually list at least some of the forces which will operate on one side or another in a given situation even when he suspects or admits that there may be other forces which he has not identified; that, in any case, the *balance* between forces which can be identified and roughly measured and those which cannot is a matter of judgement and guesswork, and that this guesswork should be undertaken by politicians who, for their part, should either shoulder the blame for mistakes or, if they shy away from that, should refrain from intervention altogether. The economist can often point out that one Government policy runs counter to or neutralises another being operated at the same time. He ought to be able to provide better than anyone else an account of what has happened in the past under what look like similar contemporary conditions; what were then the observable consequences, and what rough and preliminary conclusions might be drawn as to the causes. These limited activities will lead to propositions which may seem jejune, for fundamentally they are based on simple assumptions – such as that only a pint comes from a pint pot; that if the Government spends a part of the national income, the citizen cannot also spend it; that if the supply of money increases more rapidly than production, then inflation is inevitable and so on. But simple as such propositions may be, they will be of value if they can deter governments from blatantly acting in defiance of them and looking round for economic advisers who will undertake to pull the necessary rabbits out of hats.

It seems crucial that academics should not fall into the very errors which they condemn in others by laying down in detail practical measures and procedures which they think are likely to give effect to their own broad views of how best morality and prosperity can be fostered in western societies.

There is no need to be rigidly doctrinaire on these matters. For instance, it has been commonly accepted since the time of Adam Smith that certain essential economic functions cannot be performed through free markets and must, therefore, be conducted by the State: defence, the maintenance of justice, the general lay-out of national communications, the maintenance of stability in the value of money, the control of monopoly. In all such cases there seems to be no reason why the academic, however high may be the priority he accords to his primary duty of furthering general knowledge of the economic system, should not give the community the value of his specialised understanding in the practical management of public affairs.

If, however, he goes further than that, if he allows himself to be forced to give ground to what the politician describes as 'the art of the possible' (by which is only too often meant the art of staying in office) or if he finds his logic blocked by the assertion that such and such an act is 'unacceptable', 'unthinkable' or 'intolerable', then, as it seems to me, he is in danger of losing his credit-worthiness. I can perhaps best illustrate what I have in mind in terms of what is the most disheartening economic and social problem of modern times: the difficulties which democratic countries, and especially our own, find in controlling inflation. All those who live in these countries do not necessarily oppose inflation, indeed some may deliberately seek to foster it. Left-wingers who wish to destroy the system of private enterprise are acting quite logically when they engineer inflation by encouraging intemperate demands for wages and salaries, advocating virtually unlimited public expenditure and endangering production by fomenting industrial unrest. For then inflation, and the consequential poverty, can be attributed to the working of capitalism and the case for its abolition fortified.

In Western countries, however, the vast majority of people recognise the evils of inflation and consider the maintaining of the stability of the currency as one of the overriding responsibilities of government. One group of academic economists (whose views in large part I share) have in recent years expounded the doctrine that to prevent inflation the supply of money must be controlled. It is not a new or startling doctrine or, if so, only in the sense that it was for years ignored or denied by politicians. One can embellish and refine the doctrine. Thus historical evidence shows that attempts to treat the symptoms of inflation by the direct control of incomes and prices will, in the not very long run, be self-defeating. Or that the control of the supply of money becomes progressively more difficult if public expenditure grows beyond a certain level; that public expenditure tends almost inevitably to get out of control if the passion for equality and the welfare state is driven beyond a certain point; or that governments sliding into inflation may put off the evil day by heavy international borrowing but when that day inevitably arrives it will be the more evil.

All this leads to one ineluctable conclusion: inflation is caused by an excess in the supply of money in relation to production and any government which recognises the evils of inflation and does not take steps to strike at the cause and reduce the supply of money is a traitor to the cause of economic justice and economic prosperity.

The economists who have expounded and propagated this logic for a number of years now may have suffered the torments of watching democracies blindly drifting to possible disaster. But at least they have the consolation that as scholars they have done their duty.

Should they go further than that? It is only too obvious that the control of the supply of money will often be distasteful to politicians who recognise that the necessary measures, particularly in countries already suffering from past government misbehaviour, will be painful in the period of economic convalescence and, therefore, may well be unpopular to an electorate ignorant of, or wilfully indifferent to, its ultimate fate.

Should economists therefore spend time and thought on devising pratical rules or institutional arrangements which deter or prevent governments from misbehaving? May not economists, by stepping outside their own field, endanger their authority and even provide irresponsible governments with the means for evading issues and denying logic?

Consider, for instance, the proposal that the Government should, constitutionally, be forbidden to permit an increase in the supply of money in excess of some given percentage (x) in any one year. Even if a government in power could be persuaded to place such restraints upon itself, any determined government could, in practice, prevaricate to the point at which the system of control would be reduced to chaos. How is the supply of money to be measured? This is one of those economic concepts which is useful in its own way but is deprived of much of its practical value because of the difficulty of quantifying it. What is x to be? It might be fixed so high as to amount to a licence to the Government to print money virtually at will. It might be fixed so low that it could produce deflation and unnecessary unemployment. Suppose, as has been suggested, that x should never be increased in the hope of forcing unemployment below its 'natural' level. What is 'natural'? No one has seriously tried to define it. Is it a figure which varies from year to year or is it immutable? The same endless argument might go on about the exact relations between the money supply and public expenditure, between public expenditure and the scale of welfare services and between money supply and public borrowing, internal or international. It has been, although wrongly, argued in Britain that should public expenditure be reduced, unemployment would grow and public expenditure would once again rise to the previous level because of the need to support the unemployed. Or it can be urged that the present high level of international borrowing is justified because of a forthcoming bonanza in the shape of North Sea oil?

Take another recent suggestion for preventing governments from debauching the currency. It has been argued that the real danger lies in the excess in the supply of *legal* money, i.e. money over the supply of which the Government has the monopoly. But if this monopoly were constitutionally abolished, if there were many sources of money supply and those who used or held money were free to exchange the money of their own government for money from other sources, public or private, then good money would drive out bad. The money which, by experience, best held its value and the sources from which it emanated would be preferred to other kinds of money and sources. Any attempt on the part of a prodigal or thoughtless government to spend its way out of its problems would, it is argued, be frustrated since its money would progressively fall into disrepute. Sound money would hold the ring.

At first sight, and in theory, such a scheme seems simple and attractive and if it meant no more than binding international agreements between different governments whereby every country accepted a floating exchange rate which was kept 'clean', and if anyone anywhere had easy access to markets at which any national currency could be changed into any other national currency, it might stand a chance of acceptance and a successful life. But to go beyond this, to suggest that national governments should renounce, under the law, their right to be the sole supplier of the national currency and that private agencies should be equally free to engage themselves in this trade, would surely do more harm than good. It would be tantamount to expecting some inveterate law-breaker to frame laws to prevent his own backslidings. Beyond that, in practice, the function of money as a medium of exchange is of the highest convenience and society would be deprived of it if every individual were forced to decide every day in which of the numerous private and public currencies he could best conduct his affairs.

It may seem ungrateful to take issue, in this way, with the very economists who in recent years have done most to challenge the social evils generated by the blundering of governments. But it is important that these scholars should not endanger their public standing by exhorting and advising outside the realm in which they are at last beginning to speak with some authority.

I see no hope of ultimate safety against the destruction of western social values through inflation except along three lines. First, the economic doctrines, call them if you will dogma, which are to be observed must be framed in the simplest forms. Thus price levels must be kept stable, repeat stable. There should be no question, as so often in the past, of accepting or recommending mild doses of inflation as some kind of a 'tonic' to the economy which can be adjusted, reduced or discontinued at will and without trouble. Again, budgets should be balanced each year, I see only one acceptable exception to this. If it can be confidently assumed that a deficiency in public expenditure is raising unemployment to a level which is unnecessary, then a deficit for a time may be acceptable. But unbalanced budgets should not be tolerated on the score that problematical increases in productivity are on the way, or that export-led booms are in the offing or that the restructuring of industry by governments is an open road to prosperity. It should be recognised that the main source of social abuses in our day is to be found, not in the alleged evils of capitalism, but in the actions of governments. And that the freedom of the private individual to arrange and rearrange through time his balance between savings and spendings cannot safely be transferred to governments.

Second, in depriving governments of their powers for creating social abuses, gimmicks are useless. There is no substitute for an informed and sceptical electorate which recognises when dangerous pap is being offered to it in the name of nourishment. The primary role of the economist here is first to pursue, within the academic halls, fuller knowledge of the working of the system and then, through the education of an elite and through more popular instruction, to render the whole community highly sensitive to political moves which are little better than confidence tricks.

Third, some simple and direct deterrents on politicians might be useful. It would be rough justice, for example, to introduce in Britain a form of negative inflation-proofing whereby all ministers and members of a ruling government had their money salaries *reduced* by the same percentage as the percentage rise they permitted in the general price level. Short of that type of control, the electorate might at least be granted the opportunity of more frequently recording its judgements about economic policies by the staggering of elections, as in other countries, so that a section of constituencies could come into contention every year or two.

There can hardly ever have been an epoch when any body of men (except perhaps medical men in the first part of the last century) of such high average intelligence and guided by such commendable ambitions to do good as academic economists, should have become so much a subject, on the part of the general public, of an odd mixture of ridicule amounting almost to contempt and yet suspicion amounting almost to fear. For while it is widely believed that economists and their doctrines often lie at the root of our present troubles, yet it seems to be almost equally widely accepted that in the last resort only economists, by acquiring more knowledge and wisdom in the ways of economic society, can relieve us of some of our most painful present-day torments. Perhaps a reading of the papers in this volume will at least give the gentle reader (if, as I particularly beg him, he will carefully note the differing times and circumstances in which the various papers were produced) an idea of how economists have come to occupy their present bizarre niche in society and of how at least one economist has through the years plodded his way towards his present outlook, an outlook still not altogether without hope but less sanguine than formerly about the early arrival of the day when men will agree upon the best ways of providing for their material needs.

NOTES

1. I recall that 40 years ago, as a young University don, my research work was devoted to the decline of the textile industry, the fate of the depressed areas and the problem of juvenile unemployment – subjects which, apart from high inflation, now rank foremost in public concern.

2. Perhaps this craving of economists to become 'real' scientists goes back further than is sometimes thought. Thus Sydney Chapman, a foremost economist of the day, was in 1912 writing: 'Much modern economic science is being increasingly assimulated in form and method to the natural sciences ... to attack the ultra-abstract and mathematical economists on this account, in the supposed interest of realism, is suicidal'.

2 THE ROLE OF THE ECONOMIST

The Economist and Public Policy*

I

The science of economics has frequently passed through unhappy periods when controversy has ranged within it and public respect for its principles has, in consequence, waned. In the 20s of last century Torrens was writing of the unsettled state of the subject and looking forward, with a touching confidence that proved to be misplaced, to the early arrival of the period of unanimity. In the 60s and 70s J. E. Cairnes was deploring the numerous and fundamental divergences between economists, examining first principles again in an effort to dissolve the differences, and was vigorously defending his conception of the science against the growing opinion of many intelligent outsiders that political economy was obsolete, a useful branch of knowledge which had served its turn but was becoming an obstacle to progress. In the 80s Thorold Rogers in his lectures in Oxford was slashing energetically at what he termed the 'thorns and thistles of abstract political economy' and declaring that 'political economy is in a bad way: its authority is repudiated, its conclusions are assailed, its arguments are compared to the dissertations held in Milton's Limbo, its practical suggestions are conceived to be not much better than those of the philosophers in Laputa'.

Whilst Marshall wielded his mild and scholarly domination the skirmishing died down, although the snipings of the sociologists continued and the mutterings of the labour movement, that the dismal science stood between them and their birthright, were not wholly stilled. But between the two world wars new disputes arose within the profession and fresh doubts appeared in the minds of the public as to whether economics was much more than vigorous and ingenious hair-splitting carried on while the world was going to ruin. For mass unemployment seemed to have no remedy and the one man bold enough to hold out a cure – Keynes – was striving to give to economics a new bias of thinking which appeared iconoclastic to many of his colleagues. This was the age

*Lloyds Bank Review, April 1953.

which produced the gibe that were six economists gathered together, seven opinions would always be expressed, two belonging to Keynes.

It may appear odd to suggest that the present are anything but the palmy days of economic science. So many governments have formally accepted the responsibility for maintaining full employment, a sweeping victory for Keynesian ideas. Government offices, national and international, are crammed with economists and statisticians measuring, advising and manipulating our affairs and growing in power and status with the progressive magnification and increasing intricacy of economic problems everywhere. Vast schools and faculties have appeared for the training of young economists who are snatched away from their teachers to take on positions of responsibility and power. The flood of economic writings is at its height, the names of outstanding economists constantly before the public eye. The science has enlisted elaborate mathematical techniques and fearsome geometrical constructions through which to pursue its studies with the greater vigour and precision. Anyone, therefore, who doubts its permanent importance or its inexhaustible energy would seem to be merely perverse.

Yet it may properly be asked whether the science is not again showing the standard symptoms of malaise, uncertainty within itself and a declining prestige among informed outsiders who are beginning to wonder if the world is one degree wiser or wealthier for what economists have been doing and saying in the last two decades.

The controversies are there for all to see for, inevitably, they must go on in public and the man in the street can hardly help cocking an ear to discussions which are, after all, about him and his affairs. The two liveliest disputes centre on the part that can be played by a free price mechanism and by the process of competition in the production and distribution of goods. As to the functions of prices, the battle is most intense, at least in Great Britain, on such questions as to whether a free rate of interest has power and virtue for the allocation of capital and whether a controlled or a freely-moving rate of exchange is the better for keeping a national economy in a state of solvency as against other economies. But the real issue goes deeper: it is that of the centrally controlled as against the free economy, of automatic mechanisms against the discriminations of a central plan, of spontaneous adjustments against those socially engineered. The whole position is the more puzzling in that there are not usually clear-cut sides. A symposium of view on such questions[1] much more closely resembles a chapter from a novel of Dostoevsky than a cool and detached scientific discussion. Some hold that the free movement of prices has most benefits to confer, by its steady multitudinous pushes and pulls, when an economic system is seriously dislocated, when costs and prices are hopelessly out of line. There are others who recognise the virtues of free prices but look upon them as a kind of fair weather system of adjustment, only to be trusted when the major disruptions have been partially healed by quantitative controls. This group would advocate controls in the transition, but free prices in the long period; controls in order to attain free prices. The dilemma of this group, as it seems to me, is that they find themselves in a transition without an end. The methods they advocate seem fated to wall us up for ever within transition conditions. And there is a third group who do not believe in the virtues of a freely-moving price system and while, with great ingenuity, they stress the technical deficiences of it, really dislike the kind of society it brings about. They may be prepared to admit that direct controls are restrictive and do not always work smoothly but they believe that a system of controls is the best way of distributing resources that this evil world can offer.

A similar tangle of ideas and attitudes is to be observed on the question of monopoly and competition. Free competition is but another aspect of free prices. But, one school asks, is free competition possible, is not monopoly inevitable? When businessmen are left free to compete does that not also mean that they are free to combine and that their interests will lead them to do so? Even if they are disposed to compete, or are forced to it by state intervention, do not the technical economies of large-scale operation, the splintering of the market by the diversification of goods or by the odd habits of the consumer, inevitably create a world of monopoly? So some hold that monopoly is bad but inevitable; others that monopoly is bad and avoidable; others that monopoly does no particular harm; others that sometimes it is good and sometimes bad; others that monopoly has specific benefits to confer; others that monopoly in one part of the system is undesirable but relatively tolerable provided other monopolies exist, or can be created, to keep it in check.

The muffled sound of this discord can hardly fail to reach outside ears. But even if it did not, the intelligent observer might be wondering whether the work and the ideas of economists in the immediate past have been an entirely unmixed blessing. The past decade has seen a great victory for Keynesian ideas about the methods of maintaining full employment. Certainly, judged by the conditions of this last decade, the mass unemployment of the inter-war years appears as a fantastic nightmare from which it is good to have escaped. But, it might well be asked, do not the methods of maintaining full employment lead to dangers almost as serious as those of unemployment? Is not chronic inflation, with its destruction of a sense of security in the value of money, likely to destroy personal saving and hence block economic progress or force the State to do our savings for us and thereby create a regimented society? Were the fluctuations of the old type of trade cycle more frequent or serious than the periodic crises of balance of payments which have afflicted so many countries and particularly those which have been most successful in 'curing' unemployment? Are not the fiscal and monetary devices for maintaining employment only likely to do more good than harm where certain political and economic conditions are satisfied, conditions difficult or impossible to provide?

Or again the sceptic might ask: why is the world so increasingly preoccupied with economic problems? We know that production is greater now than at any other time in history. Industrial production is nearly double what it was in 1938; even in Europe it is one-third greater. Agricultural production is certainly no less than pre-war. Yet the western countries seem to be caught up in a hopeless tangle in making ends meet, they strain and flounder in making quite minor economic adjustments. Governments declare their aims to lie in one direction and then proceed to follow policies leading in another. They assert that they favour multilateral trade whilst they are imposing import restrictions. They favour a flexible economy while they try to freeze exchange rates and domestic price levels. They declare that they must have greater production while they increase the marginal rates of taxation, or that they must have economy while they increase their own expenditure. Of course, economists would properly reply that these things occur because their advice is neglected and statesmen point out that their apparent inconsistencies arise because they are grappling with that most formidable of all political dilemmas – the determined conviction on the part of people to enjoy a higher standard of living than is really possible. But what is happening is surely evidence that the simple principles of economic rationality are not being carefully listened to and that the mechanisms for maintaining solvency are not in high repute.

II

In these circumstances, it may not be a waste of time for economists to engage in a little self-examination: to ask whether they themselves – by the fashion in which they are seeking to build up their science, by the use to which they are putting it in political affairs, by the manner in which they are allowing it to be employed by others in the framing of policy – whether economists, by omission or commission, are not themselves responsible for some of the economic tangles which torment us.

There seem to be grounds for confession to errors both of omission and commission. First as to omission. Looking at the broad distribution of the interests of economists, do they not spend too much time in theorising and far too little in fact finding, too much in abstraction and too little in observation, too much in analysis and model-making and too little in history? One must stand in respect, envy and awe, though often in some bewilderment, before the incredible ingenuity of our economic analysts and model-makers. And all experience suggests that bodies of scientists have shown a remarkable capacity to move spontaneously from one field of interest which is being worked out to another where the chance of progress is greater. This article is certainly not advocacy for a planned science. But looking at recent economic writings as a whole one is reminded of a comment by Mark Twain. He noticed the varying estimates made by scientists of the length of the Mississippi River and he marvelled at 'the fascination of a science where one gets such wholesale returns of conjecture out of such a trifling investment of fact'. It might have been wise to take more to heart the conclusion of Marshall in 1907 that:

> Qualitative analysis has done the greater part of its work . . . Much less progress has indeed been made towards the quantitative determination of the relative strength of different economic forces. That higher and more difficult task must wait upon the slow growth of thorough realistic statistics.

There appears to be a growing gap in the study of economics between tool makers and tool users, between the theory and the applied part of the science, and the fault is not altogether on the side of the tool users. Those who spend their days, in what is often considered as activity of a lower order, in grubbing energetically among the facts of the market place, would find it easier to get on with their humble tasks if those engaged in more abstract economic speculation were always prepared to accept the following working precepts:

1. Given the complexity of economic life, the longer the chain of abstract reasoning, the greater progressively becomes the chance of some slip in logic, the omission of some factor, which renders the final hypothesis unreal.
2. Any hypothesis about the working of the economic system remains merely a hypothesis, and does not become a theory, until its truth is demonstrated.
3. Where a hypothesis is one which relates to economic quantities, the creator of it should never be satisfied until he has done everything possible to cast it in such a form that it is capable of quantitative measurement. The tool makers should try hard to put handles on their tools. They should remember that a hypothesis which is not falsifiable is not really a hypothesis at all.
4. To that end, the creators of hypotheses should themselves show more interest in subjecting their hypotheses to the facts. That is the custom in many other sciences. It should be the custom in economics. This would lead to a sense of scientific responsibility and caution. 'Hypotheses should be used as tools to uncover new facts rather than as ends in themselves.'[2]

There is a second and more specific error of omission: the surprising lack of interest in what should be the central interest of economists, the causes of the wealth of nations. We know that the standard of living varies enormously from one country to another and we do not know why. We know that some countries have passed through a period of change, commonly known as an industrial revolution, in which economic progress becomes automatic and spontaneous whilst elsewhere something has been lacking which has prevented the wheels from starting to turn. But there is no satisfactory explanation of this. When the richer countries, as at present, set themselves to help the backward areas, there is no agreement as to the points at which, and the manner in which, help can best be provided to assist these areas to help themselves. In this sense, it seems that economic science is now less of a unity than it was in the nineteenth century. There was a stage in that century in which it was regarded as commonplace 'that individuals are the best judges of their own interests; that monopolies should not be permitted in trade; that contracts should be free; that taxation should be equal and should be directed to the maintenance of the revenue, not to the guidance of commerce'[3] and in which the vast economic progress of the century was considered to arise naturally from the establishment of such rules and doctrines. The view may have been wrong or right but at least it was a tenable view about the effectiveness of an economic system. But if it is asked in these days: what economic institutions, what forms of industrial organisation, are best calculated to raise the standard of living of a community, the question is brushed aside as either unaswerable or so political as to be outside the interests of an economist. Yet, if that question cannot be directed at economists it is difficult to see to whom it can properly be addressed.

III

The major error of commission arises from the belief that economists can predict the future. It cannot be too strongly emphasised that there is nothing in economic science which enables us to foretell events. Those who claim otherwise are dragging their subject down to the level of astrology or some other of the many forms of divination that have, at various times, exerted their meretricious seductions. There is nothing in history to suggest that the expected will normally happen. For better or worse, in economic science we must, as Lecky put it, 'endure the sufferings of suspended judgement'. It would be unnecessary to repeat that truism were it not for the fact that economists have, in recent years, been disposed to overstep the limits of their discipline and to talk and act as if they knew enough about the future to advocate policy with confidence. The results have been unfortunate and are likely to bring the science into disrepute.

Before the war it was accepted by many economists, and disputed by few, that all advanced industrial countries were rapidly passing into a condition of maturity and secular stagnation. Openings for profitable investment would be restricted. The savings of these communities would be at a level which would make for extensive and chronic unemployment. It was, so the argument ran, hopeless to assume that invention could take place on a scale which would maintain the dynamic forces which had kept industrial countries going in the nineteenth century. The implications of this were obvious. Thrift and saving would cease to be virtues. The important role of governments would be to maintain and increase the level of consumption. Full employment would perhaps never again be attained in communities where investment was controlled by the expectation of private profit. Events, of course, have completely falsified these expectations. The hunger for capital is everywhere intense and nearly every government is engaged in a campaign to keep down consumption, to encourage savings, to find some space within its congested economy for the claims of investment.

Before the war, many economists were prepared to accept and even to endorse the estimates of future population which suggested that most western countries were confronted with an imminent decline in population. The most alarming pictures were painted of the effects of this decline, of the virtual impossibility of arresting it and of the menace which thereby confronted western civilization. Again the forecasts have proved unreliable. For example, in Great Britain the present population is now considerably larger than the pre-war forecasts which were based even on the 'highly optimistic' assumptions. And some countries in which alarms about underpopulation were raised before the war are now regarded, in some quarters, as being confronted with over population.

Before the war, it was widely asserted that forces were at work which would gradually reduce the volume, or the relative volume, of international trade. Some German economists, indeed, had propounded a 'law of the diminishing importance of foreign trade'. The future undoubtedly lay with self-sufficient communities. In fact, the quantum of world trade is considerably larger than before the war, every country is striving to increase that volume and, even in the case of the United States, it is clear that the dependence of one nation upon another is tending to grow rather than decline.

Before the war, it was generally accepted in Great Britain that the heavy industries had had their day and that Britain must develop rapidly the lighter consumption goods industries if she were ever to be prosperous again. The whole policy of 'balanced distribution of industry' and the restoration of the depressed areas was based upon that diagnosis. The forecast has proved to be completely wrong. It is a shortage of coal and of steel which troubles us and not a surplus. And in these days it is assumed that Britain's industrial future depends largely upon the development of the heavy industries and of engineering, upon which the export trade has come increasingly to rest.

A full list of these errors of major prognostication would indeed be a sobering one. It would tell how, in the United States in the spring of 1929, six months before the onset of the greatest industrial depression in history, a committee of high authority informed Mr Hoover that 'our situation is fortunate, our momentum is remarkable . . . in the marked balance of consumption and production . . . the control of the economic organism is increasingly evident . . . economically we have a boundless field before us'. Eighteen months later the American national income had dropped by 50 per cent. And how Mr Hoover in 1930, after consulting 200 economic experts, declared that the American depression was virtually over. It would tell how British and American economists after the war expected unemployment which never arose. Of how, in 1948, the Swedish economic experts, anticipating an American slump which never arrived, managed to plan a buoyant and healthy economic system into distress and restriction. Of how the British Annual *Economic Surveys*, year after year since 1947, failed so lamentably to pick out the crucial economic trends. Of how, over nearly half a century, economists have warned us of impending shortages of raw materials, predictions which have nearly always been falsified by new discoveries and new inventions.

Economists should make it clear that they have no special aptitude for consulting the entrails. Economic prediction as a scientific method is not merely absurd, because impossible, but dangerous, because seductive. (Indeed, on more general grounds, over-concern about the future is nothing but a source of sorrow. Carlyle once said, 'happy men are full of the present for its bounty suffices them; and wise men also, for its duties engage them'. Prediction, far from securing us against anything, is more likely to submit us to the full fury of the mood of the hour, sometimes overpessimistic, sometimes overoptimistic, and is thereby likely to prolong what might otherwise be a passing distemper within ourselves.)

Yet economists in these days are still engaged in such practices, declaring that the terms of trade have changed *permanently* against the manufacturing countries; or lending their countenance to the view that the world is confronted with a long-period shortage of food; or telling us that there will be a permanent shortage of dollars – just the kind of shots in the dark that have in the past so palpably missed the target. It does not need much thought to understand why prediction is so hazardous. It can almost be summed up in one word: invention. No one can know where pure science will take us next but we can be sure that with the recent rapid growth of scientific knowledge the chances of fruitful crossfertilisation between the different branches of science increase and, with that, the chances of new achievement in unexpected fields. No one knows what technological applications of pure science will be made, but all the recent work on the history of invention reveals how unpredictable are the darting flashes and intuitions of the seminal minds of each generation and how blind we can be to the bounties that are on the doorstep. Judged by the rate of technical innovation we are in the midst of an unprecedented industrial revolution.[4] The paradox of it is that whilst everywhere emphasis is placed upon the need for and the value of research, the purpose and result of which is to make the future unpredictable (since research consists of looking for things which may or may not exist and often of looking for one thing and finding another) there is also this neurotic hankering after prediction, the only purpose of which is to try to be sure about the future.

IV

There are, however, two possible objections to what has already been said. The answers to these objections, in my opinion, go to the heart of this question of what role the economist, strictly as an economist, should perform in society.

No advanced community could exist, and indeed no individual could lead a settled life, unless some thought were taken for the future. Each one of us must be prepared to rule his actions by allowing for the probable consequences of them. Every businessman must make decisions, particularly regarding investment, where hazard and conjecture are inherent. Every government must, at times, adopt policies upon matters regarding which all the relevant information simply does not exist. Are we not, therefore, by denying value to economics as a predicting science, removing the subject to an ivory castle in which, because it would lack immediate usefulness, it would cease to command either the interests of scientists or the respect of the public? I think not. It is, of course, clear that although no one can be sure about the future, men must by hook or by crook take thought for, and strive to be wise about the future. The role of economic science here is not to make predictions for the community. Nor is it to attempt to create the devices and techniques through which the future can be clearly foreseen. The role of economic science is, first, from its understanding of the nature of the economic scene, to make clear the inevitability and unpredictability of change; second, to suggest mechanisms and methods of measurement by which changes will be recognised as quickly as possible when they have occurred and third, and most important of all, to search for and even to recommend those institutions which will enable men and societies to adjust themselves as easily and painlessly as possible to the inescapable vicissitudes of economic life. Statesmen, businessmen, individuals may be compelled to predict. That is their burden. The economist cannot lighten that burden except by helping those who carry it to recognise their errors as soon as they are made and to build up habits and institutions best fitted for clearing up mistakes. As a great commander once entreated, 'I beseech you, in the bowels of Christ, think it possible you may be mistaken'.

The second objection to the plea for a modest and restricted role for the economist is that, if economics confers no power of prediction, and if the test of any science is that it should make prediction possible, then economics is not a science. Such a disheartening conclusion might seem an ungracious belittlement of the devoted and disinterested intellectual strivings of the great economists of the past two centuries.

The escape from such an unpalatable conclusion can be found in more directions than one. A science, to be ranked as such, need not claim predictive functions. There are many large masses of knowledge which are not directly concerned with prediction: geology, descriptive biology, observational ecology, botanical classification, some branches of anthropology, clinical medicine. Perhaps economists strive to do too much, make too great claims for their subject, partly because they are tormented, quite unnecessarily, by a sense of inferiority and un-worthiness. The student of ecology who faithfully observes and records the interplay of plant life in one small area doubtless feels that he is justifying his existence as a scientist. But the economist who devotes himself to a study of the forms of industry and the organic interrelation of units within industry is too frequently regarded by his loftier colleagues as engaged in a low-grade task. No geologist would be prepared to forecast the earthquakes of the future or feel particularly cast down because he could not do so. Yet the economist will often predict the shifts and slitherings of the economic scene or consider his failure to do so to be evidence of the painful immaturity of his science.

The second line of escape is to point out that economists, although they cannot systematically engage in prediction, can, and indeed often do, properly concern themselves with cause and effect. Studies of the past are studies of cause and effect, 'prediction backwards' as Marshall used to describe it. We would have better economics if more economic history were read and written. Economic theory is speculation under strict conditions and a knowledge of the past, of cause and effect. But, of course, the reasons why it cannot be made the basis for prediction is that what is true of the past need not be true of the future and that the conditions in the future are essentially unknowable.

V

The purpose of a science is understanding and not the power to predict.

So long, therefore, as the economist devotes himself with integrity to an *understanding* of the world around him, whether or not that provides him with the means for knowing better than the man in the street what will be the economic future, he can claim respectability for his studies. There is no real need to claim for economics a usefulness beyond that. The light it spreads and not the fruit it yields is its first aim. If it is to make a more positive contribution to policy, if it is to prove useful to those who have to make decisions within the penumbra of doubt which links together the present and the future, then it will only do so if the statesmen and the businessmen can somehow share that understanding and, as a consequence, see more clearly what they are trying to do, what are the real choices before them.

Can one go further than such general precepts? Can one indicate more exactly where economics stands as an instrument in the ordering of public affairs? Senior, although he was himself a man of affairs, once said:

> The conclusions of the economist, whatever be their generality and truth, do not authorize him in adding a single syllable of advice.

There is a whole world of difference between this attitude and that of some living economists who are ready to believe that the only purpose of economics is 'to tell the government what to do'. But need we accept either view in its entirety? Is there not something to be said for an attitude within the following rough outline?

First, the use of economics is to provide data and not decisions; it can inform but it cannot prescribe. The best parallel is that of a map. The most important function of the map is to inform the traveller where he is, to provide a frame of references. It can tell him where he will get to if he travels in one direction or another, but beyond that it is neutral as to whether he travels north, south, east or west. Every wise traveller carries a map but no sensible traveller asks the map where he should go. So, too, with economics; although it should never be forgotten that, just as men may sometimes prefer not to take the shortest route between two points on the map, so economic motives are not always, perhaps not usually, the most important promptings of the human spirit.

Within boundaries so prescribed there is an enormous range of work of immediate practical value to be performed by the economist or the economic statistician, and perhaps only by him, whether he is in a university or is working in close day-to-day contact with men of affairs. Three tasks here stand out above others. The measurement of what has happened in the past and the interpretation of its probable meaning can only be performed properly by those who have developed, by training and experience, wariness and judgement in handling economic statistics, the most slippery of all forms of evidence. Again, there are a number of vital economic mechanisms – banking systems and highly organised markets for money, capital, foreign exchange, basic commodities – about the intricate interconnections of which only the specialist can think and speak with security. And methods now exist, based upon the concept of the national income, of comprehending the economic system as a whole; these methods, whether they take the form of statistical tables or even of mechanical models, can be deployed to best effect by those who have fully grasped the imperfections and limitations of them. Advice of this kind will fortify the statesman or businessman in assessing the point at which he must depart from certainty and plunge into the relatively unknown.

Second, it seems to follow that the economist will be on safer ground in his negative injunctions than in any positive exhortations. It is nearly always easier, and still very useful, to say what cannot be done than to indicate what can be, or must be, done. No one can prevent people who are wilful or perverse from harming themselves, but it should be possible for economists to prevent them from doing harm to themselves by innocently following economic policies which are mutually frustrating, by pursuing courses which have been plotted on an erroneous conception of where they are at the moment.

Third, there are certain maxims which the economist should lose no opportunity of repeating and stressing, not because they arise from any deep learning but simply because they are true, because it needs courage to go on saying them and because they come from economists who have, or should have, no axe to grind and who still have some standing in these matters. Most of them come down to the simple proposition that one cannot have one's cake and eat it – but they can take other forms. That no government has any power to improve the lot of the people except within the limits of the power and willingness of the people to produce. That the importance which people will attach to any commodity or service is largely determined by what they must forego in order to acquire it and that, therefore, if they think they are getting it for nothing they will exercise less economy in its use. That administrative abilities of the highest kind will always be limited and that, in consequence, it will be disastrous to create an economic system which requires for its operation an unlimited supply of administrative genius. And so on.

Fourth, all our experience points to the almost terrifying momentum which can be created, in public discussion of economic organisation and policy, by the very words which are employed. Everyone must find regrettable at least some of the things which have been done in the name of 'rationalisation', 'planning', 'nationalisation', 'balanced distribution of industry', 'co-ordination', 'integration' and so on, phrases which have gripped the popular imagination and have led to headlong charges down frustrating cul-de-sacs. If this indeed is the temper in which public policy is to be discussed, then the economist surely has the responsibility for trying to throw out anchors before a drift becomes hopelessly uncontrollable, by insisting upon knowing what the words mean. As Professor D. H. Macgregor once said, 'we ought to smooth the fluctuation of thought'.

Fifth, and above all, it would be for the economist to tell us what kind of an economic world we do live in, not what kind of a world we are going to live in. When statesmen, confronted by their almost insupportable burden of decision-making, ask for help, the proper answer of the economist is that he does not know what should be done, and that it adds nothing for the blind to claim to lead the blind. But, the economist should go on, there are certain matters which seem to be beyond dispute which cannot be ignored in the making of wise decisions. The economic future is an area of vast uncertainties, technical progress has never been more rapid, the ways of best making a living have never been more fluid, the probing for new knowledge has never been so determined. Statesmen should remember, with Francis Bacon, that 'the subtlety of nature is greater many times over than the subtlety of senses and understanding and that if a man will begin with certainty he shall end in doubts; but if will be content to begin with doubts he shall end in certainty'. Economic security in the sense of freedom from change is a will-o'-the-wisp. Much that will occur will come as a surprise. Much that will be done will inevitably be mistaken. The efficiency of an economic system seems likely to depend, not upon how few mistakes are made but how quickly they are recognised and with what dexterity they are repaired. Those who plan for the future on the assumption that events will bend themselves to their wishes, those who talk of nailing colours to masts, are likely to be as completely upset as a canoeist shooting dangerous rapids who contents himself with steering by the compass. The true economic security must lie in the power for making swift and sensitive adjustments.

There, it would seem, is a field for fruitful co-operation between the scholar and the statesman: to try to determine what habits on the part of the people, what economic institutions, what international economic arrangements are most likely to guarantee that spontaneous and immediate adjustments become part of the natural order of things, that the growing points of the economic system are least impeded, that vested interests likely to resist change do not strike deep roots, that the international solvency of a community is not a matter for periodical panic efforts on the part of governments but is brought about smoothly by the decisions that individuals must make every day in their work and their purchases.

NOTES

1. See, for example, the symposium on 'The New Monetary Policy and the Problem of Credit Control'. *Bulletin of the Oxford University Institute of Statistics*, April and May, 1952.
2. W. I. B. Beveridge, *The Art of Scientific Investigation*, p. 46.
3. J. E. Cairnes, *Political Economy and Laissez Faire*, p. 238.
4. This is a case where in 1953 I myself fell into the trap of predicting too confidently. My present view (see p. 124) is that ours is an epoch of comparative technological sluggishness.

The Economist and Economic Change*

> Anticipations will be assented to much more readily than interpretations, because being deduced from a few instances, and these principally of familiar occurrence, they immediately hit the understanding and satisfy the imagination; whilst on the contrary interpretations, being deduced from various subjects, and these widely dispersed, cannot suddenly strike the understanding, so that in common estimation they must appear difficult and discordant, and almost like the mysteries of faith.
>
> Francis Bacon: *Novum Organum*, Book 1, Aphorism 28

I

Some time ago I published an article in which I pleaded that economists should not claim for their science powers that it did not possess, particularly the power to predict.[1] The economists, to whom it was directly addressed, received it somewhat coldly; which was perhaps not very surprising. Of the few commendations it received, the greater part came from those actively engaged in economic planning, from which I deduced that their experiences in placing whole-hearted confidence in the predictions of economists had not been altogether happy. To me the significant thing was that the article was, in effect, ignored. For whatever may have been in depression in the past few months, there has been a great boom in predictive activity. And since I believe that such behaviour is likely to undermine the status of economics and the public standing of economists, which has some importance, and is further likely to do damage to our economic affairs, which has great importance, I thought I might take this opportunity of developing further my ideas. My subject can, therefore, be defined as follows: How best can economic science and the methods of thought that go with it be utilised in furthering the aims of the community? In what directions do we find the best opportunities of applying the accepted principles of economics and the skills of economists, the formalised understanding and the less spectacular know-how, so that we can at all times maintain our rights as experts but never permit ourselves to behave as charlatans? I ought to

*Lecture given before the Brookings Institution, Washington, DC, 1954.

add, in parenthesis, that in my opinion even if economics were completely useless in the narrow sense there would still be a case to be made out for its study so long as economists were concerned with truth and retained their integrity. I see no reason why they should not, in these matters, be given at least equal treatment with archeologists, astronomers, historians or philologists.

II

On the negative side, I submit that economists cannot, without stepping outside their discipline, predict in the sense of telling us what will happen in the future. It might appear quite unnecessary to make this point but for the tenacious hold that contrary ideas now seem to have gained. I listened the other day to a television programme – it was in this country but I fear it might have been anywhere else – in which a group of questioners were taunting a man of public affairs who was also a distinguished economist: 'If you really are an economist, then predict to us'.

The grounds for rejecting prediction as an activity proper to economic science can be put in general form or displayed as a series of detailed objections although, in fact, these are merely different ways of establishing the same conclusion. In the most general sense, there is, indeed, no such thing as the *economic* future. There is only *the* future in which economic factors are bound together, inextricably and quite without hope of separate identification, with the whole universe of forces determining the course of events. This pattern of causes and consequences, even when looked at after the event as history, almost paralyses the mind with its intricacy. Anyone who proposes to look at it before the event must take as his province the whole of experience and knowledge. He must cease to behave as a specialist, which means that he must cease to behave as an economist.

The economist's claim to predictive authority must be false in that it leads to a palpable absurdity. If the economic future can, indeed, be described, why not also the scientific future, the political future, the social future, the future in each and every sense? Why should we not be able to plumb all the mysteries of future time? Now the economist might argue either that, in his own sphere, he possesses techniques for forecasting superior to those possessed by scientists in other disciplines or that, in the interplay of economic forces, the link between the past and the present and the future is simpler to understand than in other subjects. But I see no reason for economists to assume that their task is less complex than that of others. Some sociologists, indeed, have claimed that they, too, can usefully predict inventions and technical progress. There are historians prepared to believe that history repeats itself, that by discovering congruent past and present sets of circumstances, the future can be foreseen. I know of no means of disputing such claims by scholars in other fields except by reasoning which also cuts the ground from under the feet of the economist. It is, incidentally, worth while noting that one group is frequently highly sceptical about the work of other groups of forecasters. In this case a prophet *is* without honour save in his own country.

Even if it be granted that the economist possesses a time telescope, which other students of society have not been able to construct, we are not at the end of the difficulties. The economic future will be determined partly by the predictions themselves. The future then is the compounded result of the economic forces, which would have operated in any case, and the influences exercised by the predictions. The prophets must then be prepared to claim that they comprehend not only the inevitable consequences of current economic forces but also the effect upon the minds of everyone else of what they themselves have to say. There are only two possible lines of escape from this conclusion. It might be said that economists' predictions have *no* influence upon the course of affairs, that nobody listens to them. Scientifically, this might make prediction more respectable but only at the expense of completely destroying its usefulness. The intrinsic interest in making guesses and putting them into sealed envelopes would seem to be small; much less, for example, than in picking the winners of horse races without backing horses, and I know of no economist who spends his time in this way. The second escape route, sometimes followed by economists who find their forecasts incorrect, is to claim that the warning inherent in the prediction has been so much taken to heart that people have been led to modify their intended actions and thus have falsified the prediction. Therefore it has been said that the scarifying pre-war predictions of an imminent, inevitable, and rapid fall in population in most western countries, predictions generated by or accepted by many economists, have proved woefully wrong simply because people took the appropriate action to avoid the disaster. In my opinion, however, that is not where babies come from. If each time the meterologist predicted rain this had the effect of increasing or decreasing the rain that would fall, then the virtues of the forecast as a basis for action would be destroyed. That seems to me to be true also in economics.

The weapons that can be employed for economic prediction are two: economic laws, the fundamental logic of the science, and the facts of the past. Of the first I shall speak in a moment. As for the second, we can, of course, predict upon the assumption that past trends continue or have a continuing momentum of their own, that established regularities will not change. If such assumptions prove correct, the predictions will be correct. But if the universe of facts changes, the predictions will fail. That is to say, the power to predict is most reliable when it is least necessary, when the conservative rule of thinking about tomorrow as if it were today is most likely to be sound. When the circumstances change, on the other hand, the more strictly the rules for prediction have been adhered to, the grosser will be the errors.

These general conclusions can, I think, be supported by glancing at the outcome of recent prediction. First, the forecasts are not always correct. There is no need to enlarge on this fact. The long list of appalling errors is by now well known. There are economists in Great Britain and even in the United States who have given the best years of their lives to a stubborn reiteration of the view that *the* American depression has at last arrived. Perhaps one of the most extraordinary of recent predictions was that a shortage of food would be permanent in the post-war world. If it can be considered a consolation, the predictions of the sociologists as to invention and the like have been just as inaccurate as those of the economists. Of course some predictions do come true. If all had been wrong, a method of accurate prediction would exist: to assume that the course of events will be the opposite of the predictions. On the whole, however, it seems that this perverse method would, in the past decade, have yielded many more successes than have in fact been achieved by economists.

Second, there is evidence to suggest that economists, like other scientists, are biased – of course unconsciously. I think it can be established, for example, that economists are on the whole a pessimistic lot. There are very good reasons why this should be our occupational disease. I consider that it is almost impossible for us, at some point, not to inject into our thoughts about the future vague impressions that we would not care to defend. Most of us will have gone through that agonising experience of scrutinising a curve of past performance that seems to reveal a trend but that, towards its end, shows some tantalising short-period divergencies from the trend; of wondering where the line will go next; of extrapolating on different sets of assumptions; of reaching very different conclusions on the basis of the different assumptions and rejecting the outsize results, without any good reason, just because they are outsize. Perhaps the most famous case is the series of predictions made by the European Commission for Economic Co-operation as to whether there was surplus capacity in the European steel industry. In all such cases, it seems to me impossible that the guesses will not be tipped one way or another by irrelevant factors. On the whole, for example, it is socialists who have predicted most incorrectly about the onset of *the* American depression, and who were most gloomy about the future of Germany, with its new economic policy, until the facts swamped their doubts. On the whole, those who advocate the virtues of free markets have, in their forecasts, been unnecessarily pessimistic about the future of output in Great Britain.

Third, it is clear that different economists looking at the same

evidence frequently reach very different conclusions about the future.
This is particularly disturbing. It is no answer to say that there are some
good economists and some bad ones. It is of the essence of a science that
there is a body of universally accepted principles and presuppositions
and that, in regard to these at least, all scientists are good scientists.

There are other minor indications of the essentially unscientific
nature of these predictions. One is the practice of employing obscure
words by which those who use them try to say something significant
without being tied down to any statement that can be checked. Hence
the evasive distinctions between 'depression', 'recession', 'decline',
'readjustment', 'downturn', and so on. Another is to provide a prediction without a time scale so that the day of reckoning never arises.
Another is to claim that while predictions about the near future are likely to be incorrect, predictions about the remote future are likely to be
right. It is quite extraordinary how many people there are who know
that they do not know what will happen next month but appear confident about what will have happened five years hence.

In view of these truisms it may be asked why these predictions continue on such a wide scale. The simple answer is that there is a market, a
demand, for them. Nearly everyone of us has to take action that is
coloured by our guesses about the future. Certainly every business and
every government is in that difficult position, and it is not surprising that
they should be prepared to clutch at straws. It is melancholy that men
and communities should be exposed to the anxieties and dangers of the
unknowable future. But that is one of the facts of life. It is my thesis that,
in the last resort, the burdens that fall upon the men of action cannot, in
fact, be lifted off their shoulders by economists who hold themselves out
as capable of providing a service that they cannot, in fact, perform. On
the supply side, economists are perhaps tempted to predict because the
risks attendant upon failure are slight, the premiums on success great. A
long string of quite incorrect predictions will be completely overlooked
if the economist makes one isolated guess correctly. There is a danger,
indeed, that a kind of Gresham's Law will operate by which the more
spectacular predictions will drive out the less. What is more natural than
that an economist who believes that serious economic dangers confront
us and who passionately thinks that he knows the way to avoid them,
should utter his warnings in an exceptionally stident and alarming form
in order to get a hearing at all? There may be a special peril awaiting
society just because economists have the interests of mankind so closely
at heart.

Although there is little danger of it, in an assembly of this kind, I do
not want to be understood to imply that the men who must make the
economic decisions cannot derive great and indeed absolutely necessary
assistance from those who are trained in ways of economic thought. This
is a point I enlarged upon in my earlier article.[2] The golden rule here is

that the economic expert should be most scrupulous in setting down all his assumptions and indicating the degree of probability that attaches to each one. The wise man of action, in assessing the importance of the advice tendered to him, will always insist that this is done. For, as a general rule, when economists go wrong, it is not because of any failure of logic but because of some defect in the data or the assumptions from which they start.

My second explanatory word is that I do not deny the value of economic logic. Misunderstanding here is very common because of the different uses to which the word 'prediction' can be put. When it is said that *if* the supply of money increases by 100 per cent, everything else remaining equal, prices will rise, no one will demur. If it is declared on such a basis that economists can 'predict', there can be no objection, although it would have to be pointed out that this kind of 'prediction' is not what I have been talking about. I think it would be better to describe it as economic logic. And there are, of course, a large set of propositions in our logic which enormously increase understanding of the economic world. But we ought to recognise their limitations. When it is said, without any conditions being attached, that if the supply of money increases by 100 per cent next year then prices will rise next year, even then perhaps I would not protest. But with an apology for stating the obvious, I would remind you that we are always uncertain whether the *ifs* will come true; we are always uncertain whether the *other things remaining unchanged* will be true; we are often uncertain whether the *ifs* are really consistent with the *other things remaining unchanged*. We must further recognise that the generalisations of economic logic become progressively less valuable for action the smaller the changes being considered. A statement, for instance, that, if the supply of money increases next year by 5 per cent, prices will rise, is clearly a shot in the dark.

III

I come now to the more positive side of my suggestions. The activities of economists may be misplaced either because they do harm or because they are devoted to less important things before more important things. Both statements may be true, but anyone who makes the second can properly be expected to indicate what tasks, in his opinion, economists are unduly neglecting.

The most important task in economics is that of strengthening and extending the range of economic laws. Difficult as it is even how to define the scope of economics, the subject would become an unsystematic hotchpotch of transient and disconnected interests but for the cohesive power of its fundamental logic. This centralising body of doctrine accounts for the continuity of modern economic thinking over the

past two centuries and explains why so many of the most fertile and subtle thinkers have devoted themselves with such absorption to the subject.
Lacking familiarity with this logic, it is amost impossible to escape
helpless floundering among the innumerable economic fallacies to
which the human mind can be subject.

Despite this there can be no doubt that in recent years the authority of
economic theory has declined. The scholars in many important
branches of the social sciences related to economics do not even deem it
worth while to acquaint themselves with the economist's techniques.
Those who make the important economic decisions of the world often
brush off the simpler truths of economics as irrelevant or even misleading. The very mention of economic laws generally arouses a restive
feeling that some very old, utterly uninteresting, and entirely obsolete
incantation is being mumbled. A study of the causes of this loss of
prestige would take me too far afield. But there are among them two
that are relevant to my thesis.

The first is that the obvious next steps in the development of
economic theory present appalling intellectual difficulties. Up to now
our economic laws have concerned themselves with static conditions.
Although it is true that such laws are in many ways useful and, in any
case, are all that we possess in thinking about economic change, it is also
true that the speed and ubiquity of technical change, the frequency with
which the data alter, make it highly desirable that the element of innovation should be embodied in the system of thought. If, for instance, we
concern ourselves with the optimum distribution of economic resources
not at a moment of time but over a period, what part of our resources
should be devoted to the process of innovation itself? Has economic
theory anything at all to tell us about the right rate of investment in industrial or scientific research, or even about the right proportion
between the two? Are there rates of economic expansion that, of
themselves, provide greater stability in growth than others? These
questions have only to be posed to make clear how little we know about
them and how difficult it will be ever to theorise about them. Although
these are subjects to which some of the best minds in the profession
devote themselves, I suspect that the feelings of being up against a blank
wall is damping to enthusiasm and confidence.

A second reason why economic theory has lost prestige is, I think, the
fault of economists themselves. While they have been searching for a
more advanced theory applicable to dynamic conditions and delivering
themselves of opinions about the future for which no support can be
found in economic theory, many of them have, paradoxically enough,
taken the lead in belittling those older and simpler forms of economic
logic that, up to now, would seem most reliable and most useful in the
framing of policy. It is almost as if a mathematician became so deeply
involved in the abstract theory of numbers that he began to doubt that

two and two made four and thereby led his poor wife to falsify the domestic accounts. Thus, in recent years, at various times and in various quarters, some economists have argued, or even purported to prove by appeal to facts, that the rate of interest has little or no influence upon business policy; or that the behaviour of the business man cannot usefully be studied on the assumption that he is seeking to maximise profits; even that a shortage of the currency of one country suffered by another country cannot be rectified by movements in the rate of exchange. It would not surprise me if, one of these days, some economist comes out with the idea, based on a small public opinion poll, that consumers are not really trying to maximise their satisfaction. These agonising second thoughts about the ABC of their subject doubtless help to explain why economists since the end of the last war have so frequently been reluctant to recommend the processes of the free market, the forces of supply and demand, as the most effective system for correcting economic maladjustments, or restoring economic balance. I very much doubt whether, if action had depended upon a consensus among economists, we would have seen the revival of Germany under their new economic policy, the successful employment of monetary policy as an anti-inflationary measure in Great Britain, or the restoration of much freer economies in other European countries. The attitude taken up at the present time towards the convertibility of currencies seems to me another case in point. There are economists who believe that convertibility will never be possible or desirable, there are others who believe it desirable but who continue to believe that the time is not ripe, there are others who attach almost unsatisfiable conditions to a return to free international markets in currency. There are few who have real confidence in the powers of the market, including the speculative market, to create a balancing system.

The aim of economic science is to reduce the number of uncertainties in a world that, in its totality, will never be knowable. The first function of economists is, therefore, to speak firmly in terms of these certainties they claim to have established. If these claims have, in fact, been dropped, this should be frankly admitted, and we should go into sack cloth and ashes and take up other work. In my opinion, however, the old claims are still good, and economists should constantly be striving to widen the area of certainty in this form, however bleak and difficult that task may seem.

My second suggestion is that economists should become more historically minded both in the sense of devoting more time to studying the work of economic historians (who in my opinion are far too small a band for the work they have to do) and in the sense of engaging themselves in historical studies. No one will doubt, from what I have already said, that I do not hold history to be a science. But there is a *sense* of history, a knowledge of the kind of things that *can* happen, a feeling of what fits with what, a comprehension of how a multitude of tiny interlocking events make up the whole, always possessed by the wise and cultured scholar. I suspect that what we speak of as economic judgement is a talent of the same kind, to be cultivated in much the same way. Many years ago Keynes spoke of this gift when he said 'the theory of economics does not furnish a body of settled conclusions immediately applicable to a policy. It is a method rather than a doctrine, an apparatus of the mind, a technique of thinking which helps its possessor to draw correct conclusions'. Economic judgement is bound up with a sturdy disposition not to allow current affairs to bulk too large, however insistently these affairs seem to press upon the mind and the imagination; with the caution that comes from the knowledge that everything under the sun is both old and new; with the power to absorb other men's experiences at other times almost as if they were our personal experiences; with a confidence about what will probably not happen which remains unshaken although the future is a dark mystery. You may call this commonsense or a sense of the practicable, the feasible, or cool scepticism, or middle-of-the-road thinking. But it seems to me most likely to flourish among those who are aware of the past, and aware of it because they have rubbed up against the facts of history, sought to place themselves in other men's minds, watched the frustration of expectations, the occurrence of the unlikely, the failure of the probable, the collapse of well-laid plans, and the constant emergence of some new pattern out of standard and familiar elements.

A closer working contact with history might bring a double bonus of economic understanding. It would give ballast to conclusions reached through formal analytical reasoning. Foolish results may, and do, emerge from economic theorising, as a consequence of a slip in one of the steps or neglect of one of the assumptions, unless the theory is steadily confronted with the facts. And it would help to clear up errors about the past. Some notable recent historical and statistical studies have thrown a flood of new light upon the economic events of the past 150 years. Ashton[3] and other writers have shown that the nineteenth century was not the bleak age of falling standards of living, exploitation, and progressive misery that so many had supposed. Stigler[4] and Nutter[5] have thrown serious doubts upon the widely accepted view that industrial monopoly has been steadily increasing since the beginning of this century. Weston[6] has challenged the contention that industrial mergers have, since 1900, contributed greatly to industrial concentration. Adelman[7] has given us grounds for believing that industrial concentration has not been increasing in this century. And the work of Kaplan on the large corporation has provided for us a new conception of the pervasiveness of competition and the precarious hold on the market possessed even by the biggest and apparently most firmly established corporations. It is not too much to say, in view of these results, that a good deal of thinking and writing about the Industrial Age is now obsolete. It is not fanciful to suppose that, if this knowledge had been possessed earlier, western societies might have been spared much toil and trouble.

There remain many tasks of the same kind. For example, a study is badly needed of the British economy between the two world wars. The popular opinion that this was a period of falling standards of living, of decreasing productivity, of backward industries, is palpably incorrect. Again, much more study should be made of the character and the consequences of technical progress, a subject on which opinion swings about in the most puzzling fashion. Up to 1924, it was generally assumed that invention and technical improvement were highly desirable features of any economy, even though doubts were expressed about the distribution of the resultant increase of income or about the more general consequences of a highly mechanised economy. The heavy unemployment in Great Britain after that year and the world crisis after 1930 led to the view that there could be too much technical progress, that it might produce uncontrollable disturbances. The age of 'technocracy', however, did not last long. By 1939 the popular theory was that there would probably be too little technical progress. The theory of the mature economy, of secular stagnation, implied that there would not be sufficient inventions to provide profitable outlets for the savings of a community in full employment. Now, in the post-war period, the popular view has once again changed. We are told that technical progress is a guarantee both of improving standards of living and economic stability, that providentially there will never be any shortage of profitable invention, that technical progress has become automatic, that the process of invention has now been invented. These views cannot all be correct. Clearly here is a subject well worth study.

My third and my last suggestion is that there ought to be a rich field for economists, or for some economists since we must have specialisation, in the study, or even the invention if they happened to be gadget-minded, of economic institutions, the administrative devices through which economic forces operate and can be harnessed to the best effect. It is arguable that economic progress in the nineteenth century was just as much to be attributed to the discovery and improvement of such institutions – banking systems, the gold standard in various forms, the joint stock company with limited liability, the organised produce markets, the stock exchange, employment exchanges, the patent system – as it was to the brute effect of technical progress. I am not, of course, suggesting that all these ingenious ideas were produced by economists. But economists were closely associated with many of them, and at least they were interested in all of them.

Now I can well imagine some of my listeners hotly denying that economists have lost their ingenuity, asking who invented the budget deficit as a device for maintaining employment, and asserting that in-genuity of that kind is misplaced if not actually wicked. But leaving this awkward exception on one side, I submit that there has been a strange lack of curiosity on the part of economists about some extremely impor-tant social experiments of our times. Take, for example, the British National Health Service. The important economic question about the scheme was this: if there is a service the demand for which at zero price is almost infinitely great, if no steps are taken to increase the supply, if the cost curve is rising rapidly, if every citizen is guaranteed by law the best possible medical service, and if there is no obvious method of rationing, what will happen? I do not recall any British economist, before the event, asking these simple questions and, after the event, it is the doctors themselves and not primarily the economists who have raised these questions. Or take the British Nationalisation Schemes that, whether they have been good or bad, have been very important in-stitutional experiments. The systematic examination of them, before or after the event, has been surprisingly perfunctory. Or take the very im-portant matter of the relation between the size of, or the degree of monopoly possessed by, industrial organisations and the frequency of invention and industrial development. There are economists (I fear I am one of these) prepared to deliver themselves of generalisations on the subject. Yet we have practically no systematic knowledge in this field and only a handful of workers interested in it. Or take the patent system: on the one side, it is described as essential for industrial progress, on the other, it is condemned as obsolete. But how much attention have economists devoted to this very important subject in the past quarter of a century?

I find it equally surprising that, although our profession absorbs at least its due proportion of the natural intelligence of each generation, economists have produced in recent years only a thin trickle of ideas for automatically operating schemes and devices as stops and stabilisers in the economy. That point may be illustrated merely by listing some of the main anxieties of our times. It is widely believed that chronic inflation is one of the grave dangers of western democracies. But where is the flow of bright ideas, from which statesmen could pick and choose, as to how best communities could set a watch on themselves so that they do not thoughtlessly drift into conditions that they will regret? Again if it is true (I am myself doubtful about this but I recognise I am in a minority) that, as between two countries with vastly different levels of efficiency and rates of technical progress, balance of payments difficulties will in-evitably arise, have we to assume that there is *no* kind of market for currency that will obviate the need for the State manipulation of trade and currency transactions? If it is recognised, as I think it is now widely recognised, that a Welfare State runs the risk that the more 'welfare' provided the more will be demanded and that, ideally, welfare schemes should be automatically self-liquidating, what actual recommendations are before us to how help can best be provided for the unfortunate in such a way as to destroy the need for such help in the future, as to how 'we might emphasise the goal of greater equality in earning capacity rather than greater equality in the distribution of results'.[8] If we accept the view that progressive taxation is so seductive a concept that once we start along that course there seems nothing to prevent democracies pursuing it to the point of actual income equality (which few would really like), can economists not tell us where roughly the danger point is to be found and how the brake might be imposed when we approach it? If a budget deficit, properly handled, can assist us in maintaining employment, is it possible to put the use of this weapon into an automatic form that will avoid the confusing political squabbles that will otherwise arise on every occasion that the weapon is employed? Note that the problem in each one of these cases is the same: there are certain changes that are innocuous or even desirable provided they go on at a certain speed and to a limited degree and are not irreversible; but that are disastrous if permitted to exceed that speed or degree and thereby become irreversible. The danger exists so long as the critical points have not been identified.

Now some economists, of course, may not be overworried by the prospect of inflation, of controlled exchanges, or everwidening welfare schemes, of progressive taxation pushed to its logical conclusion, of increasing national debts through deficit financing. Others who are anxious perhaps comfort themselves with the thought (which I am not prepared to declare foolish) that the worst never happens, that the expected never occurs, that trees do not grow up to the sky. There are others who believe that there is no need for new social and economic gadgets, that the stricter adherence to well-known economic truths and the freer operation of well-tried economic devices should suffice. But I wonder whether there is not something more to be said here. I wonder whether many economists have not in a sense lost heart because they have been driven to the belief that, in Western democratic communities, political forces and the pressure of vested interests are so powerful and can be so blind that the economist, if faithful to the traditions of science, can never do more than whisper in the thunder of an elemental gale. I hope we shall not weary in that way. For in the squalls that drive first one way and then another will always come breaks in the storm when societies must rest to count their self-inflicted wounds and to take stock of those who led unwisely. In those lulls nations may be inclined to listen to restrained and consistent voices. And therein may be the opportunity of the economists provided, but only provided, that they have not in the meantime allowed their authority completely to lapse by seeking to bluster a way into the ranks of the politicians through making bogus claims for the power of their science.

NOTES

1. *Lloyds Bank Review*, April 1953.
2. See pp. 12–25.
3. T. S. Ashton, *Capitalism and the Historians*, ed. F. A. Hayek, Chaps. 1 and 4.
4. George J. Stigler, 'Competition in the United States, *Five Lectures on Economic Problems*, 1950.
5. G. Warren Nutter, *The Extent of Enterprise Monopoly in the United States, 1899–1939*, 1951.
6. J. Fred Weston, *The Role of Mergers in the Growth of Large Firms*, 1953.
7. M. A. Adelman 'The Measurement of Industrial Concentration', *Review of Economics and Statistics*, Vol. XXXIII, November 1951.
8. Aaron Director, 'The Parity of the Economic Market Place', Conference on Freedom and the Law, University of Chicago, May 1953.

3 THE GOVERNMENT AND EMPLOYMENT POLICY

A Defence of the White Paper on Employment Policy 1944*

I

In the past 50 years remarkable turns have occurred in economic theorising about the influence which governments can exercise upon the level of employment. In the 1920s it was the conventional wisdom that government intervention could do little or nothing to create additional employment. Mr Churchill, relying upon the advice of his Treasury officials, in his Budget Speech in 1929 had said:

> It is the orthodox Treasury dogma steadfastly held that, whatever might be the political and social advantages, very little additional employment and no permanent additional employment can, in fact and as a general rule, be created by State borrowing and State expenditure.

This declaration was not seriously challenged at the time.

In the 1930s, however, it was challenged by Keynes and, by 1939, it had become widely accepted by economists that the Government, through appropriate changes in the Budget and money supply, with their reactions upon public expenditure, could in large measure control the volume of employment.

When, therefore, as part of the plans for post-war reconstruction in Britain, the White Paper on Employment Policy was presented to the nation in 1944 by the Coalition Government there was a formal undertaking that, for the future,

> The Government accept as one of their primary aims and responsibilities the maintenance of a high and stable level of employment after the war.

In this White Paper the conditions which would have to be satisfied if Governments were to be able to honour this undertaking were carefully

* Published here for the first time.

laid down and the dangers of ignoring the declared warnings were fully spelled out.

For almost a quarter of a century, between 1945 and 1970, unemployment in Britain remained very low, rarely rising above 2½ per cent, without incurring any danger of serious inflation. Neither at the time nor since has anyone offered any conclusive explanation of what must now be looked upon as an economic bonanza in those 25 years. But the good times had two unfortunate consequences. First, it came to be generally accepted that such a low rate of unemployment was normal; that anything worse was neither politically nor socially tolerable. Second, that what was happening could be attributed to the policies laid down in the White Paper. The conditions and warnings in the White Paper were forgotten or ignored.

When, therefore, in 1969 unemployment began to rise well above the 'tolerable' limit, the reflex action of successive Governments was to try to spend their way out of the difficulties by running budget deficits and by increasing public expenditure. These measures did not provide the expected relief. And although the remedial measures laid down in the White Paper were now being applied under conditions which rendered them useless or dangerous the White Paper itself was now condemned as erroneous both as to principle and practice.

From 1970 onwards there has been another turn in the circle. The views of the 'monetarists' have commanded increasing support. The contention of these economists is that there are conditions (conditions which in fact were ruling in Britain after 1970) under which any attempt to reduce unemployment by increasing public expenditure would be self-frustrating, for the result would be an increase in the supply of money which would lead to more inflation and even more unemployment, especially when steps were finally taken to restrict the money supply in order to avoid the final evil of uncontrolled hyper-inflation.

Although the 'monetarists' have certainly won the intellectual battle, they really have said little that cannot be found in the White Paper of 1944. And the less thoughtful of the monetarists may be running us into another set of errors by assuming that there can *never* be an occasion when increased public expenditure may be desirable in order to stimulate employment and by suggesting that there is a simple set of arithmetical rules which could enable Governments to specify, and measure and control exactly, the supply of money in order to keep unemployment at the level below which it should not fall and above which it need not rise.

The following defence of the 1944 White Paper is really a plea that if, today, it were carefully read again, it might provide the basis for a sensible employment policy which the two main political parties could both accept. I have ventured to set up this defence because I was associated with the original drafting of the White Paper and I early became uneasy about the dangers inherent in the way it might be misrepresented. Also I now feel that there are in the White Paper warnings and reservations that some of the less cautious monetarists might do well to heed.[1]

II

I will recount briefly my recollections of how the White Paper came to be written and of the ideas in the minds of those who had a hand in framing it.

It appears that sometime in 1942 Dennis Robertson,[2] at that time in the Treasury, was persuaded to produce the first draft of a paper on employment policy. It may be that his heart was not in the task for he had an intuitive perception of the pitfalls in government economic management; it may be that his habit of making references to Alice in Wonderland were not deemed appropriate in a White Paper. Whatever the reason, his draft was quietly abandoned. But the then Members of the Economic Section of the War Cabinet Secretariat were convinced of the need for a formally expounded and publicly declared employment policy and they continued their work on the subject.[3]

In the event the final form of the White Paper was prepared in the Office of the Minister of Reconstruction. The Minister was Lord Woolton who had, in November 1943, been given the task by Mr Churchill of drawing together the numerous major schemes and plans for post-war policies which were then being widely and anxiously discussed. Lord Woolton had, by his own insistence, quite a small staff headed by Norman Brook[4] with John Maud,[5] Alec Johnston,[6] Sylvester Gates[7] and myself as his senior aides. In the actual wording of the White Paper, Norman Brook and especially Sylvester Gates played the major part. The latter had been seconded from the Ministry of Information. After the war he became a successful businessman and had a distinguished career in banking, but he was not a professionally trained economist. He listened with a fascination approaching incredulity as the economists discussed matters in their own particular cherokee. (I once heard him quizzically remark that 'economists sometimes remind me of medieval theologians'.) But with a mind of extraordinary agility he was quick to see what the economists were driving at and he was a superb draughtsman. Of course the White Paper went through many versions and corrections, exposed as it was to the comments of numerous departments and criticisms at many meetings at different levels. But it was Gates who produced many of the clear and forthright sentences of the Paper, for which everybody seemed to be grateful.[8]

The White Paper was scrutinised by the Reconstruction Committee of the War Cabinet, of which Lord Woolton was Chairman, and presented by him to his colleagues in Cabinet and later to the House of Lords. But the thinking which lay behind the Paper, and the intellectual standing thereby guaranteed to it, came from the Economic Section of the War Cabinet Secretariat, the responsible Minister for which was Sir John Anderson.[9] The Economic Section was then headed by Lionel Robbins[10] and the distinguished men who worked most closely with him on this Paper were James Meade,[11] Stanley Dennison,[12] Marcus Fleming[13] and Ronald Tress.[14] They, in turn, worked closely with Lord Woolton's staff. I was perhaps the most direct link with the Economic Section since I had been a member of it in 1940–2 until, after a spell in the Ministry of Aircraft Production, I went back to work under Norman Brook.

Brooding over the whole of the enterprise which finally produced the White Paper was the great Maynard Keynes himself. He rarely intervened directly. I can recall only one occasion when, at a later stage in the preparation of the Paper, there was a meeting of Keynes, Hubert Henderson,[15] Lionel Robbins, Sir Richard Hopkins[16] and myself. Keynes said little; he was certainly not critical of the White Paper as it stood. He may well have thought the Paper was an oversimplified effort. But it has to be remembered that by now the Paper had been running the gauntlet of corrections and criticism from Ministers of different political views in a coalition government and qualifying phrases had had to be introduced to meet all comers. But, as far as my recollection goes, if Keynes was not interfering a great deal, he was accepting the White Paper as the best that, in the circumstances, could be got through with a coalition government. And Sir Richard Hopkins seemed equally ready to let it pass.

It would be idle to deny that the White Paper was a 'Keynesian' document.[17] Keynes was, after all, the major prophet of the idea that governments could, by increasing aggregate demand, reduce unemployment. Some of those who collaborated in the preparation of the White Paper had been his pupils or had long been his followers. Those who had resisted some of his ideas before the war had later gained an enormous respect for and confidence in him as they watched, and collaborated in, his superbly dextrous negotiations with the American Government and its economic officials. Those who had perhaps been most suspicious of the pre-war ideas of Keynes (I was among these) had seen at first hand the horrible consequences of the pre-war high rates of unemployment in the depressed areas especially among juveniles and were only too ready to concede that, if the doctrine of the White Paper could be made to work, the post-war world might be a safer and more humane place.

III

To repeat, the first, and what was to become the most famous sentence in the Paper, ran:

> The Government accept as one of their primary aims and respon-
> sibilities the maintenance of a high and stable level of employment
> after the war.

Note that there is no mention here of 'full employment'.[18] It was, as I
recall, Robbins who most constantly insisted that such a term would
create overambitious expectations which might easily lead to frustration
and disillusionment. 'A high and stable level of employment' it had to
be. The danger that if the sights were set too high, overheating in the
economy and consequential unemployment could easily be the result
was clearly perceived by Lord Woolton himself. In his *Memoirs* (p. 282 *et
seq*) he says:

> I had studied the books and works [of Lord Keynes] for many years.
> He had a persuasive prose style that made his views so easy to accept
> but I always felt it necessary to approach them with a hostile mind . . .'

> Few things have given me more satisfaction than the presentation to
> Parliament of a White Paper on Employment Policy . . . *I never asked
> for 'full employment' for everyone. All that I asked for was a 'a high and stable
> level of employment'.*

He foresaw clearly the social and economic dangers of inflation:

> Over-employment, where there are so many more jobs than there are
> men and women to fill them, then the temptation arises for people
> not to consider seriously whether, in fact, they are giving society a fair
> return for the wages they are paid. When the demand for goods, as
> well as for employment, is so high that management does not have to
> consider costs, when the standard of wages continues to rise – not
> because of increased productivity but because the manufacturers can
> always pass the increased wages on to the consumers, then the whole
> economic fabric of society is in danger . . . Money and savings lose
> their value and employment becomes gravely imperilled by inflation.

And yet the seductive phrase 'Government commitment to full employment' with all its potential mischief became inseparably linked with the
White Paper.[19]

No one, as far as I know, has ever provided a generally accepted
definition of what was meant by 'full employment'. By the same token,
however, it is only right to point out that the White Paper nowhere indicated what was meant by 'high' or 'stable' in the phrase 'a high and
stable level of employment'. Of course essays were prepared in the

Economic Section on this subject and rough figures suggested. But none of them found a way into the Paper itself. My (confident) guess is that the absence of precision here was due simply to the fact that the White Paper was a document of a coalition government and that the Reconstruction Committee contained right-wing ministers anxious not to set too high a target and left-wing ministers determined not to set it too low.

I would, however, be equally confident that most of those who were concerned with the preparation and the final approval of the Paper and its submission to Parliament had in their minds a target figure, a trigger point at which the Government should intervene to increase aggregate demand and check further increases in unemployment, which was much higher than the rates of unemployment which in fact ruled in Britain from 1945–68 and perhaps as high even as those of the present day. I submit the following, necessarily circumstantial, evidence in support of this hunch:

1. I am sure the White Paper was written under the general impression that, perhaps after a short interim period, there was a real possibility of very high rates of unemployment. This was a wise and reasonable assumption to make. High unemployment had appeared after the first World War. More relevant, between 1922 and 1938 the number of unemployed in the United Kingdom had never fallen below 1,200,000 (10 per cent); had risen to more than 2,000,000 in five of the years and had averaged nearly 1,800,000 (14 per cent). The year 1938, with unemployment at 1,800,000, had come to be regarded as something of a boom year. If, in 1944, anyone had suggested that between 1945 and 1969 unemployment would have remained around 2 per cent he would have been laughed out of court.

2. Even the Labour ministers, and especially Ernest Bevin, with his massive commonsense, had recognised that the manipulation of aggregate demand was not an instrument enabling governments to engage in the 'fine tuning' of the economy (to use a phrase which came into popularity only much later). It was a back-stop, it was not a cure-all. Ernest Bevin stressed the need for special action for the depressed areas and was largely responsible for the lengthy references in the White Paper to 'a balanced distribution of industry'.[20]

3. In 1944 Lord Beveridge had published a book *Full Employment in a Free Society*. It was apparently started and certainly published later than the White Paper. Beveridge was highly critical of the White Paper as timid and non-comprehensive – all of which is perhaps understandable since at that time he was much influenced by the extraordinary popular success of the earlier volume *Report on Social Insurance and Allied Services*, produced by an official Committee of which he was the dominating Chairman. He was recommending, as a part of *his* employment policy:

abolition of want; collective outlay to provide good houses, food, fuel and other necessities plus a free National Health Service for all; extension of the public sector of industry; national control of the location of industry; the organised mobility of labour; controlled marketing of primary products; and international trading agreements: a set of measures, to my mind, ideally designed, despite his good intentions and his protests to the contrary, to bring us, by a short cut, to a collective society. On the specific question of 'Full Employment' he stipulated that there should always be more vacancies than jobs and that *average* unemployment rates might well be kept to about 3 per cent without incurring danger of inflation (presumably an average of 3 per cent would not in his mind have ruled out substantial variations between one year and another). At the time the Beveridge employment plans were generally regarded as unattainable and his indicated tolerable maximum rate of unemployment was attacked by many experts.[21] I may perhaps quote what I myself wrote around that time expressing views which I think were shared by many of those associated with the White Paper:

There is a very serious danger that the second half of the twentieth century may be the age of inflation just as the first half was the age of mass unemployment. We may, that is to say, jump from the frying pan into the fire. For the prevention of general unemployment calls for the maintenance of national expenditure up to, but not beyond, the critical point at which inflation results. If democratic communities are to use the technique for preventing unemployment with discretion and are not to throw away the important social values which distinguish them from the totalitarian states, they will be called upon to exercise their democratic virtues in the economic sphere as already they have revealed their power to exercise them in the political . . . It would be unwise to try to exceed, by the manipulation of national expenditure, a level of about 94% or 95% of employment, i.e. 5% or 6% of unemployment. We cannot work to finer limits than that. Used beyond that point increasing national expenditure is almost certain to slip over the edge into inflation and everything it involves.

(*Ordeal By Planning*, 1948, pp. 78–9)

The White Paper carried other warnings. The measurement of unemployment to fine limits was a pretty hopeless task. Unemployment constituted the relatively small residual between two greater magnitudes: the employable population and the employed population, small changes in either of which would produce big percentage changes in the residual. Hence the preference in the White Paper for relying upon measurements of the level and stability of *employment*. Unless wages were related, not merely nationally but also as between different industries, to productivity then inflation and unemployment were inescapable.[22] Difficult as it might be, the identification and separation for treatment of structural unemployment on the one hand, and unemployment due to cyclical or sporadic forces on the other, was necessary if government policy was to be soundly based. Government attempts to increase employment could be frustrated by monopolies which could absorb any increased purchasing power pumped into the system. In a changing world, especially for an economy significantly dependent upon exports, mobility of labour was the price that would have to be paid for restraining unemployment.[23]

And finally, it may be pointed out, the White Paper in no way suggested that maintaining a high and stable level of employment implied comprehensive central economic planning.[24] This is how I put it nearly thirty years ago:

> The essence of the programme was that of allowing the market economy to run without hindrance or interference unless private and normal Government expenditure seemed likely to be inadequate. The Government action would be sufficiently tentative and its weapons sufficiently flexible to enable it to adjust its own activities if its estimates of 'normal' national expenditure proved unsound. There is nothing here of programmes for individual firms or industries, nothing of the establishment of social priorities which would bind the consumer or producer, nothing, in fact, of what is normally understood as comprehensive planning by the modern Socialist. The policy is one of trying to control the economic climate rather than of telling each citizen when he should put up and down his umbrella, when he should don and doff his overcoat.
>
> *(Ordeal By Planning, 1948, p. 64)*

I conclude that the view that the publication of the White Paper on Employment Policy of 1944 can properly be held to be one source of our present troubles, that it might have been better if it had never been published,[25] is, in my opinion, incorrect. The Paper was a cautious statement, promulgated by the famous wartime coalition government, thought out and written by a group of middle-of-the-road economists, accepted by Keynes himself and formulating a way of maintaining rough stability of employment and prices through the manipulation of aggregate demand but also embodying a set of clear warnings of the conditions to be satisfied if adverse reactions, and especially inflation, were to be avoided. The criticisms of the White Paper, therefore, seem to be based either upon ignorance of what was in the White Paper (which I suspect has frequently been the case) or a misunderstanding of its meaning.

IV

It is one of the most remarkable events in recent economic history that between 1946 and 1970 the conditions which might have called for the introduction of the programmes prepared in the White Paper never appeared. In those years unemployment in the United Kingdom only once rose above 3 per cent and in 15 of these years it was 2 per cent or less. In that period the number of persons employed never changed by more than 2 per cent between one year and another. We had, unexpectedly, been blessed with a period of high and stable employment.

Many conflicting ideas have been advanced to explain the almost startling contrast between conditions prevailing between the two world wars and those during 1946–70. Although much maligned for it at the time, Mr Macmillan was certainly right when he protested in the 60s 'we have never had it so good'. Each and every theory for this happy state of affairs advanced by one expert has been challenged by another of equal eminence.[26]

V

When in 1970 unemployment began to rise and was to reach 5 per cent in 1975, successive governments ignored or defined the warnings laid down in the White Paper, and, in fact, produced the very evils of inflation and more unemployment against which Lord Woolton and his servants had been warning more than 30 years earlier.

1. Attempts to spend a way out of unemployment were made while unemployment rates were still far too low for so-called 'demand management' to have any effect. Indeed the level of unemployment below which public spending was likely to produce beneficial results was probably higher than had been thought in 1944, because of social and economic changes likely to increase normal rates of unemployment. For, in the interim, more generous provision for the unemployed had considerably narrowed the margin between the income of an employed and an unemployed person, and thus reduced the concern of the average man to keep his job, to find another when unemployed or to accept a fall in earnings in order to get back into work.

2. Over the years Governments have bundled together different types of 'unemployment' and thus attributed unfounded meanings to figures of total unemployment. Mr John Wood, in his two important papers 'How Much Unemployment', 1972, and 'How Little Unemployment', 1975, has performed a national service in analysing the official unemployment figures and revealing their many weaknesses. As he says:

The unimaginative presentation and misleading use of statistics about unemployment must bear a large responsibility for the appalling mismanagement of the British economy since the end of the war.

Perhaps the most perverse attitude of government has been grossly to neglect the collection of reliable and comprehensive figures of job vacancies, and to continue to publish figures of vacancies which, admittedly, were perhaps only one-third or one-quarter of the correct total. To seek to maintain a balance in the field of employment by using unemployment figures which were excessive and vacancy figures which were gross underestimates must be one of the most remarkably clumsy government exercises in economic management of all time.

3. The mobility of labour has been impeded by governments in many ways. With the rents of council houses below the market rate and complete security of tenure, workers become reluctant to move. The system of redundancy payments; extensive legislation for 'protecting' workers; higher national insurance contributions as additional costs upon employment; the rigid enforcement of equality between the wages of men and women; the erosion of differentials under incomes policies: all these measures have slowed down the process by which workers move from jobs where they are less needed to jobs where they are more needed.

4. Ernest Bevin, when rather proudly introducing the White Paper to the House of Commons on 21 June 1944, said that, with a high and stable level of employment, 'The general level of wages ought to be related to productivity'. This injunction has been ignored. Between 1970 and 1975 output per person in industry increased by less than 10 per cent; average earnings by about 130 per cent and labour costs per unit of output by about 100 per cent. The increased militancy of the trade unions has been fostered by the practice of providing from public funds supplementary benefits for the families of strikers and by the introduction of so-called 'productivity agreements' which amounted merely to increases in earnings. In the two industries where trade union power was used to greatest effect to increase wages – coalmining and production of motor vehicles – output per head lagged most.

5. The White Paper had stressed the need to recognise 'structural unemployment' and, where it was discerned, to accept the inevitable and provide all possible government help to expedite change by retraining labour, facilitating transfers and so on. Instead, however, governments have sought to bolster up industries revealing obvious signs of decay and have, therefore, been forced to place heavier burdens on firms and industries showing greater promise of viability and expansion.

6. The White Paper recognised that exports, however important, will always be one of the great uncertainties in our national accounts whereas, today, governments place unfounded confidence in the in-

crease and stability of the export trade for maintaining employment.

If blame has to be attached for the continuing obsession with 'full employment' since the war and for the intellectual ideas which have mis-directed governments into paths leading inevitably to inflation, then the fault should lie with those, such as Beveridge and his colleagues, in their insistence that maintaining employment involved a whole set of fresh arrangements changing the whole character of the market system, and such bodies as the National Institute of Economic and Social Research, which for many years misinterpreted the statistics of unemployment and vacancies and the mechanics of 'reflation without inflation' and insisted upon its own peculiar social valuations of the relative evils of unemploy-ment and inflation.[27]

VI

This defence of the White Paper, however, also carries with it a warning to the 'monetarists' who, quite properly, have been active in exposing the dangers of 'crude Keynesianism'. For my own part, I accept the view that the supply of money, over which the government possesses the ul-timate power, is the prime determinant of the price level. But the way in which the monetarists present their case and the terms they employ sometimes lead to counter-complaints about 'crude monetarists'.[28] The wiser of the monetarists know that when they speak of 'the natural rate' of unemployment, as the index in terms of which the supply of money should be controlled, they are using a useful concept but one the *quan-titative* meaning of which depends at any one time upon the interaction of a complex set of economic, social and other institutional factors con-stantly varying and incapable of exact measurement. Yet in the more popular writings about monetary policy the impression is being created that, in order to prevent inflation, all that is necessary is for the Govern-ment to determine 'the natural rate' of unemployment and then to fix, perhaps by law, the correspondingly appropriate supply of money and all will be well.[29]

The monetarists will not weaken their (fundamentally powerful) case by giving some ground to those who at present do not go all the way with them. We have all been so taken aback, and still remain perplexed about, what at times has really happened since 1945, that other surprises and novel conditions might be in store for us. It may be that in order to maintain or improve real standards of living and to free ourselves from the social rot which follows from inflation, higher rates of unemploy-ment will have to be tolerated than those normal after 1945 and than those envisaged by the present-day calculators of the 'natural rate'. It may then be that greater emphasis will have to be placed in the search for a high and stable level of employment, on the need for greater mobility and everything that encourages it, and on the dependence of improved earnings upon increased productivity. Then the doctrines of the White Paper would be highly relevant.

NOTES

1. I may perhaps mention 'Second Thoughts on the British White Paper on Employment Policy', a paper read before the 25th Anniversary Meeting of the National Bureau of Economic Research, Washington, DC, 1946 and Chapter IV 'Is Mass Unemployment Inevitable in a Free Economy' in *Ordeal By Planning,* 1948.
2. Sir Dennis Robertson, 1890–1963.
3. Lord Robbins, *Autobiography of an Economist*, p. 188, has said: 'John Jewkes (when still Director of the Economic Section) suggested that a paper should be drawn up in which the lines of practical policy for maintaining a high level of employment should be set forth and this was done with characteristic lucidity and logical force by James Meade'. To which I would only add that James Meade needed little or no encouragement to undertake the task, for that gentle spirit had been roused by the thought of the suffering and waste of unemployment.
4. Later Lord Normanbrook, 1902–65.
5. Lord Redcliffe-Maud.
6. Sir Alexander Johnston.
7. S. G. Gates, 1901–72.
8. It may perhaps be added that the Treasury were responsible for the more slippery sentences, especially as they related to the possibility of even temporarily unbalanced Budgets.
9. Lord Waverley, 1882–1958.
10. Lord Robbins.
11. Professor James Meade.
12. Mr Stanley R. Dennison, Vice-Chancellor of the University of Hull.
13. Mr John Marcus Fleming of the International Monetary Fund.
14. Mr Ronald C. Tress, Master of Birbeck College, University of London.
15. Sir Hubert Henderson, 1890–1952. Henderson was, as it seemed to me, suspicious of the White Paper. He was, I think, always wondering what was wrong with the simpler idea of stimulating employment by public works or even by placing public contracts for the manufacture of commodities. I imagine it was his doubts, and their rejection, which led to para. 73 of the White Paper: It might be suggested that the Government should go further and should place orders for consumer goods which are not required for Government use with a view to meeting a temporary deficiency in demand. But ... there would be a risk that Government stocks overhanging the market would create uncertainty and cause traders to reduce or postpone their orders for these goods.
16. Sir Richard Hopkins, 1880–1955, at that time Second Secretary of the Treasury in charge of finance.

17. Although it has to be said that some economists believe that if Keynes had lived longer he might, in the changed circumstances, have been anti-Keynesian. Thus F. A. Hayek, *A Tiger by the Tail*, p. 103, I.E.A. Hobart Paper: 'I have little doubt that we owe much of the post-war inflation to the great influence of ... over-simplified Keynesianism. Not that Keynes himself would have approved of this. Indeed, I am fairly certain that, if he had lived, he would in that period have been one of the most determined fighters against inflation.'

18. It has to be confessed, as Beveridge pointed out later, that the term 'full employment' does actually occur in two places in the White Paper although in neither case was it related to any 'commitment' on the part of the government. Even so, I cannot imagine how these words slipped in under the eagle eye of Lord Woolton, Robbins and, I may perhaps add, myself.

19. On 21 June 1944 Ernest Bevin introduced the White Paper in the House of Commons. On 22 June *The Times* leader on the subject was already talking of a commitment to 'full employment'.

20. The White Paper, para. 24: 'It will not be enough to rely upon the general maintenance of purchasing power to solve all the problems of local unemployment'.

21. Beveridge was oddly possessive about *his* employment policy. In his book he made an attack on an earlier interesting private document 'The Problem of Unemployment' issued by Unilever Ltd; a document much nearer in spirit to the White Paper and equally prophetic in the warnings about the dangers of too optimistic a view of what constituted 'full employment'.

22. The White Paper, para. 54:
The principle of stability means that increases in the general level of wage rates must be related to increased productivity due to increased efficiency and effort.

23. The White Paper, para. 56:
If an expansion of total expenditure were applied to cure unemployment of a type due, not to absence of jobs, but a failure of workers to move to places and occupations where they were needed, the policy of the Government would be frustrated and a dangerous rise in prices might follow.

24. Ernest Bevin in the House of Commons, 21 June 1944: 'The White Paper is not a "blue print", and the ownership of industry, public or private, was not prejudiced by it.'

25. Some economists of a later generation have recently taken up the cudgels on behalf of the White Paper. Mr John Wood ('How Little Unemployment', p. 61) has said: 'We are really back to the now much maligned White Paper on Employment Policy of 1944, which anticipated many of these difficulties and warned us against the traps into which we have so eagerly fallen'.
And Mr Peter Jay ('Inflation: Causes, Consequences, Cures', IEA Readings, 14, pp. 108, 109): 'The dangers (of ignoring the appropriate warnings) were fully appreciated and carefully spelled out in the wartime Coalition Government's Employment Policy of May 1944'.

26. Sir John Hicks, *The Crisis in Keynesian Economics*, p. 3, confesses that he cannot answer the question: 'That is a major question, one of the largest questions for which the world is at present confronted ... I do not suppose that I am able to answer it' although he has put forward some rather unconvincing efforts to provide an answer. R. G. O. Matthews, in his article 'Why Has

Britain had Full Employment since the War?', *Economic Journal,* September 1968, argued that the low unemployment was not to be attributed to deficit financing by government, the main cause being a high level of investment, especially private investment and exports.

But G. B. Stafford, 'Full Employment Since the War: Comment', *Economic Journal*, March 1970, using much the same material, reached the opposite conclusion: that the boom was due to an increase in public expenditure.

27. See 'Short-Term Forecasting: A Case Study' by George Polanyi, I.E.A. Background Memorandum 4.

28. Hicks, in 'Crisis '75?', I.E.A. Occasional Paper Special 43, has declared bluntly although, in my opinion, mistakenly: 'The first thing that needs to be said about our present troubles is that they are not of a monetary character, and are not to be cured by monetary means.'

29. I confess I was rather taken aback when Professor David Laidlaw, ('Unemployment v. Inflation', I.E.A. Occasional Paper 44, pp. 42, 45) in a paper of otherwise impeccable theoretical reasoning, suddenly revealed his own social valuation that a 5 per cent unemployment rate by 1980 would be 'too much unemployment for too long', and his mention that research in his own department suggests that 'the natural rate' of unemployment in Britain 'is perhaps a little less than 2%, although such an estimate is necessarily subject to a wide margin of error'. Of course everything turns on how wide is wide. But my own feeling would be that, given the kind of Chancellors of the Exchequer we are likely to have in the next few years, to mention to them 'a natural rate' of 2 per cent would be a sure signpost to hyper-inflation.

4 THE GOVERNMENT AND PLANNING

The Perils of Planning*

If ever the history of economic hallucinations comes to be written, the idea that governments possess the knowledge and power positively to determine the rate of economic growth through the technique of central economic planning will be revealed as one of the most widespread, tenacious and harmful of errors. In the long term, experience will doubtless make this clear; in the interim, the damage likely to be done by it may be considerable, depending upon the scale on which the fallacy gains a hold over public opinion and the persistency of the designers and operators of the economic plan in the face of failure. Some tragic cases immediately come to mind. The present parlous economic condition of India is attributable in no small degree to government planning which has led to massive misdirection of resources into grandiose schemes for capital investment, to the relative neglect of the primary task of food production, to the erosion of international reserves and the dependance of India each year upon the charitable whims of the West. In Russia, such planning has, since 1917, been enforced at untold cost in the shape of human freedom and now, after half a century of economic vicissitudes, Russia is generally recognised as a country still of low general standards of living.

In western countries, with their better informed public opinion and free comment, matters are not likely to reach such a pass. Even here, however, wrong economic ideas may result in loss and disillusionment which were better avoided. And in Britain particularly, in my opinion, we are now in danger of economic decline not so much because of incompetent management, lazy workers, lethargic salesmen, unimaginative technologists or unequipped scientists, but much more because successive Governments have in recent years naïvely aspired to determine our general standard of living although lacking the knowledge or the competence to do so.

It is fortunate that this subject can now be discussed without reference to politics or personalities. It was a Labour government which, in 1945, gave Britain its first peace-time experience of central economic

*The *Three Banks Review*, June 1965.

planning; an experiment in which aims and methods were so grotesquely unrelated and the failure so complete that no one ever now refers to it. It was a Conservative government which, in 1962, set out upon the second course of central planning and no one, least of all those who initiated it, is prepared to claim it as a success. It is a Labour government which is, at the time of writing, engaged upon a third effort in the same direction, with new groups of planners, new committees and new words for very old ideas. It is well to remember that it was not organised Labour in 1962 which was pressing most strongly for central planning; it was British business men through their Federations. It has been suggested that this melancholy record over the past 20 years in itself should relieve us of anxiety. Will not time itself quickly check these aberrations of thought? Where the impossible is being attempted, can any harm arise except to those foolish enough to waste their time on hopeless quests? I cannot help but feel that this attitude is escapist. For if, as I shall try to show later, central planning does positive harm, then the sooner it is checked the better. Beyond that, it is by no means certain that, in the future, the failure of central planning will so readily lead to its abandonment as in earlier days. Vested interests are now growing up around it. The careers of many public servants depend upon its continuance. Many economists have reached the conclusion that the only function of their science is to improve the methods by which governments can enlarge their activities and take a stronger grip upon the economy. The road back from central economic planning may not be so easy as in the past.

There is one thought that should be ever-present in any discussion of the part that the State can play in encouraging economic growth. It is the simple, central and, to my mind, unchallengeable fact that whilst the various forces and conditions which are more or less intimately associated with economic growth can be listed, yet there is not (and it may be there never can be) any adequate understanding of the exact way in which these forces act together to bring about the results observable after the event. Of course it is known that the scale of investment, the rate of innovation, the level of knowledge, the skill of the workman, the ability of the entrepreneur, the level of demand and many other major or minor factors will help to determine whether a country is to be rich or poor. But to assume that those who draw up such a list have thereby equipped themselves with the power systematically to determine or even sensibly to influence the rate of economic growth is as grave an oversimplification as it would be to list the different parts of the human body and then assume that the secret of human life itself had been revealed.

The intellectual error that in the economic system are to be found certain key points at which governments can bring pressure to bear and thereby determine economic growth has led to much waste and confusion in recent years. For example, in many undeveloped, and in some

not so undeveloped, countries public policy has been based on the principle that there was a well-established and reasonably reliable connection between the scale of investment and output and that to increase the
former might fairly confidently be expected to produce an expansion of
the latter. But the work of Colin Clark and others has shown that the
theory based on the capital–output ratio is something of a myth, that the
ratio varies from time to time and country to country, that to press on
with investment when other conditions are not favourable can be a potent
cause of waste. There was a phase, through which we have perhaps not
yet finally passed, during which it was believed that expenditure on
scientific research was the vital clue to expansion. But, unfortunately for
this thesis, the two countries which have spent most, proportionately, on
science – the United States and Great Britain – have in recent years
shown the slowest rates of industrial growth. More recently, the secret
has been thought to reside in the scale of expenditure on education and
some pretty rickety statistical correlations have been appealed to in support of this idea. But even those who fully accept the social and cultural
case for wider and better education, ought not to conceal from
themselves the possibility that, after a point, further education may
render the individual less competent, or less interested in, those activities which will increase the national income. Education not merely
changes the power of people to do different things, it may also change
their views as to what is worth while doing. Some economic luminaries
have sought to establish, through international studies, that the
maintenance of a very high level of demand pressing constantly upon
existing resources accounts for economic success. But when they turn to
the case of Britain, where the pressure of demand has been more consistently maintained since 1945 than possibly in any other major western
country, a striking exception to this doctrine is found.

Great devotion, enormous energy and almost endless ingenuity have
been shown by economists in recent years in their efforts to solve the
riddle of economic growth. This is all to the good and does much credit
to the profession always provided it is recognised that, as in any other
science, about 95 per cent of the hypotheses will prove to be without
foundation. The standards of living of whole communities are too important to be entrusted to the latest untried ideas of back-room boys
fascinated by the elegance of their latest economic models or to
politicians feigning powers of controlling economic affairs.

This article, however, is mainly concerned with another device for
stimulating economic growth. As employed in Britain in recent years it
falls into three stages. First, some general rate of growth for the whole
economy is fixed upon. Then the implications of this general growth are
worked out: for example, what rate of growth of exports or imports is
consistent with the general figure. Then, if it appears that some of the
implications are not likely to be achieved, special efforts may be made to

bring about at these points a better performance than would otherwise be expected. Now at each one of these stages the government may make mistakes. It may fix upon a general rate of growth higher than is really attainable (it must always fix a rate higher than it thinks could be attained in the absence of a central economic plan, otherwise there would be no point in going to the trouble of preparing such a plan). Or it may make mistakes in working out the implications of the general rate; in which case its own actions may contribute to a surplus of some goods or lead to a shortage of others which, in itself, will endanger the achievement of the general rate of growth. Or it may miscalculate the possibility of improving performance at the point where the implications seem to demand it, in which case once again the general rate will not be achieved. But errors at the second and third stages, although by no means to be ruled out, are perhaps less likely than at the first crucial stage and what happens at this stage can conveniently be studied in the light of experience in Britain since 1962 under first a Conservative and then a Labour government.

When in 1962 the Conservative government set forth its first five-year economic plan, it declared that this was centred on an annual average rate of growth in the economy of 4 per cent. Those most closely associated with the design and the carrying out of the plan declared that this procedure amounted to a revolution in thought, based upon what was described as the 'dynamic concept of change'. But, despite these sweeping claims, the nature, purpose and function of this figure of 4 per cent has always remained shrouded in mystery. What is meant by the figure? Was it an increase which it was thought would occur; or was hoped would occur; or was feared would not be achieved unless the Government itself engaged in these special measures? In the early days of 1962, the National Economic Development Council would go no further than to say that 'the implications of a 4 per cent rate of growth should be studied'. Later, we were informed that 'Britain's economic policy is geared to a 4 per cent rate of growth'. Clearly, unless the choice of one figure rather than another was a wholly capricious act and the study of its implications a matter of idle curiosity, it ought to have been possible to describe the peculiar significance of this figure. But this was never done. In fact, it came to be widely accepted that this rate of growth could be achieved, would be achieved and should be generally accepted by everybody in the community as what would occur.

The choice of the figure of 4 per cent seems to have been oddly arbitrary and unscientific. It represented a rate of growth half as fast again as that which had occurred in the United Kingdom in the 1950s and twice as fast as the average for the first half of this century. Why then was a figure chosen which was so out of line with past experience? Could any new factors be pointed to which were likely to make history in these matters irrelevant? Nothing of that kind was indicated by the Government. A further mystery was that apparently it did not matter whether the central economic plan was wrong or right in this respect. For as the Director-General of NEDC put it

> Deviations will occur and it does not reduce the value of forward assessments that market conditions may produce results different from those expected. An examination of the reasons for the difference between the result and the expectation can be of great value in helping to overcome difficulties.

The forward assessments must either have had some influence or no influence on the action of people. If they had no influence, could there be any purpose in the plan? If they had some influence, would the existence of an incorrect forward assessment not have tended to lead people to behave in a wrong way and thus contributed to economic distortion?

In fact, as we now know, the 4 per cent increase was not achieved and had fallen into disrepute by the time of the Conservative Party lost power. This plan had covered a period which had seen a most serious balance of payments crisis; yet the plan had given no indication that this was likely to happen.

Strictly speaking, it is not possible to say that the economic planning of the Conservative Government failed since, in the absence of any clear-cut idea of what purpose the plan was intended to serve, no obvious test of success or failure presents itself. But it can at least be said that the plan was abortive in the sense that it proved to be out of step with reality. If the plan, however, had done no positive harm little more would need to be said about it. But, to my mind, the plan can be held to have been harmful, to have contributed to the economic troubles of 1963 and 1964, in three ways:

1. It led the trade unions, naturally enough, to think in terms of bigger annual wage increases than were consistent, without creating inflation, with the actual growth of the economy.

2. It led to the uncritical acceptance of bigger increases in the scale of government expenditure, especially in the social services, than would have gone unchallenged if it could have been known, before the event, that the 4 per cent figure would not in fact be achieved.

3. Whilst it is probably true that the vast majority of business men did not, as a consequence of the promulgation of the 4 per cent annual rate of increase, do anything different from what they otherwise would have done, it seems more than likely that certain public and semi-public institutions, searching for grounds on which to base their claims to expansion, seized upon the 4 per cent figure in order to plan rates of growth for themselves larger than would have been justified by a less sanguine

view of the national economic future. This was especially the case with electricity and coal.

When the Labour Party came into power the Conservative economic plan was scrapped. New and more elaborate administrative machinery for economic planning was created. The Government declared their intention of issuing, as soon as possible, a new plan. But, subject to the one qualification mentioned below, no new plan has yet been presented to the public. The intention seems to be that a new final economic plan will be presented in the 'late summer or the autumn'. On these more recent events, therefore, it is possible only to make general comments.

1. The nation presumably is to be without a published plan for nearly a year, from October 1964 to the 'late summer or autumn' of 1965. But if the country can carry on for such a long period without a plan, does this not throw doubt upon the need for it at all?

2. The qualification to be made to this first point is that, early in February 1965, Mr Brown suggested that 'we should aim at 25 per cent growth in national product by the year 1970'. At that time he deprecated the breaking down of this long-period figure into annual targets but he did point out, what indeed is the simple arithmetic of the matter, that since 25 per cent in five years represents on average about 4¼ per cent each year and since growth at the present time is running at less than 4 per cent, his figure of 25 per cent implied that towards the end of 1970 annual rate of growth would be in excess of 4¼ per cent. Another straw in the wind is that, on 22 February, Mr Callaghan announced that, up to 1970, the Government intended to increase public expenditure by 4¼ per cent per annum. What can be deduced from all this? It appears that the present Government is beginning to doubt the value to industry of annual figures of predicted growth. That would be a move towards realism. But if the future over a relatively short period cannot be predicted with confidence, on what grounds can it be assumed that predictions will be safer over a much longer period? Surely over the longer period the chance will be greater of important unsuspected elements exercising an influence upon events. Again, whilst it appears that the present Government is disposed to deny some of the virtues claimed for economic planning by the preceding Conservative Government, nevertheless Mr Brown, in the form in which he has already presented his statistics, is exposing national economic policy to the more serious dangers inherent in this device for attempting to stimulate economic growth. Once the figure of a 25 per cent increase in five years has passed into the currency of economic talk, then the belief has been generated that there will be more jam tomorrow than there is today. Under those circumstances it is perfectly reasonable for all those who stand to gain by the prevalence of this belief to take full advantage of it.

Trade union organisations, in making long period agreements, would be foolish if they did not do so. And, as mentioned above, already the Government has committed itself to a 4¼ per cent increase in public expenditure so that if national production does not rise at this average rate, then the proportion of public expenditure to national income will steadily increase.

3. Suppose the 4¼ per cent annual rate of increase up to 1970 does not happen? If in fact it is too high it will have helped to build inflation into the economic system. If, on the other hand, too low a target has been fixed, then it may well result in a standard of living less favourable than might otherwise have been possible.

4. One ominous reaction, which might well have been foreseen, of the use of this planning device is that the exercise may cease to be an effort rationally to examine the economic system and its potentialities and become more of a field for political manoeuvring. For if the Conservative Government offered the country a 4 per cent annual rate of increase, even though they failed in their aim, is it not likely that the public will regard the offer of anything less than 4 per cent by the present Government as something of a confession of failure? Already cynical observers of the present scheme, who regard a 4 per cent rate of increase as beyond the national capacity, are beginning to feel a morbid fasincation in watching what will happen when the party in power finds it politically impossible to withdraw from a position which is economically untenable. This is perhaps the most dispiriting consequence of this kind of economic experimentation. It is launched with the claim to be a revolutionary and more scientific approach to the handling of economic affairs and it gradually degenerates into the defence of myths and into political casuistry.

The moral to be drawn is not complicated; nor is it dependent upon complex and highly sophisticated economic analysis. It is simply that the cure for bad planning of this type is not better planning but no planning. The prospects of improvements in the standard of living of the people will be more favourable if we drop the belief that, by thinking of numbers, we can do much to improve our lot. The wiser course for any government to follow is to do whatever it can to create a general environment conducive to growth and then leave the rate of growth to settle itself, recognising that this is a highly unpredictable world and that to tie oneself to one figure is likely to be more embarrassing than helpful.

Of course it will be objected that such an attitude is negative and outmoded, that not to accept economic planning is to reject a purposive and coherent design enabling men to be masters of their destiny in favour of a neutralist, not to say nihilist, conception of the working of the economic machine. Nothing, however, could be further from the truth. Does anyone really believe that in Britain the period 1962–65, with its economic bolts from the blue and the babble of conflicting theories about the cause of economic growth, was one of purposive and coherent economic planning?

There are, indeed, many ways in which governments, and governments alone, can help to build up a vigorous, flexible and resilient economic system. Unfortunately, in most of these tasks they will be obstructed, if not wholly frustrated, by the practices of economic planning. It is, for example, accepted in all quarters in Britain that more competition in industry would work to the general benefit. What does competition involve? It means that each and every firm must be prepared to back its own view of future market possibilities, to take the risks of making mistakes, to be sanguine about the chances of outstripping its competitors. How can this happen if, under economic planning, the firms in an industry are being encouraged to think of policies in common, especially of investment policies, and are expected to follow the guiding lines laid down from above about the chances of expansion?

Again, whilst governments may not be particularly effective in initiating and stimulating economic change and innovation, yet they have a crucial role to play in facilitating such change and in mitigating the pains associated with it. This calls for active public intervention in the collection and publishing of statistical and other forms of information, in retraining of workers, in meeting the costs of transfer, in encouraging mobility, in providing promptly the public services and especially the communications which are needed for each unexpected change of direction in industrial expansion. But can a government devote itself wholeheartedly to the service of the community in these ways unless it takes for granted the fact that needs will be constantly changing in a world perpetually in transition? And is not this interpretation of the world around us wholly at variance with the doctrine that a government can predict, or can control, or can in detail determine, the future course of economic events?

Variety Among the Planners*

In an economy where the functions of the State are limited economic relations are impersonal and individual decisions are made by reference to a framework of prices. A mechanism of this kind cannot be substantially influenced by any one individual. Its study is in the nature of a science. In a community subject to an 'overall economic plan' economic analysis is more diffuse and less scientific. An overall plan implies that, in the last resort, one man, or a few, make the decisions for the many. The personal opinions, idiosyncrasies or even prejudices of the supreme planners may then become of great importance in determining the form and purpose of the economic system. There may be many different suggested plans since planners tend to be strongly individualistic.[1] The varying conceptions of the overall plan may thus lead, particularly in the early stages of its development, to significant conflicts of ideas. The objective study of this important social process is, perhaps, not primarily work for the economist. It would seem to be more properly the task of the student of administration or of the psychologist. The economist may, however, be able to make some minor contribution. In this article an examination is made of the recent utterances of public men regarding the overall plan to which the British economy is now being subjected. The purpose is to try to make a rough classification of contemporaneous views of overall planning in order to open out the field for later workers. The article, of course, does not concern itself with the merits or demerits of overall planning as such.

There seems little doubt that the members of the British Government believe that they have created, or are in the process of creating, a centrally planned economy. They frequently speak of the social and economic revolution through which we are passing. They contrast the British type of economy with that found in the United States. Mr Attlee has put this point beyond doubt by his declaration that 'in matters of economic planning we agree with Soviet Russia'.[2]

The Manchester School, 1947.

I

Perhaps the most important question to ask about an overall plan is this: does it express a purpose, something which the planners intend to make happen? Or is it something far less substantial than that, an estimate of what might happen, a prayer for what ought to happen? The fundamental difference between these two approaches has been well put by Monsieur Stalin.[3] 'Admittedly they (i.e. under the capitalistic system) too have something akin to plans. But these plans are prognosis, guess plans which bind nobody, and on the basis of which it is impossible to direct a country's economy. Things are different with us. Our plans are not prognosis, guess plans, but *instructions* which are *compulsory* for all managements and which determine the future course of the economic development of our *entire* country. You see that this implies a difference of principle'. Into which group does the British plan fall?

Although a close examination of their own words suggest that there are very subtle, not to say perplexing, nuances between the ideas of the supreme planners, at least six main conflicting strands of thought are to be discerned in current discussions. This classification cannot, of course, be watertight: some ministers, indeed, seem to belong to more than one group. In any case, the vocabulary of planning has now become so opulent and varied as almost to defy the efforts of the neat cataloguer.

PLANNING WITH A PURPOSE

There are first the planners with a purpose. They believe, with Monsieur Stalin, that men are masters of their economic environment, that they can lay down in advance what should happen and then proceed to make it happen. Sir Stafford Cripps is perhaps the leading figure in this group. He has said[4] 'I was delighted with the general measure of agreement that we should plan, and having a plan that we should try to carry out the plan'. He is anxious to follow the Russian model and get the kind of results achieved in Russia although, of course, he would not wish to use the hideous suppression of human rights which have been employed in the Soviet Union. He has said[5]

The truth is that we as a Government and as a nation, have set out upon what most of us always realised was a new and difficult task: we are attempting, without the extreme compulsions of totalitarianism, to plan and organise our production so as to give a higher and more equal standard of life to our people. The fact that we do not apply extreme compulsions means that it will take rather longer, but the delay is, in our view, well worth while if we preserve our democratic freedom as we are determined to do.

It is to be noted that this sort of planned economy leaves one very important question unanswered. What is to happen if we fail in the difficult task? Will we scrap the policy of overall planning or will we get rid of democratic freedom?

The significant point about planning with a purpose is that, once the plan has been set, then the supreme planners tend to fall into the frame of mind in which they are prepared to make any 'sacrifice', or more exactly force any 'sacrifice' on others, in order to achieve the plan. So that a plan laid out for promoting the interests of the consumers often leads to the deliberate and implacable sacrifice of those interests. This could only be regarded as logical if the attainment of the plan, independently of the economic consequences of fulfilling the plan, were regarded as an end in itself. Broadly speaking, any plan with calls for 'sacrifices' should be subject to suspicion since the purpose of a plan (except perhaps in the case of war or threatened war) should be to lessen sacrifices and not increase them. A very pertinent illustration of this point is provided by the recent compaign to raise our exports to 75 per cent over pre-war levels. That figure saw the light of day as a rough estimate of the export target we must reach if we were to enjoy the pre-war standard of living. But in the minds of the planners with a purpose it is rapidly becoming a target to be reached for its own sake even if, in order to attain it, we have to cut down our standard of living below the level it might reach with a lower level of exports. A close analogy would be that of a relieving force which sets out to bring food supplies to a besieged and starving garrison. The relieving force meets unexpected difficulties and is compelled to consume both its own food and that intended for the garrison. But with blind courage the relieving force presses forward and gloriously reaches its objective but only, of course, to add to the sufferings of the garrison by increasing the number of people to be maintained on the garrison's depleted resources.

GUESS PLANNING

The second group of planners, to employ Monsieur Stalin's phrase, are the guess planners.[6] They recognise that events will be determined by forces at least partly outside their control. They are interested in what is likely to happen in the future but they recognise the fallibility of economic forecasting. Mr Attlee himself seems to fall into this group. He has said 'although we may have to plan without having all the data, it is better than having no plan at all. We must make some kind of economic forecast'.[7] So long as the guess planners do nothing which binds anyone, their activities are of no great significance. But the state of being a guess planner seems to be a highly transitional one. For if their prognosis is a gloomy one the guess planners are easily led on to try to avoid by positive action what they believe, rightly or wrongly, they see in the future. If their prognosis is favourable they will be tempted to try to bring about the desirable conditions much earlier than they could normally be expected. Indeed it seems to be a generaly working rule among many planners: 'find out what is going to happen and then make it happen more quickly'. In both cases guess planning is transmuted into planning with a purpose.

FLEXIBLE PLANNING

The third group are the flexible planners. They attach great importance to keeping the plan so flexible and altering it so swiftly that reality will never falsify the plan. Thus Mr Dalton has said[8] 'These plans must not be mere essays. They must be consistent with practical possibilities. They must not be too rigid or hidebound. They must be capable of continuous adjustment in the light of changing conditions. We shall never be able to sit back as some planners imagine and close our eyes and let the plan take charge, like one of the automatic pilots in an aeroplane . . . Eternal vigilance is the price of successful planning'. This type of planner may easily become a menace to logical thought because, if he is successful in changing his plans sufficiently quickly to fit the facts, then he comes to believe that he is controlling the economic system when he is really controlling only the statistics in his own plan. This wastes effort just as it would be wasted by a man who took great pains to keep his watch scrupulously correct so that the movements of the sun should not be held up.

OPPORTUNIST PLANNING

Fourthly there is a group which may be described as opportunist planners who, whilst continuing to claim merits for the overall plan, would use the plan sporadically, dodging in with the plan from time to time and from place to place as opportunity suggested. Mr Bevan is perhaps the chief exponent of this technique. In dealing with the building of houses he has expressed himself strongly against the use of 'programmes'. On various occasions he has said: 'I am not going to do any crystal gazing. We have had too many programmes. It is time we had houses'.[9] 'I refuse to give a target because I am content rather to rest upon performance than promise'.[10] The people of this country do not want promises which can only be based on guesswork . . . Long-term national targets in the form of figures give no psychological stimulus'.[11] This form of planning must be very attractive to Ministers who have a specific administrative task to carry through. If there is no target they cannot then be challenged on their achievements. One refinement of this method is to plan all the resources which go to the making of the final commodity but not to plan the output of the final commodity itself. Thus Mr Bevan: 'The Government hoped to be able to produce at the end of each month . . . a full statement of the production of building materials . . . Having provided the industry with the materials the labour and the contracts, it would be the responsibility of the builders to answer the critics . . . It would then no longer be the Government who would be the Aunt Sally—it would be the industry'.[12]

PLANNING THROUGH DISLOCATION

There is, fifthly, a group of thinkers who would appear to push opportunism to the point at which they deny the very purpose of the overall plan. Whatever disagreement there may be on other points, most people would consider it axiomatic that an overall plan should strive so to distribute national resources that the efforts of the different co-ordinated pieces of the system would fit snugly together. The different flows of raw materials, labour and capacity should be adjusted so that the pre-determined flow of consumers goods should issue without stoppages or wastage at any point. But some planners seem positively to welcome the waste of 'bottlenecks' (i.e. of shortages of supply of one thing in relation to others) and indeed to consider that the plan makes this inevitable. Thus Mr Morrison addressing the Labour Party Regional Council at Leeds on 30 November, speaking of the many bottlenecks in the economic system, said 'it is not at all my view that this array of bottlenecks is a cause for gloom or discouragement. On the contrary, the fact that we see so many bottlenecks is evidence that we are expanding our economy. Let us be realistic and recognise these bottlenecks not as reasons for alarm and inertia but as challenges to our resource and initiative . . . In a full employment world where the bad old practice of wasting plant and labour and materials is frowned upon, we must expect that the higher level of demand and the fuller use of resources will constantly thrust this bottleneck problem upon us'. But if, as is indicated above, 'the bottleneck problem' is simply the problem of having to waste one lot of resources because they have not been properly matched in the plan with other sets of resources then it would seem that there is little to choose between the bad old world and the brave new world.[13]

This point can perhaps be made clearer by taking a parallel case in an ordinary business. If a business man planned his production, acquired his labour, machines and raw materials and then discovered that, unfortunately, he could not operate because he had forgotten to acquire a supply of lubricating oil, we should naturally consider this as a breakdown of planning. Any attempt at robust blustering on his part that 'this kind of thing is inevitable' would properly be looked upon as pure make-believe. But when national overall planners make such mistakes we are expected to welcome the dislocation as evidence of the expansionist tempo.

There is a second point in Mr Morrison's statement which seems to defy the principles of elementary economic logic. A 'bottleneck' is the item which ultimately is holding up everything else. That is to say there cannot be several bottlenecks simultaneously because there cannot be several items all in shortest supply at the same time. A man who is mixing mortar cannot be shortest of cement and sand at at the same time. When Mr Morrison speaks of simultaneous bottlenecks in manpower of all kinds, raw materials, coal, electricity and gas, he can only mean either one of two things. Either that the plan has been drawn up in defiance of the facts upon which the plan should have been based, that the plan is far too large to be carried out. Or that whilst there is an adequate supply in total of (say) raw materials they have been distributed to the wrong points, i.e. that the distribution side of the plan has broken down. In neither case does there appear to be cause for self-congratulation.

FREE PLANNING

Sixthly, there is a group perhaps best described as free planners, partly because they contemplate the possibility that the plan may leave room for some private enterprise, partly because they intend that the plan should be approved by the whole community, partly because they emphasise the need for planning for 'freedom'. Mr Morrison, for example, has said that: 'if only nationalization will secure the results required then we must nationalize. But if private enterprise can do it, well then let private enterprise remain'. 'We in Britain stand for free planning and in planning for freedom'.[14] This is strangely at variance with the views of those planners who squarely recognise that planning involves a risk to freedom but think the risk worth taking. It will be interesting to watch the elaboration of the technique of planning for freedom. Clearly it is still in an embryonic state.[15]

II

Another main bone of contention between the planners is the form that the plan should take. Most planners think of it as a very large document (similar to the fat volumes embodying the various five-year plans of the Soviet Union) which would lay down in detail the output of each commodity and would prescribe the allocations of raw materials, capacity and labour for each specific final commodity. This would go along with a group of *physical controls* exercised by the State which would steer resources into the correct channels. That is to say there should be *a* plan continuously controlled in detail. Sir Stafford Cripps appears to hold this view.[16] 'Our objective is to carry through a planned economy without compulsion of labour. The general idea is that we should use a number of controls in order to guide production into the necessary channels, according to the plan we have formulated. The principal controls will be financial, including price control and taxation, materials control, building control, machinery and exports control'. Sir Stafford, however, seems recently to have been changing his ground somewhat, perhaps because of a growing realisation of the administrative impossibility of co-ordinating a mass of physical controls. On 21 November 1946, he said in the House of Commons: '. . . a great many controls have been removed . . . This process is continually going on and will continue until we have been able to get rid of a great many in the future'. He thought that 'if all these controls were to be removed in the present circumstances, there would be a completely chaotic situation'. It seems, however, that he is putting increasing emphasis on the planning of the distribution of manpower as the fundamental instrument of planning. On the same occasion he said: 'the planning of the choice of products . . . carries with it the planning of the distribution of man-power'. The same idea seems to have been in the mind of Mr Marquand, Parliamentary Secretary to the Board of Trade, who is reported as saying on 29 October 1946: 'there are limits in which detailed State intervention give you no long-term advantage. You can dispense with the intervention of officials so long as you can lay down a broad economic plan'.

To try to carry out an overall plan through the allocation of manpower is to employ the crudest of all weapons of control. For labour control is the most intractible of all the physical controls. No compulsion is to be exercised over labour.[17] How then is the labour to be distributed in the proportions necessary to implement the plan? Sir Stafford Cripps argues that we must 'persuade and induce' labour into the right channels. But how precisely? Differential wages, which most people would regard as the main inducement, he is doubtful about. 'They (the British people) deserve and need reasonable remuneration for their work . . . But beyond that it is good working conditions and team work that will produce the results we want. The idea of an ever rising spiral of inducement wages is one which makes me shudder at the economic consequences that might come'.[18] There seems here a danger that detailed planning through the physical controls may become somewhat flaccid and mean very little more than competition between industries in shortening hours (which might also lead one to shudder); a drive for works' canteens, etc., and vague exhortations to pull together.

If the central plan is to be based on a detailed manpower budget and no labour compulsion is to be tolerated another dilemma immediately arises to which no public answer seems yet to have been given. Is the plan to be based on the labour allocations which the supreme planners regard as ideal? Or is it to be based on labour allocations which are regarded as practicable in view of the 'stickiness' of the labour supply? If the former then the plan becomes a pious aspiration, if the latter, then somebody will have to make an estimate of the probable effect of government propaganda. For example, if the Minister of Supply believes that another 20,000 foundry workers are vitally necessary and he starts a drive to get these workers (without using the incentive of 'inducement-wages') will the plan assume that he will or will not get these workers for the foundries? How are such estimates to be made?

III

Unfortunately, just at the time when Great Birtain is embarking upon an overall plan under the guidance of a group of thinkers who favour *a* plan and the instrument of physical controls for carrying it through, another group, the real intellectuals of the planning movement, are cutting the ground from under the feet of the first by attacking the idea of *a* plan, sometimes on the grounds that it will not work, sometimes because they fear the destruction of democratic liberties in the process. Mr Durbin, for example, has stated quite specifically: 'Planning does not in the least imply the existence of *a* Plan – in the sense of an arbitrary industrial budget which lays down in advance the volume of output for different industries'.[19] Other thinkers in this group, such as Mr Lerner,[20] have swung even further from the old line and would seek to combine the benefits of the capitalist economy and the collectivist economy in a sort of 'mixed' economy. But they all contemplate a system in which the State would make a few major economic decisions and, thence forward, the distribution of production factors would be carried out by a socialist 'pricing system'.

Theoretically, many of the logical and administrative problems bound up with central planning can be avoided by the use of a price system operating within a framework of major economic decisions by the supreme planners. Progressively intricate discussions on this subject are now going on among the economic experts.[21] It is not to be assumed that they have yet reached agreement or that their findings prescribe practical measures for the running of a controlled economy. In particular, they appear to ignore, in their theoretical working models, most formidable problems associated with incentive. But they are all agreed, as far as I can understand them, on two points: first, that the price mechanism must be allowed to operate sufficiently extensively to leave to the individual a great mass of detailed decisions which the old-fashioned planners now in charge in Great Britain would leave to the State; second, that the consumer must be free to distribute his income as he wishes and that the productive system must be free, within the framework of the major economic decisions, to adjust itself to the consumers' wishes. Whether the ingenuity of the academics will ever produce a scheme of thought which will provide a solid basis for practical policy only time can decide. We certainly need not hasten to implement their findings until these have reached a more advanced stage of precision and are more widely accepted.

Even if they ever do reach final agreement their ideas will be obstructed first by the inherent attraction of planning through the physical controls mentioned above and second by an almost pathological dread among many of the older type of planners of the working of the price system.[22] This in itself is causing a great deal of confusion. The two main functions of price movements are to bring about necessary changes in supply and to distribute goods among potential consumers. But Mr Strachey, the Minister of Food, for example, seems to reject both these functions. On 19 August 1946, speaking of the Wheat Agreement with Canada, he is reported as having said 'he had been criticized on the ground that in two or three years the price of wheat might have dropped. Even if there was a great slump in wheat prices again he said, quite frankly, that they could buy from the Canadian farmers too cheaply. If they got their wheat from them at the price of sawdust, the Canadian farmers were ruined, which was not a very nice or fraternal or good thing.' (Incidentally it may be noted that the Ministry of Food has fixed prices for Danish agricultural produce at a level which, the Danes allege, involve losses for the Danish farmers). Mr Strachey further rejects the price mechanism as a device for rationing (without coupons, queues or black markets) the available goods between consumers. In the House of Commons on 18 July 1946, he described a rise in the price of bread as the traditional method of rationing such a commodity. He indignantly rejected the idea that the Government would resort to it. He is reported on 27 October 1946, referring to the varying consumption of meat, eggs, butter and milk by rich and poor people before the war, as saying: 'that was rationing all right for the poor family. It was the most vicious, pernicious, vilely unfair kind of rationing that you can imagine – rationing in which the rich got three times as much as the poor. That is the kind of rationing to which we will never go back.' Now, unless Mr Strachey has in mind a policy of completely equal distribution of income (which it is difficult to imagine is the case in view of government policy regarding the salaries of Ministers, M.P.s, officials of Public Boards, etc.) this must mean that he regards 'rationing by income' as inconsistent with his conception of a planned economy. If this is really correct those who are working on the possibility of a 'socialist price system' are wasting their time.[23]

There is, indeed, a curiously close association, in the minds of many people, between 'overall planning' and equality in the distribution of income. This in itself raises questions which few seem yet to have considered. If income is distributed equally, through what processes will labour be properly disposed over the various industries? If, on the other hand, income is allowed to be unequally distributed what would be the purpose of it if consumers are not permitted to buy unequal quantities of goods?

IV

There are other directions in which British Ministers have not yet achieved the lucidity of thought and singleness of purpose which undoubtedly they are striving for and which is essential if the ordinary citizen is ever to understand what it is he is being asked to approve. There is space here to refer only to two of the most important. Mr Bevan apparently thinks of planning in terms of a technique which no other Minister has mentioned. He prefers to have *two* different plans at one and the same time – a plan built up out of 'programmes' and a plan built up out of 'targets'. 'The building industry was now entitled to receive a clearer picture of its future prospects and he intended to invite the leaders of the industry to meet him and hear what the Government's programme was likely to be. It has been impossible for him in the first year to provide the industry with a target; but there was all the difference in the world between a target and a programme. The industry was entitled to expect from the Government an estimate of the flow of materials it could have in 1947, the number of houses it could build, and an estimate of the labour force that would be available. It would be foolish to regard that as a target because there were a number of things which were still doubtful.'[24] Does this presage a double plan, a plan-within-a-plan? If so, all the problems of the scientific co-ordination of the plans become enormously increased.

There is a similar suggestion that one plan is not enough in Sir Stafford Cripps' speech in the House of Commons on 21 November 1946: 'Planning is, of course, only one part of the general scheme. Side by side with it goes the question of the tackling of those major industrial difficulties which private enterprise has proved itself wholly unable to tackle in the past; such as, for instance, the coal-mining problem, the transport problem, the problem of power and light and heat, and so on.' This seems to mean that 'planning', the nationalisation of industries and the attainment of efficiency are independent things. 'We want to get an integration of partnership between the Government as the overall planners and the employers in industry as the executors of the plan, whether the employers happen to be a national board, as in the case of coal, or private employers, as in the case of cotton.' This suggests that planning and execution are two different things, that a policy is framed and then, only after that, is the attempt made to determine whether it can be carried out. More light is urgently needed on this point since, to the superficial observer, it would appear that the important element in planning has here been omitted and that the relation between thoughts and deeds is being left to the blind ravages of chance.[25]

V

These fundamental confusions about domestic economic policy are naturally leading, particularly among the planners, to anxiety, impatience and criticism and thus are tending to undermine public confidence. It is probable in the past that all economies with an overall plan have suffered in this respect. But in these cases, as Sir Stafford Cripps has rightly observed, their teething troubles have been eased by the employment of 'the extreme compulsions of totalitarianism'. In Germany and Russia it was quite logical and proper, so long as the attainment of an overall plan was regarded as possessing overriding priority, to stifle the critics and murder the recalcitrants. Where free speech and respect for other human rights still obtain, the embarrassments to the establishment of the overall plan may be serious or even decisive. Under such conditions the danger to be feared is that of a growing disillusionment with the overall plan. This disillusionment may be expected to pass through three stages.

First, the more robust believers in planning begin to criticise the existing form of planning and to call for their own particular ideas of planning to be put into operation. This is already beginning. Mr Tanner,[26] the President of the Amalgamated Engineering Union, has advocated an 'Engineering Advisory Board' with a full-time chairman and staff which would have day-to-day contact with departmental officials and provide the closest possible link between those with executive responsibilities and those engaged in the industry whose practical advice and co-operation are indispensable. He went on 'this reciprocity would transform planning from the *present rather vague and academic exercise* [my italics] into a practical technique to get more of the right products in the correct order out of an engineering industry purposefully shaped more fully to meet national requirements.'

Every planner, not at the centre, sees his own industry as the 'basic' industry which should be put right first so that everything else may follow in proper sequence. Mr Tanner says with much point: 'It is because engineering is the basic industry on which almost every other depends, and is the key to successful planning and increased output in a period of re-equipment, that we engineers are so concerned about practical planning for our own industry.' Others, of course, can argue with just as much force and coal-mining or iron and steel,[27] or transport, etc., is the 'basic' industry.

As a consequence, therefore, of the failure of the Government to produce an overall plan which satisfies all the planners, a large crop of planning schemes pour into the centre from the periphery. The sectional planners are anxious to put purpose into the overall plan. From their knowledge of their immediate economic environment they see clearly that, as far as their own section is concerned, the overall plan is defective. They conclude that the first step required is for the Central Government to put their section right and they cannot understand why this should not be proceeded with forthwith. What they do not see is that their sectional plans might well conflict with other sectional plans or with the necessary character of the co-ordinating agency at the centre. On the other hand the central co-ordinating agency is not in a position to chop the sectional plans about in order to make them fit together, partly because it cannot know enough to do so, partly because the number of possible permutations between combinations of sectional schemes is infinitely large. So whilst those at the centre plead patience, those outside cry forward. All this may tend to add to the original confusion.

The second stage of confusion may be expected to take the form of growing clamour of 'Where is the Overall Plan?' The *Economist*[28] has already raised this issue. 'No visible signs of any general plan have appeared but it had been faintly hoped that one might be being made somewhere in the depths of the Cabinet Offices. Now such hopes are dashed and one is brought up once more against the bold fact that the headquarters command are not commanding and that innumerable minor offensives are taking place with no grand strategy.' A group of Labour members tabled on 30 January 1947, a motion that 'a five-year plan should be prepared . . . also plans for each industry . . . to fit into the national plan.'

Once this clamour attains a certain intensity it probably cannot be stilled except by visible and concrete evidence of the existence of the plan. The planners are now out for red meat; they are not likely to be fobbed off with what will appear to them as the somewhat anaemic offer of a Socialist pricing system. At this stage it is, therefore, very likely that a fat planning book must be produced and exhibited if dwindling faiths are to be sustained and revived. The supreme central planners may search for a breathing space to perfect their plans by:

(a) Declaring that the plan cannot be properly formed until much more information has been collected. Thus Sir Stafford Cripps.[20] 'It is no good doing any more to-day because no plan can be any more than an approximation. The statistics do not exist yet.'

(b) Complaining that there is 'a shortage of administrative talent'.

(c) Complaining that some members of the community are trying to obstruct the plan.

(d) Challenging, as has Mr Bevan, the value of having a plan at all 'at this stage'.

Finally, however, the Government must presumably pull out and display the plan. The present Government has promised to do this early in 1947. It will be interesting to see whether this satisfies most planners as a visible, concrete embodiment of the overall national plan.

The third, final stage in the disillusionment may well come in the form of a widespread recognition that there is in fact no overall plan. What happens after that only time can tell. It might well become increasingly believed, as some apparently already believe, that there cannot be a national overall plan in a free society, that it is an administrative impossibility, a contradiction in terms, a will-o'-the-wisp. Or, alternatively, a more determined effort might be made to create and impose an overall plan. For where the concept of overall planning has taken possession of an individual, the apparent failure of an overall plan will always be attributed either to the fact that the planning was 'bad' in the past and must be made 'good' in the future, or to the fact that the planning was not really extensive enough and must be made even more 'overall' or, more simply, to the fact that sabotage is prevalent and can no longer be tolerated. If this view gains the day we would expect more of the limited supply of the nation's economic intelligence to be drawn into the Civil Service, more time to be devoted by ministers and civil servants to the task of making the plan, more powers to be taken by the State to bring the various elements of the community into line with the plan, more emphasis placed upon producing what it is decided to produce with less regard for the needs of the consumers (at least of the consumers in the home market). It is then that the social scientist would have the interesting task of watching the tug-of-war between the alleged advantages of an overall plan and the claims for elementary liberties for the individual.

NOTES

1. Planners often complain that their opponents are discussing not their kind of planning but somebody else's. Mr Durbin, in the *Economic Journal*, December 1945, takes Professor Hayek to task because the Professor bases his understanding of 'economic planning' only upon modern references to

students of government and sociology and such socialist economists as
Marx, Engels, Shaw and the Webbs and ignores the writings of 'those of us
who are now both practicing economists and also socialists'.

2. House of Commons, 18 November 1946.
3. Quoted from Baykov, *Soviet Economic System*, p. 424.
4. House of Commons, 26 February 1946.
5. House of Commons, 21 November 1946.
6. Some authorities prefer to describe this as 'wish' planning or even 'dream'
   planning. Actually the most striking cases of wishful thinking are found not
   in Great Britain but in other countries. Thus in the French 'Monnet' Plan
   enormous increases in productivity per head are wished into the plan. The
   Czechoslovakian plan is based upon the unlikely assumption that very large
   foreign loans will be available. A recent interesting case of 'wish' planning
   in Great Britain was revealed when Sir Stafford Cripps announced on 13
   January 1947, that the allocations of coal to industries would be roughly
   halved but that this would not necessarily reduce the amount of coal which
   would actually be received since the old allocations had been on an
   'unrealistic' basis.
7. House of Commons, 26 February 1946.
8. House of Commons, 5 February 1946.
9. House of Commons, 17 October 1945.
10. House of Commons, 30 July 1946.
11. Reported in the *Observer*, 22 September 1946.
12. Reported in *The Times*, 21 November 1946. Since the above was written Mr
    Bevan has produced his 'Housing Programme for 1947' which strongly
    suggests that he has graduated into the guess planning group. 'The rate of
    building will be reduced if it proves impracticable to obtain increased im-
    ports of soft wood timber. It has not been thought right, however, to lower
    the estimate on account of uncertainty in regard to a single factor.' But he
    then goes on (para. 14) to say that 'production during 1947 is dependent
    upon *many* [my italics] uncertain factors ... the supply of fuel ... the
    recruitment of further labour ... the possibility of finding alternatives for
    certain scarcer raw materials.' It is interesting to note that on the very day
    that this Housing Programme was produced, showing that the output of
    houses depended on the production of coal, Mr Isaacs, in the House of
    Commons, was saying that the use of Polish miners, which would help to
    determine the output of coal, was dependent upon housing. This suggests
    another possible group of 'vicious circle' planning.
13. The *Manchester Guardian* has perhaps given the most enthusiastic welcome to
    the policy of 'Strength through Shortages.' This will be found in the leader
    of 1 August 1946. Speaking of the policy of house building they say: 'The
    Minister's chief concern must be to allow (or stimulate) just so much
    building that the demand for materials and the components will press close-
    ly, but not to the stalling point – on a supply that is as copious, well
    balanced and steady as good organisation can make it. Whilst this supply
    remains inevitably smaller than *the available labour and management capacity
    could handle* [my italics] there must always be a critical shortage of one com-
    ponent or another.' That is to say, the plan must tolerate the inadequate use
    of labour and managerial capacity in the building trade in order to provide
    a stimulus to the expansion of the supply of building materials. Surely a

plan should strive to avoid bottlenecks, not to create them.

14. Reported in the *Manchester Guardian*, 18 October 1946.

15. Thus in 1946 the Government took the whole nation into its confidence regarding the need for exports. But, unless I have missed something, the Government did not consult the citizens about the distribution of the national income between consumption and investment – which is generally regarded as the crucial planning decision.

16. House of Commons, 26 February 1946.

17. Sir Stafford Cripps, House of Commons, 26 February 1946: 'no country in the world, so far as I know, has yet succeeded in carrying through a planned economy without compulsion of labour. Our objective is to carry through a planned economy without compulsion of labour.'

18. House of Commons, 21 November 1946.

19. *Economic Journal*, December 1945.

20. 'Economics of Control', p. 1.

21. See Lerner, 'Economics of Control; Meade, *Economic Journal*, April 1945; Wilson, *Economic Journal*, December 1945; Fleming, *The Manchester School*, September 1946.

22. The head-on conflict of principle is perhaps seen most clearly in the application of the marginal principle. Thus the modern planners insist upon the importance of the rule that marginal cost should equal price which, in cases of increasing returns, would imply that a concern as a whole would run at a loss. But the old-fashioned planners who were responsible for the recent bill to nationalise the British transport industry will have none of this. They assert (Clause 3) that the enterprise must cover its total costs.

It would take us too far afield to examine the causes of the psychological suspicion of the price system. But, undoubtedly, it is closely bound up with the irritation felt by those who like to think in terms of the 'broad national interest of the well-being of the community as a whole', when they are confronted with the controlling influence of economic costs. Sir George Schuster (*Observer*, 8 December 1946) has spoken most frankly on this point. Dealing with the Lancashire Cotton Industry, he advocated a bold policy of re-equipment and went on 'many firms have their machinery written down to very low figures on their books and, taking into account the cost of capital charges for interest and depreciation on new machinery, it may well be doubtful for an individual firm whether it will pay to put in new machinery. But we must export to live. If we could double the volume of production, even with a slightly higher cost of manufacture, it would be to the national interest to do so. It is, therefore, a case where . . . the State must intervene for the sake of the community.' It is, however, difficult to see how exports can be increased, over any significant period, by increasing costs or how the community can gain by using resources to make new equipment as a result of the use of which costs would rise.

23. There are many other instances of the belittling of the function of prices. Thus Mr Shinwell in the House of Commons, 9 October 1945, announcing the shortage of petrol which prevented him from increasing rations was asked why, in these circumstances, he had recently reduced the price of petrol. He said 'petrol rationing is a distinctive question with nothing whatever to do with the price level'.

24. Reported in *The Times*, 21 November 1947.

25. At the time of going to press another type of planning is to be observed – 'planning on the past'. Thus Sir Stafford Cripps is reported as saying on 22 January 1947: 'in the first instance our aim was a normal peaceful existence with the average standard that we had in 1938 to be attained as rapidly as possible, but that average to be more equitably spread among all the people'. Planners are inclined to pride themselves upon looking forward but when they get into serious difficulties they are often disposed to clutch at the past for guidance. This, however, does not really help them since the problem remains of how to decide whether future conditions really justify the nostalgic determination to re-create the old conditions.
26. In a letter to *The Times*, 9 November 1946.
27. The steel industry appears to have a budget for 1947 (see the *Manchester Guardian*, 6 January 1947). It would be interesting to know whether this was based upon the Government allocations of coal then ruling and what changes have been called for in this budget by the severe cutting of these allocations on 13 January.
28. 23 November 1946.
29. House of Commons, 26 February 1946.

5 THE GOVERNMENT AND HEALTH

Frustrations in the British National Health Service*

I

No new scheme for social welfare can ever have been launched with such acclaim and high hopes as the British National Health Service in 1948. It constituted a government undertaking to provide in full medical services of all kinds to all citizens (and indeed to foreigners) without charge. It was, in the euphoria of the day, prematurely described as 'the envy of the world'. In the event it had, by 1976, proved to be almost the opposite of this. For the National Health Service was frequently being described as on the point of breakdown. Despite the steadfast work of a body of devoted doctors and nurses, the medical services available were certainly inferior to those obtainable in a number of other countries; conflict had developed between the government and the medical profession; friction was rampant in hospitals between doctors and ancillary staff. Perhaps most lasting and tragic of all, the country had apparently riveted upon itself a system from which it is difficult, if not impossible, to escape. For no political party seems prepared to retrace steps, to challenge the faulty reasoning underlying the creation of the Health Service or to face the inevitable consequences of the system and to take those unpopular (at least temporarily) steps to correct past errors.

This is indeed a cautionary tale. It goes far to provide, in one vitally important case, an answer to the question (never asked in 1948 by anyone): if there is a service the demand for which at zero price is almost infinitely great; if no steps are taken to increase the supply; if the cost

*This paper is based partly on: Royal Commission on Doctors' and Dentists' Remuneration 1957–60. Memorandum of Dissent: J. Jewkes, HMSO, 1960. J. & S. Jewkes 'The Genesis of the British National Health Service', Blackwell, 1961. J. & S. Jewkes 'Value for Money in Medicine', Blackwell, 1963. J. & S. Jewkes 'Britain Out of Step' in 'Monopoly or Choice in Health Services?', I.E.A. Occasional Paper 3, 1964. A Review by J. Jewkes of Enoch Powell's 'A New Look at Medicine and Politics', *British Medical Journal*, November, 1966.

curve is rising rapidly; if every citizen is guaranteed by law the best possible service; and if there is no obvious method of rationing, what is likely to happen? In the following paragraphs an attempt is made to provide an answer in the light of experience.

II

The main purpose of medical services is the mitigation of suffering. People are less prepared than of old to tolerate pain and discomfort and, with the advance of medicine, it becomes increasingly possible technically to meet these demands. It is therefore strange that people in many western countries, whilst attaching such a high priority to health services, should apparently have become more and more reluctant to pay directly for them. It is no answer to point out that health services become more costly since many other services and commodities of desired quality have also risen substantially in cost and, for these, people are ready to pay quite happily (the veterinary services for their domestic pets are a case in point).

In western countries the cost of health services are met in a variety of ways: by direct payment by individuals for some or all health services; by voluntary private insurance; by compulsory insurance through private agencies or the State; by a combination of these arrangements or, in the extreme case as in Britain, by the complete take-over and organisation by the State of the means to provide free of charge all medical facilities and services.

Why have governments so frequently become involved in such provision, in one form or another? It can be argued that it is a proper function of government to undertake for a community those services which, whilst generally regarded as desirable, individuals cannot or will not provide for themselves. At first sight, this would seem to restrict the functions of the State to preventive medicine, funds for medical research and, although more debatable, the provision of capital equipment for such purposes as the building of hospitals. But further than this, it is argued, some especially unfortunate people will have serious illnesses or accidents, the cost of which will be so high that these costs must be spread over the whole community. Oddly enough, however, the total expenditure on health services as a proportion of national income tends to be lower in those countries where the State tries to do most, as in Britain, than in those where private initiative and voluntary insurance are encouraged and State action is limited to the covering of certain groups, or to providing funds for research and general capital equipment, as for instance, in the United States.

The British system is almost unique in the western world in that it provides all medical services free and the costs have thus to be paid out of general taxation.

The main arguments which finally brought about the establishment of the National Health Service in Britain in 1948 were:

(a) That the British medical system before the Second World War was seriously defective and that nothing short of a centrally controlled free system could provide appropriate remedies.
(b) That increased expenditure on health services would be a sound economic investment because, by reducing ill-health, it would not only increase production but it would, for the future, steadily improve the health of the community and thus reduce the costs of medical services.
(c) That social justice called for identical and the best possible medical services for each and every citizen.

III

The first of these arguments was examined and challenged in 'The Genesis of the British National Health Service' published in 1961. There is, indeed, no detailed statistical information of the scale on which medical services were provided before the Second World War. The National Health Insurance Scheme, started in 1911, by 1939 covered about half of the population. The Scheme was insurance, although compulsory insurance; it excluded dependants of insured workers; it applied an income limit and provided only for a limited range of medical care. Those who were in need of hospital treatment, and could not afford it, received it free either in the voluntary or in municipal hospitals; others were expected to pay what they could afford. Many voluntary funds existed which gave working people access to the hospitals as of right. In addition, the outpatient departments of hospitals provided services for those who did not wish for, or could not afford, the services of the general practitioner. And it is reasonable to suppose that, even without a National Health Service, Britain would have enjoyed after 1948 medical services more ample and better distributed than those which existed before the war. All experience in western countries suggests that when general incomes rise the community will spend increased sums on medical services. Natural growth might well have taken the form of widening compulsory insurance to include dependants and an increase in voluntary insurance among the better-off.

Thus it will come as no surprise to find that Lord Horder was claiming in 1939 that 'it is universally acknowledged that our health services are the best in the world' and that the Deputy Chief Medical Officer of the Ministry of Health has pointed out:

It is sometimes suggested ... that the nature of the medical care available to our population changed abruptly in July 1948. This is quite untrue since a complete range of medical and allied services was available before the National Health Service was introduced. What the Service did was to change the ways in which people would obtain and pay for the care that they needed. Indeed one might almost say that the only services that were new on 5 July 1948 were the availability of specialists' consultations in the patient's own home, and home helps for households in which there was illness. Even these had been present to some extent before.

(G. E. Goder, 'Health Services – Past, Present and Future' *Lancet*, July, 1958).

This then was a great social change advocated and introduced by wrongly picturing it as the inevitable reaction against ancient and no longer tolerable evils. The Beveridge Report, published in 1942, is often regarded as having fostered an irresistible public demand for a free health service. But even this Report warned:

The State in organising security should not stifle incentive, opportunity, responsibility; in establishing a national minimum, it should leave room and encouragement for voluntary action by each individual to provide more than that minimum for himself and his family.

But when the White Paper on Health Services was published in 1944 the Government revealed a vital switch in policy: from the public provision of a minimum service to the provision of the best possible health service for all:

The Government ... want to ensure that in future every man and woman and child can rely on getting all the advice and treatment and care which they may need in matters of personal health; that what they get shall be the best medical and other facilities available; that their getting these shall not depend on whether they can pay for them, or on any other factor irrelevant to the real need ...

Thus at a stroke the need for self-help, consumers' preference and the use of the price system for encouraging economy were all rejected.

If the centralised State organisation of Health Services of the British type had justified itself one could have expected that the medical services thereby provided would in the long run have outstripped in quantity and quality those found in other advanced western countries. Of course, straight exact international comparisons on this subject are not feasible. But two statements can be made with confidence. In other countries, the

United States, Canada, New Zealand, Germany, various mixtures of public and private medicine are to be found. But no country has copied in full the British system. Again, there is no evidence that medical services are there inferior to those in Britain – most factual material points in the opposite direction.

IV

I turn now to the claim that the National Health Service would justify itself as a good investment and that, as a result of the improved health and productivity of people, the cost of the health services would progressively fall and even be offset by economic gains. So that, in effect, the country would get the National Health Service for nothing. This idea was properly described by Mr Enoch Powell, when he was Minister of Health, as 'a miscalculation of sublime dimensions'.

It is easy to see why this was so and to pick out the consequences of the fallacy. There is no such thing as perfect health. The extent to which the individual will deem it necessary or desirable to call upon professional medical help will depend not only upon his physical condition but the stoicism he shows towards a physical trouble. The demand for medical services will automatically increase if nothing has to be paid for them directly. There is no limit to 'the best possible' medical service. It is always conceivable that any patient would benefit from the attention and consultation between more doctors, the care of more nurses, the widespread use of rare and highly expensive equipment. Moreover, as Dr Ffrangcon Roberts brilliantly argued in 1952 in 'The Cost of Health', the more successful medical services are, the more expensive they will become. By its promise to provide without charge the 'best possible' medical service to all, the Government was inducing an open-ended demand which, in the nature of things, could not be and could never have been met.

The results were as could only have been expected. Since the Government in 1948 was clearly unaware of the implications of the undertaking it had entered into and had made no prior arrangements to expand the medical services, the inevitable increase in demand came as a shock, threw a sudden heavy burden on the medical profession, led to long waiting lists and efforts on the part of one group of overstretched doctors, the general practitioners, to unload more work upon another group, the hospital doctors. This condition of general shortage has continued. Since 1948 successive British governments have fought a constant battle against rising costs. At the inception of the National Health Service it was assumed that the annual cost would be about £200 million. Within a short period costs were rising rapidly and Sir Stafford Cripps, alarmed at this, fixed a ceiling of £400 million per annum. This held the line for a time but inevitably costs began to increase again. In 1975 the total cost was in excess of £5000 million. Despite this there never seems to be enough money to meet demands, therefore successive governments have been forced to seek for economies in different ways: by neglecting the casualty services, by imposing (usually derisory) charges for certain services, by forcing down expenditure on capital equipment such as hospitals,[1] by making use of a very large number of junior doctors from abroad, often from poorer countries where medical services were extremely scanty – in brief, by reneging on the promises made originally in 1948.

There is little evidence that the National Health Service has increased economic productivity. Of course, medical advance largely through research in this and many other countries has brought its benefits. But absence from work through sickness has certainly not declined, and the demand for medical services has not fallen off. And it is noticeable that government economies have tended to fall more heavily on those forms of expenditure which might have been expected to bring quicker, bigger or more direct economic returns than others. Thus low priority has been given to preventive medicine rather than curative; medical services designed to reduce the loss of working time in industry; spending on capital equipment to reduce operating costs; special forms of health care for the young; and medical research. For such economies were likely to arouse less public resistance and be less noticeable than restrictions by imposing charges for doctors' service, the supply of drugs or hospital care.

V

Probably the most powerful drive towards this unique British social experiment came from the almost neurotic pursuit of equality: the doctrine that all men, rich and poor alike, should have full and free access to all known types of medical care. It was considered as fundamentally immoral that 'the cash nexus' should come between a citizen and his inalienable right to health, or even survival. The whole vast social question of equality can perhaps more pertinently be examined in terms of medical services than in terms of any other kind of commodity or service.

Why should medicine ever have been regarded as 'different'? Why should a free-for-all provision of medical services have been regarded as more important than similar arrangements for other goods and services? Food, heating, clothing and shelter are just as much needed for comfort and survival as medicine, in some ways even more so. Yet food, heating, clothing and shelter are, for a greater part of the population, provided through a market system. It is true that the incidence of bouts of serious ill-health may be unpredictable, but not more so than other risks: fire, accidents or acts of God. This kind of uncertainty is normally, and best, provided through insurance and left to the judgement and circumstances of the individual.

The campaign for a free-for-all in medicine, as for other kinds of absolute equality – in income, education or housing – reveals that no rational definition of equality is available; that even if a watertight concept could be found it would be virtually impossible to give it practical shape; and that, by the very attempts to achieve what is impossible, egalitarian aims are defeated since they tend to create new forms of inequality and lower the standards of excellence in the Service itself.

What is meant by equality of medical service between one citizen and another? Of two people with exactly the same physical complaint, if the one is more demanding of medical attention than the other, does equality mean granting to him the same or unequal treatment? If there are two people who have equal incomes and who, if left free to make their own choice, would devote unequal proportions of those incomes to medical services, on what grounds can it be claimed that the government should properly step in to insist that, in effect, they spend the same proportion on medical services? As with all men of skill, doctors vary greatly in knowledge and aptitude. But no one can work more than 24 hours in a day. If a doctor becomes recognised as outstanding and is swamped with demands for his services, how can he decide which patient to treat and which to reject? In Britain, as the result of the enormous influx of doctors from abroad, many of whom have long been recognised, for one reason or another, as not really as competent as the average, it is largely a matter of chance whether a patient under the medical service is treated by a doctor of more or less than average ability. In any case, does not 'equality' become a very odd thing in a system such as the National Health Service where, in effect, people with small incomes who are rarely sick may nevertheless be paying taxes which subsidise people with much larger incomes who frequently fall ill and make large demands on the Health Service?

Is there any sense in which the National Health Service has since 1948 established greater equality? It can be expected that there is now a more equal geographical distribution of hospital services and of consultants than formerly. But it can hardly be doubted that, as is true in other countries with no such National Health Service, rising standards of living in the poorer parts of Britain would have benefited more than others even if private medicine had been the rule. Nearly 30 years after the inception of the National Health Service, the Government of the day is still claiming that great inequality exists and that further steps should be taken to cure this. Well-to-do Britishers can still go abroad to obtain private services; doctors in Britain can still establish private institutions which, because of their reputation, are patronised by rich foreigners. Only an innocent would deny that, under the National Health Service, 'important' patients with good political, medical or academic connections do receive prompter and better treatment than others and that the gap between them and those who patiently sit in crowded waiting rooms and queues is not becoming noticeably narrower.

As with the pursuit of equality in other unattainable forms, the attempt to impose the ethics of the queue through the National Health Service has brought its own adverse social and economic side-reactions. A search for equality in medicine threatens to restrict equality and freedom in other ways. If there is to be the same number of doctors per 100 of the population, or per square mile, then the government must enforce this distribution, must be prepared to deprive doctors of freedom to operate in the district of their own choice, except in the sense that they can exercise it through emigration. The tactics of the egalitarians may reduce efficiency. It has always been argued by the medical profession itself (which although it cannot be disinterested can properly claim to be better informed than anyone else on such matters) that some private practice is inseparable from the maintenance and improvement of the highest standards of medicine. The massive, and it would appear the increasingly cumbrous, administrative set-up of the National Health Service is in part required for the enforcement of equality. It was indeed a Regius Professor of Medicine in Oxford who declared:

> Since hospitals came under Ministry control committees have spawned and it has become increasingly difficult for senior men like myself to get any work done.

In the search for methods of enforcing equality the administrators of the National Health Service must always be tempted to seek to establish uniformities in treatment. This the profession has stoutly resisted but its defence has not improved the relations between professionals and administrators. To be healthy, the medical system in any country will always have special centres of excellence, mainly to be found in the great teaching hospitals. This, of course, immediately confers special benefits upon the population within the catchment area of such hospitals. Recently in Britain the government has proposed to make cuts in the famous London teaching hospitals, partly in order to reduce national expenditure but partly also to reallocate National Health Service resources from relatively well-off to relatively deprived parts of the country.

Another adverse side-reaction of the National Health Service, not frequently remarked upon, has been the creation of friction between the profession and the government, especially as to conditions of work and salaries; friction which has at times become so bitter as to lead to the threat of mass withdrawal of services. When the Health Service was introduced the doctors were much divided and confused about it, especially about their future independence, rights to private practice and the level and form of remuneration. But, understandably, they were untaught in the art of dealing with politicians and they were finally cajoled and bullied into acceptance by Aneurin Bevan, a past master in such tactics, who perhaps clinched his victory with the claim, made at the Labour Party Conference in 1945, that 'If we were rich enough we would not want to have free medical services; we could pay the doctors.' For this, if words meant anything, left the impression that the National Health Service was a temporary expedient which could be jettisoned as prosperity returned.

The squabbling, however, has had no end. The Government was forced in 1957 to set up a Royal Commission on Doctors' and Dentists' Remuneration which reported in 1960. This Commission recommended a package deal which was presented by the Government to the profession for acceptance or rejection as a whole, no negotiations being allowed. The profession was really in no position to do anything but accept, perhaps believing that the special Review Body which was to be set up would discover ways, acceptable to both sides, of determining doctors' incomes.[2]

That hope has been frustrated. The training of new doctors at home has never been high enough to meet shortages. The Service has been saved from even more serious collapse by a remarkable influx of young doctors from abroad and by the gross overworking of junior hospital doctors. At the same time more senior British doctors have been tempted by the much higher salaries available in other, and especially English-speaking, countries, to emigrate. The Conservative Government of 1970–4 alarmed and antagonised the profession by a drastic reorganisation of the administration of the Health Service which seems to have done little good and has complicated and increased the cost of the Service. And with the coming into power of a Labour Government in 1974, fresh disputes broke out both regarding pay and the arrangements controlling the extent of private practice. This has led to the setting up of another Royal Commission on the National Health Service, which still has to make its Report. One of the questions put to this latest Royal Commission is

> Whether it would be possible or advantageous for the National Health Service to be taken 'out of politics' by putting it under the control of an apolitical central agency.

What, however, is becoming increasingly evident is that, in the setting up of the National Health Service, British governments have taken upon themselves a task for which there may be no satisfactory solution: how to work out a harmonious relation with a great profession which will guarantee the independence of the profession and the conditions of work and pay likely to evoke an adequate supply of doctors.

Of course all professions have in some way to solve these equations. There is, however, a critical difference between the British medical profession now and most other professions. In the other professions there is a relatively free market; there are numerous employers; there is more than one way of entering the profession; if there are shortages or surpluses spontaneous adjustments can be expected in the level of earnings. That is no longer true of the medical profession in Britain. The State is very largely a monopoly employer; it exercises an influence upon the demand for medical and dental services and therefore upon the demand for doctors and dentists themselves in various ways. It fixes the charges (if any) to be imposed for the treatments and drugs received by patients. It determines the size of the hospital establishments. By fixing the maximum size of list for the general practitioner, it fixes the minimum and influences the maximum requirements for such practitioners. Doctors and dentists can enter the profession only by passing through a university training followed, in the case of doctors, by a compulsory period of hospital experience. The upper limit to the doctors and dentists who can be trained is fixed by the number and size of the medical and dental schools and the cost of any increase here would have to be met by the government. The responsible government departments are therefore in the extraordinary, and perhaps unique, position that they largely control the demand for, the supply of, and the price offered for, the services of the medical and dental professions. It is a position at once both powerful and delicate. Powerful because all the important levers lie in the hands of the government. Delicate in the sense that unless it maintains the proper co-ordination between the variables, maladjustments will occur as indeed they have occurred on more than one occasion since 1948.

On the other hand lies the bargaining weakness of doctors because they are members of a profession, and the essence of a profession lies in its adherence to a sense of social responsibility. They have taken the Hippocratic Oath; they are thus deterred from the threat of mass action or, if driven to such threats, from making them real, by their own sense of duty.

It is this grip of the Government which explains why the profession has spent so much time, inevitably so far without success, in the search for a formula which would in perpetuity protect it against arbitrary action on the part of the State. For the same reason it is only to be expected that, in any new major settlement with the profession, doctors and dentists will not be wholly, nor perhaps even primarily, concerned with the new level of earnings established. They will also be vitally interested in the light thrown by these decisions, in terms of works and not of words, upon the view which the Government holds as to the place of the medical profession in society and the degree to which it is to be allowed to share in any increase in the general prosperity of the whole community.

Such dilemmas do not arise, or not to the same degree, in countries where medical services are provided in much greater measure outside a government-organised and controlled system.

VI

The British people, with their governments, have created for themselves through the National Health Service a medical system which seems doomed to remain second- or third-rate. It was based upon national self-deception. It has failed to command the respect and loyalty of the medical profession. In the absence of any control over demand, every part of the Service regards itself as short of money; no part, therefore, dares to do anything but denigrate its own performance. Confronted with the choice between an inferior service which is 'free' and a superior service which involves sacrifices of other things, the public opt for the worse. Medicine and politics become hopelessly entangled, so that governments, in any efforts to economy, tend to make cuts at points which will be least easily identified in the short term by the electorate, although often will do most harm to the long-term efficiency of the Service. The National Health Service is an outstanding manifestation of those social and economic attitudes which have come to be comprehensively described as the 'British sickness'.

Is there no way in which Britain can dig itself out of this pit? Why is it impossible to reorganise the medical service so that the Government would restrict itself to providing preventive medicine, medical research, free medical services for those who demonstrably could not afford them and perhaps a large measure of support for capital expenditures, thus leaving the great mass of the people to pay for their own services to a profession largely operating independently of government? Why should private voluntary insurance not relieve the majority of the people of the stresses associated with the unpredictability of ill-health? Why should Britain not simply follow the examples of other countries, none of which has copied our extreme system and many of which regard our experiment as a sombre warning?

One would have to be sanguine to suppose that any such significant changes will occur in the near future. Indeed Socialist Governments since 1974 have been driving hard in the opposite direction and have been seeking to weaken what private medicine still remains. Fresh legislation has been introduced to phase out pay-beds in Health Service hospitals. Contributions by employers to private medical insurance on behalf of their workers or pensioners are to be taxable. The Government has not hesitated to engage in confrontation with the medical profession over salaries and conditions and has been prepared to watch, with equanimity, the increasing emigration of some of the more senior and best qualified British doctors.

It seems utopian to hope that any British political party would propose changes designed to bring about a marked and continuing rise in private medicine to cover perhaps one-half or two-thirds of the population and substantially reduce public expenditure. All political parties since 1948 have, at best, ignored or neglected the various bodies providing voluntary medical insurance. Mr Enoch Powell (Minister of Health between 1960 and 1963, when he sought actively to repair some of the damage caused to medical services since 1948 through the virtual strangulation of capital expenditure) is universally recognised as one of the most perceptive and courageous defenders of free market and individual initiative. He has brilliantly diagnosed the weaknesses of the National Health Service.[3] But, after asking the question 'is there really no practical escape from the circle in which medicine and politics are imprisoned by the National Health Service?' he has sadly confessed that 'the very contemplation of denationalising the Service is enough to daunt the stoutest political heart'.

Even such a thorough student of the weaknesses of the National Health Service as Mr Arthur Seldon who, given the logic of the matter, has dared to hope that 'the days of a "free", tax-financed National Health Service are numbered'[4] probably now feels that, until the slow-moving British people finally recognise how much damage they are doing to themselves, there can be no great urgency in specifying too exactly how freedom of choice can be restored to individuals and more independence granted to the medical profession – through voluntary or compulsory insurance, or through cash payments or vouchers, or a system of negative income tax for the needy.

NOTES

1. From 1948–58 capital costs were virtually non-existent: no new hospital was built and no new medical school established. This compared unfavourably with what happened in other countries such as the United States and Switzerland. Not until 1965 did capital costs reach even 10 per cent of current costs.
2. As a member of this Royal Commission I felt compelled to produce a Memorandum of Dissent since I believed that the level of the award suggested by the majority was unfairly low and, what was perhaps more serious, was too low to provide a sufficiently large inflow of doctors into the profession.
3. 'A New Look at Medicine and Politics', 1966.
4. Arthur Seldon, 'After the NHS', 1968.

6 GOVERNMENT, SCIENCE AND TECHNOLOGY

How much Science?*

I

It is frequently said that Great Britain is suffering from a shortage of scientists and technologists and of the means for conducting research and development and, since the study of shortages is the main interest of the economist, I propose to examine the reasons usually given for making this statement and to speculate a little about how a community can satisfy itself that it is devoting sufficient of its efforts to scientific and technical matters. As I shall try to explain in a moment, the scale of scientific activities in the country is determined by a very puzzling combination of public and private views, public and private action and, in the last resort, the striking of a right balance will inevitably be a matter of judgement and of intuition. Those who take sides too strongly, therefore, are not likely to give good advice, and I fear that, in recent years, some of those who have taken a vigorous part in the campaign for 'selling science to the Establishment' have been prone, with the best intentions in the world, to muddle up good arguments with bad and, paradoxically enough, to push the claims of science against the humane studies by making questionable use of history, economics, statistics and even perhaps educational theory.

I begin with some matters mainly of definition. It has become fashionable to speak of 'science and technology' in the singular as if what was true of one was inevitably true of the other. But the generalisations that can be made about the two in common are few. In purpose, method and appropriate scale of operation they can best be discussed separately and, although they may frequently have to be discussed as one, that is nearly always evidence of the limitations of our knowledge about them. The practice of bundling the two together has had some very odd results in recent years: for example, when the Russians, by a highly competent piece of engineering, put the first sputnik into orbit, this was used as a proof that more money should be spent on

*Presidential Address delivered to Section F (Economics) on 4 September 1959, at the York Meeting of the British Association, printed in the *Economic Journal*, March 1960.

science in Great Britain.

A second truism. If we train in the univerisities more people in the sciences or in techology, then there will be fewer of the ablest segment of the community trained in the other disciplines. This would be untrue only if the universities were at present failing in their task of selection, which I do not believe to be the case. If we decide to have more scientists we must pay the price for it. It is an evasion to suggest that we can have more scientists, more technologists, more historians, more doctors, more economists and so on all at the same time. For the question of quality immediately comes in. The proportion of university graduates who fail even now is high (and incidently it is higher in science and technology than in other subjects). To scrape the bottom of the barrel more vigorously, to set out to produce what is sometimes described as a 'scientific proletariat' would further increase the proportion of failures; unless, of course, university standards are lowered. The right term, therefore, in which to discuss this whole question is whether the community will gain by having more scientists or more technologists trained at the expense of non-scientists. Some eminent scientists have declared themselves in very forthright fashion on this subject.[1] Whether they were right or wrong they were certainly, to my mind, discussing the right question.

The most important matter of definition, however, relates to the meaning of the word 'shortage'. For the economist, a shortage exists when at the prevailing price the demand is greater than the supply. There is a shortage of scientists when, at existing salaries, schools, universities, government laboratories, research associations and industrial firms cannot get as many of these people as they would be prepared to engage. In these circumstances it is to be expected that salaries of scientists would rise because of the competition for them. What would be needed and what would follow sooner or later in anything like a free market would be a boost in supply. I propose hereafter to use the word 'shortage' in this sense: it is a condition of the market.

There is, however, a second, much hazier, meaning given to the word in present-day discussion. There is said to be a shortage when those individuals and institutions which actually exercise the demand for scientists – those same schools, universities, public laboratories, industrial firms mentioned above – are not demanding enough of them, are making mistakes in not rating sufficiently highly the contribution that such workers can make to the profits of individual businesses or to the national welfare, are not sufficiently 'science-conscious'. In this sense it is not merely the supply but also the demand for scientists which is inadequate. For this situation I propse to use the term 'unmet need'.

As I say, this 'unmet need' is a vague and perplexing concept (although I am not prepared to argue that it is entirely without meaning). It implies that those people and institutions responsible for exercising the demand for scientists do not really know their job as well as some other group of people who have no responsibility for action or for risk-taking but claim to be able to draw upon some source of higher wisdom. For instance, if a statesman or an economist declares that industry would gain greatly from the employment of more scientists, how does he know? Why should he know better than the industrialist? If he is confident of his conclusions why should he not go into industry himself and make the large profits which the existing industralists are neglecting to make? A second reason why 'unmet need' is so slippery an idea is that it is bound up with the distinction between private gain and social gain. It is possible to argue that even if the employment of more scientists by one particular firm will not increase the profits of that firm, yet it will increase the national income. But social gains and social costs are the most difficult things to measure even in a rough and ready fashion.

II

Let us try now, as an exercise, to answer the questions: what evidence is there of (a) a market shortage, and (b) an unmet need for scientists in Great Britain? By scientists I mean (following the classification of the Ministry of Labour) persons trained to university levels in biology, chemistry (other than pharmacy), geology, mathematics, physics and general science.

Let us take market supply and demand first. The number of scientists being turned out by British universities is on the increase. In 1956–7 the number of degrees and diplomas obtained in pure science was more than twice as great as in 1938–9 and 11 per cent greater than in 1949–50. Between 1955 and 1958 the number of full-time students entering university institutions for the first time in order to pursue courses in pure science increased by 25 per cent. The output of science graduates is, therefore, certain to move upwards in the next three years. And still further increases are being planned for later years. In the three years 1956–9 the total output of scientists from British universities was in the neighbourhood of 18,000. This was the supply. What was the demand? Fortunately we have a rough idea of that, because in 1956 the Ministry of Labour undertook an inquiry[2] in order to determine the number of scientists already employed in industry, government and education and the number of additional scientists that,in the view of those who employed scientists, would be required in the following three years. The conclusions reached was that by 1959 the net additional demand for scientists would be about 9500. Even after making any reasonable allowance for death, retirement and emigration, it seems fairly certain that in these three years scientists were being produced by the universities at a rate commensurate with the increase in demand as estimated by those who can be supposed to be in the best position to judge.[3]

Have there in recent years been increases in the salaries of scientists disproportionate to the changes in the salaries in other professions, which might have been expected if there had been a shortage? The evidence is very scrappy. In the PEP Report, *Salaries of Graduates in Industry*, 1957, where a study was made of the salaries paid to a random sample of some 4000 graduates of 1950, the general conclusion was that there was little difference between the earnings of graduates in arts, science and technology. The Report goes on to point out that the pattern of earnings was 'not well calculated to encourage men to read science and technology rather than history or languages or some other non-technical subject'. By 1959 the median salary of all corporate members of the Royal Institute of Chemistry had reached about £1700, a 45 per cent increase in the six years 1953–9.[4] By 1956 the median salary of Fellows of the Institute of Physics reached about £1950, which represented an increase of 35 per cent in the five years 1951–6.[5] In comparison, the average annual salary in manufacturing industry increased by 55 per cent between 1950 and 1958 and the average annual wage by 72 per cent. We must await more figures before reaching a final conclusion. My impression is that the earnings of scientists are still not outstanding in the professional hierarchy; on the other hand, the rapid rate of increase in very recent years may presage big changes.

Even if there is no market shortage is there nevertheless an unsatisfied social need for more scientists? At least four different reasons are given why the community should have more science and more scientists. First, it is said that, quite independently of what kind of career young people may subsequently wish to follow, they should be taught more science in schools and universities as a part of a good general education. We ought to try to raise the level of scientific literacy. Secondly, it is suggested that more scientific resources should be made available for the purpose of extending man's knowledge of the nature of the physical universe, even if no material advantage could be expected. 'The picture we form in our minds of nature will be the more beautiful for being brightly lit.' Thirdly, it is claimed that more science is needed in order to strengthen our national defences. And finally, it is stated that more science is a necessity for improving economic standards.

It immediately becomes obvious that the chance of determining 'needs' of this kind by methods which would possess a commanding logic or find general acceptance seems to be extremely remote. There are great differences of opinion, even between experts, as to the proper place of science in our general scheme of education. How does a community make up its mind what it wishes to spend on the acquiring of pure scientific knowledge which may or may not have usefulness in the narrow sense? It is customary to suggest that the extent to which science should be subsidised for the purpose of national defence is a matter which can be left to military experts. In fact, that is not the case; military needs have no limit and there must be some point at which, as military expenditure increases, the economy as a whole is so weakened that this expenditure becomes self-defeating. Presumably the decisions under the fourth head can be more exactly determined, or at least they can be left to business men, each deciding on the merits of his own particular case whether increased expenditure on science seems worth while. But even there it is not easy to discern any very clear pattern of business behaviour.

Difficult as it may be to reach a convincing decision about needs on any one of these four grounds, when they are looked at together the complexities multiply quickly. The different needs may be in conflict. In the short period, if the community wants more teachers of science it must content itself with fewer scientists for work in industrial laboratories. Or, in the longer period, if the community decides that it attaches value to extend knowledge of the cosmos, it may be necessary to sacrifice material standards of living for that purpose. More radio telescopes mean fewer private television sets.

Must we, then, resign ourselves to the idea that the decisions made can never be rational; that action will always have to be taken on but a fragment of all the evidence needed for logical behaviour; and that, having taken decisions, it will never be possible to know whether they were correct or not? Or, on the contrary, can we be confident that, although there can be no precise determination of how much science there should be ideally, yet at the moment there is certainly too little; that although we do not know how far we should go, we can feel confident that we are moving in the right direction? It always seems to me to be an additional enigma of this subject that, despite all its mysteries, outstanding writers and institutions manage, by somewhat mystical processes, to reach confident conclusions that one line of action is palpably preferable to another.[6]

In the next section of this paper I examine the broad tests which, at various times and places, have been applied in order to determine whether sufficient emphasis is being placed on science. Before doing that, however, it is worth while pointing out that some well-informed observers have suggested that Great Britain is not suffering from an unmet need for more scientists.[7] That view gains support from comparisons between the United States and Great Britain.

In the Appendix, I compare in detail the annual output and the existing stock of scientists in Great Britain and the United States. The conclusions to be drawn (and this is indicative of the grave difficulties of making these comparisons even in the most favourable circumstances) depend crucially upon the view that is taken of the relative standing of science degrees in the two countries. If the first science degree is taken as equivalent in Britain and the United States, then America possesses, and is annually producing, about twice as many scientists in relation to population as Britain. If, on the other hand, the first science degree in Britain is regarded as equivalent to the second science degree taken in the United States, then the advantage would lie heavily with Great Britain. I suggest that, surrounded with all these doubts, a reasonable compromise conclusion is that the two countries are roughly in the same position.

I repeat that I have in this section been dealing with scientists alone. It would be useful if one could prepare a similar analysis for technologists, which roughly means engineers of all kinds. The existing information is not adequate to support conclusions. For the moment it is intriguing to note that in 1955–6 the median earnings of professional engineers was slightly below £1200.[8]

III

What tests have been applied to determine whether the resources devoted to science and to technology are adequate? The extensive literature on the subject reveals four ways in which writers have sought to establish their case:

1. International comparisons: thus it is frequently asserted that Great Britain is lagging behind other countries, notably the United States and Russia.

2. Industrial comparisons: if one industry is devoting less effort to science and technology than others, it is presumed that this is evidence of failure on the part of that industry.

3. The establishment of positive correlations between industrial output and the number of scientists and engineers employed in industry. The presumption, then, is that an increase in the number of scientists and engineers will increase industrial production.

4. The measurement of the net return, for specific inventions or for particular industries or countries, of investment on research and development.

INTERNATIONAL COMPARISONS

Although there are honourable exceptions, recent international comparisons of the scale of scientific effort must rank among the most reckless of all statistical exercises ever made. (Indeed, they suggest that what we are most short of are competent and responsible statisticians.) The common argument is that Great Britain is falling behind the United

States and the United States is falling behind Russia. But why should it be assumed that Russia is doing the right thing and the other two countries the wrong? From experience of the last quarter of a century it surely cannot be denied that Russia is capable of inflicting upon herself massive misdirections of her resources. Why not in this case?

What is meant by the statement that one country is falling behind another? What is the right basis for comparison? For example, I have already suggested that, if some allowances are made for differences in educational standards, the number of scientists being turned out annually by American universities per thousand of the total population may not be very much higher than in Great Britain. But these statistics of graduates can be looked at in other ways. For example, in 1956, 25 per cent of those who graduated with the bachelor's degree in Great Britain graduated with science degrees; whilst in the United States only 4 per cent of those who took the first degree took a science degree. The reason for this is simple one: the annual output of university graduates in the United States in non-scientific subjects, in proportion to the population, far outstrips that in Great Britain. Is Great Britain, then, in a more or less favourable position than the United States?

Or again, it seems to be roughly true that the money expenditure in Great Britain on industrial research and development as a proportion of national income is about as high as in the United States. Does this mean that the British position is satisfactory? Some may argue so. But others may argue that the British proportion is relatively high only because the national income is low, and the national income is low only because insufficient funds in total are devoted to research and development. The suggestion would be that if Great Britain spent more on research and development then its national income would increase at least *pari passu*, and the proportion between expenditure on research and development and the national income would still remain the same. If there is anything in this line of reasoning, then the present situation in Britain could be regarded as highly unsatisfactory. In any case, is it safe to regard the *costs* of research and development as a proper measure of fruitful results? How much truth is there, for instance, in the statement often heard that research in America is carried out on a much more lavish and perhaps even wasteful scale than in Great Britain?

I will not elaborate on the other statistical snags in these measurements. What is a scientist or an engineer? To what extent is a man who 'comes up the hard way' necessarily inferior to a formally trained man? These difficulties are great enough when comparing two countries, such as the United States and Britain, which are similar in many respects. But when we bring into the comparisons Russia, where social institutions are so different, where independent observers are not allowed to move freely (and where, of course, a good Marxist, by definition, would not be above the use of statistics for the purpose of

misleading the decadent bourgeois), then the foundations for conclusions
become even more rickety.

But taking the figures most commonly employed, there are some formidable obstacles in extracting real meaning from them. For example, it
is said that Russia and the United States have about the same number of
qualified engineers. It is also said that the total industrial output in
Russia is, at most, about half that of the United States. It follows
arithmetically that industrial output, per qualified engineer, is twice as
great in the United States as in Russia. Does this mean that Russia makes
a prodigal use of qualified engineers or that its engineers are inefficient?
Or is it that there is some inherent weakness in the Russian industrial
system which makes it essential to employ more qualified engineers per
unit of output than in other western countries?

THE CORRELATION BETWEEN INDUSTRIAL OUTPUT AND THE NUMBER OF SCIENTISTS AND TECHNOLOGISTS

The only attempt known to me to establish a link between the number of
scientists and engineers in employment and the growth of the economy
and, in this way, to predict the future need for scientists and
technologists is that of the Committee on Scientific Manpower.[9] Its
argument is worthy of close scrutiny. There are three stages in it which
can be set down in the words of the Committee's Report:

1. There is a definable relationship between the rate of increase of industrial production on the one hand, and the number of trained scientists and engineers employed by industry on the other.[10]

2. It is more reasonable to base our projections of the likely need for
scientific manpower on the assumption that demand within each industry will, on the average, increase in direct proportion to increases in
industrial output than on some even more arbitrarily chosen
relationship.

3. It would be appropriate to work on the basis of an average increase of industrial production at the rate of 4 per cent per annum.

If, therefore, the number of scientists and technologists is linked to industrial production in this way and if industrial production is to increase at the rate of 4 per cent per annum, then a basis exists for determining the need for the number of scientists and technologists in the
future.

This approach is perplexing for more than one reason. Which is supposed to be cause and which effect in this correlation? Is it being
suggested that the number of scientists and technologists is the crucial
determining factor in economic growth, so that if we do not have a 4 per

cent increase in the number of scientists and technologists we cannot possibly enjoy a 4 per cent increase in industrial production? Actually the annual percentage increase in industrial production between 1955 and 1958 was not 4 per cent; production did not increase at all in this period. But the number of scientists and technologists certainly increased. Does this mean that too many scientists and technologists were produced in the period? If not, what becomes of the assumption that there is a definable relationship? If so, and if the crucial mistake made was in the assumption of a 4 per cent increase in industrial production per annum, what is the point of trying to predict the future annual requirements of scientists and technologists by basing it upon another prediction, that of the probable increase in industrial production, which is no easier to make than a straight prediction out of the blue of the number of scientists and technologists required?

An even more puzzling point is that this Committee, along with other authorities, accepts by implication one assumption for which there appears to be little evidence and which is highly pessimistic in character. The assumption is that, since the number of scientists and technologists moves in step with industrial production, output per head of scientists and technologists will never improve, that whatever economies are made in the future they will not be in that particular type of labour. If this were true it would be a striking fact that scientists and technologists could economise in everything but themselves. I do not see why this assumption is made. And I suggest it is pessimistic because, if we accept the idea of a 4 per cent annual increase in industrial production, a short calculation shows that the number of scientists and engineers in Great Britain will have to increase from about 120,000 in 1955 to 5,171,000 in 2050. That is a lot of scientists and technologists.

INTER-INDUSTRY COMPARISONS

Some authorities[11] seek to establish a case for more extensive industrial research and development by pointing out that some industries spend less than others on research and development and by assuming that all industries would gain by raising themselves to the standards of the highest. Now different industries vary greatly in almost every imaginable sense: in capital investment per head; in the raw materials consumed per unit of output; in the types of labour employed; in the methods of financing new expansion; in the extent to which they buy finished or semi-finished parts from other industries; and so on. Nobody doubts that these variations represent the proper responses of different industries to the different circumstances which face them. Why, then, should it be assumed that it is a golden rule, an inflexible uniformity, that, in proportion to size, every industry should spend the same proportion on research and development or devote the same proportion of its labour force to these ends?

THE MEASUREMENT OF THE NET GAIN ARISING FROM RESEARCH AND DEVELOPMENT

In much recent writing the practice has been common of quoting the *costs* of research and development as a measure of the returns to them, a practice all the more illegitimate because it is in the case of research and development that costs and returns are most uncertain and most likely to fluctuate from time to time and case to case. There have, however, been one or two recent commendable efforts to strike the balance between costs and returns. Thus Z. Griliches, in the *Journal of Political Economy*, October 1958, 'Research Costs and Social Returns: Hybrid Corn and Related Innovations', has carried out a fascinating study of the history of the introduction of hybrid corn in the United States and, after trying to determine, on the one hand, the whole of the costs of the research and development which led to it and, on the other, the net increase in the value of the corn crop as a consequence of this innovation, has reached the conclusion that the social rate of return on the research and development of hybrid corn was not less than 700 per cent. There is a fertile field for other similar studies, but the inherent difficulties of generalising from such cases must always be borne in mind. In any specific case the costs may be so widespread, both in space and time, that it is virtually impossible to identify and total all of them; correspondingly the net advantages of an innovation may spread out in so many directions as to defy measurement. More important, one cannot judge of the general effect of research and development by adding up the successes; there are many more failures than successes.

Nevertheless, as it seems to me, we have here the right kind of question to ask. If nothing had been spent directly on technical progress in the past two decades how much poorer would we be than we actually are? We can, of course, never give a precise answer because it is not possible to isolate from many other forces the specific influence of technical innovation. But orders of magnitude, bearing a rough similarity to the conditions that exist in some Western countries, can be indicated. Let it be assumed that net national output per head is increasing at 2 per cent per annum and that the national expenditure on scientific research and development is of the order of 2 per cent of this output. The causes of the increase in output are various: the use of more capital equipment; improved organisation of existing resources; increased efficiency of labour quite apart from any increase in the use of equipment and, finally, technical innovation. If one-fifth of the annual increase in national output could be attributed to innovation, then the rate of return on the expenditure on research and development would be 20 per cent; if one-tenth of the increase in output would be attributed to this factor, then the return on expenditure would be 10 per cent; if one-twentieth, then the return would be 5 per cent. We cannot make a choice with any great confidence between these different possible answers. But, before we too readily accept the higher, optimistic figures, some sobering facts should be kept in mind.

One is that although there has been an enormous increase in the United States in the sums expended on industrial research and development since 1930, when the modern industrial research laboratories began to make their appearance, there does not seem to be any strong evidence that this has made steeper the general upward trend in output per head.[12] And the second is that if we compare the experiences of the different industrial countries in the period since 1945, or in any part of that period, there does not seem to be any very obvious correlation between the rate of industrial expansion and the resources devoted to scientific and technological effort. In relation to their size, the United States and Great Britain have probably spent most on research and development; but they have not been the leaders in the rate of economic growth. Conversely, Germany and Japan and some other European countries have shown the biggest increases in industrial production per head, although, from any information available, they have not distinguished themselves in scientific and technical expenditures.

IV

My principal conclusion is that we should go on searching for better criteria for determining how much the community should devote to science and to technology. I have no doubt that when everything that can be done has been done in devising objective tests for guiding public policy, much room will still be left for intuition, for judgement, for common sense. I would be the first to admit that the process of shuffling resources about until something like the correct balance is struck is not, in itself, a scientific procedure and certainly not one in which scientists should be allowed the last word.

If, however, there have to be guesses, the more informed they can be the better. To my mind we derive no help from such statements as that 'modern science and technology is the greatest force for good or ill in the world today' or that 'scientists and technologists have a special responsibility, since it is their genius and their skill which alone can bring the material basis of happiness within the reach of all'. These are surely myopic misinterpretations of our world in which religious, political and social (and not scientific) ideas are the great moulding forces.

For those whose task is to put science and technology on the proper map and in its proper place, the following points are perhaps worth considering:

1. Whilst no one would wish to deny that technology and science (in that order) have contributed much to the raising of standards of living in the last two centuries, there is a disposition in these days to exaggerate the contribution they have made and to underestimate that made by new social organisations and institutions. New ways of collecting capital for investment; new systems of controlling currency and banking; new market organisations for bringing goods and services to the right places at the right times; new conceptions of the virtues of free trading; new legal codes and systems of arbitration enabling trade to be carried on more securely and more speedily; in their totality these social discoveries may have contributed just as much as the technical inventions and scientific discoveries of the period.

2. Much loose talk about 'the second industrial revolution' is leading up to overstress the potential material benefits of recent scientific discoveries. Atomic energy, to take the most spectacular case of all, must still rank as a very heavy debit in this scale. For, as a result of it, fearful peoples everywhere are sacrificing their standards of living for the purpose of creating modern weapons of war or systems of defence against them. As for the peace-time uses of atomic energy, all we have are promises, which in recent months have become increasingly tentative, that, at some unidentified future moment, electricity will thus be generated at a cost as low as the present cost of producing electricity by burning oil or coal under boilers.

3. It is by no means clear that for those countries with urgent short-period economic problems, such as intractable balance-of-payment difficulties or levels of poverty which are politically explosive, more science and technology should have the highest priority. It is usually said that for increasing the British export trade the first need is for more vigorous and better-trained salesmen. It is rarely if ever said that British products are failing to sell abroad because of the lack of qualities which they might have possessed if our science had been more advanced or our technology more progressive. In the other field I doubt whether the first need of the undeveloped parts of the world is for more science and technology; indeed, they cannot utilise fully the existing stock of knowledge. On the contrary, what they need above all are more men of the administrative and managerial type and the pervasive spread of specialised skills of all kinds which western countries take for granted.[13] India, in particular, seems to me an area where administrative acumen and not more science is the top priority; certainly in that country in recent years the shortage of economists who understood properly the limitations and pitfalls of central economic planning has exposed the economic system to violent stresses that it could well have done without.

4. When something is in short supply the most useful immediate step that can be taken is to economist to the utmost in the use of it. It is, therefore, of extreme importance that the scientists and technologists we already have should be employed to the best effect. I wonder whether that has been true in the recent past in Great Britain.

5. Striking the right balance as to the number of scientists and technologists calls, as I have said, for both public and for private decisions. Errors, carrying with them serious possible consequences, may arise if both types of decision are not made with an eye on the market. Governments may make provision to encourage more young people to train as scientists, but, in the last analysis, it will be business men who will have to employ most of them. There are reasons for supposing that, as a result of a shortage, the demand for scientists may snowball in a way which will make likely a surplus in the future. If, for example, there is a sudden increase in the demand for scientists in industry, then, since the total supply cannot increase instantaneously, the first direct consequence would probably be that scientists teaching in schools and universities would be drawn into industry by the higher salaries offered there. So that just at the time when more science teachers were required to augment the annual supply, fewer would be available. The boom would be intensified. And if efforts are made to meet the shortage quickly, then the annual output of new scientists might easily be raised to the point which was too large to meet normal requirements when the backlog had been satisfied.

Allow me to illustrate what I mean by 'keeping an eye on the market'. First, it is a good working rule to suppose that a business man knows his business better than anybody else. It is to be feared that the vigorous propaganda from outside for more science and scientists in industry, especially when firms can set costs against taxation at high rates, has sometimes led to industrial research laboratories being established which have had little purpose or value. Second, if the demand for scientists does increase, it is desirable that the salaries of scientists should be allowed to rise: for this at once tends to damp down demand and to increase supply. In this connection I cannot help but feel that the general policy in British universities of striving to maintain income equality among the various faculties is short-sighted and indeed self-frustrating. *If* the universities accept the contention that there *is* a shortage of scientists and that there is a case for swinging the balance somewhat in favour of science in the universities, then it is inconsistent to prevent the salaries of scientists from rising in relation to other university salaries. The principle of equality, of trying to pursue a given policy in defiance of the market, is also self-defeating, for it means that the universities, for a given salary, will get lower-quality people in the faculties short of teachers than in other faculties. Third, if government departments and businesses really consider themselves short of scientists they should be prepared to narrow the margin between scientists' salaries and the higher salaries usually given to administrators (often scientists turned administrators); conversely, if they deem it wise not to narrow this margin, they should accept the logic that it is administrators who are in short supply and not scientists.

6. The recent boosting of science has taken the form of arguments which might easily be fatal in the long run to the autonomy of science. The doctrine has been widely spread that, even where scientific investigation is not directed towards some specified, materially useful end, yet it can be confidently assumed that it will more often than not have such a result. If the public, acting through its Government, succumbs to such appeal and puts down its money for what has been offered as a sound investment, it will not unnaturally look forward to a return. It will expect scientists to devote themselves largely to those investigations most likely to lead to material gains and to accept public guidance and control. In 'seeking to sell science to the Establishment' scientists may also sell themselves to the Establishment. In fact, the overwhelming mass of scientific thought and observation in the western world was never designed to bring, has not brought, and is highly unlikely ever to bring the slightest improvement in material standards of living. This, of course, is not a confession of failure. It is simply one way of asserting that the ultimate purpose of science is not to cater for the lower claims of material progress, where indeed its yield is uncertain, fluctuating and sometimes even negative, but to satisfy the higher needs of knowledge for its own sake, where its returns can hardly ever fail to be positive.

Appendix

1. THE STOCK AND THE ANNUAL PRODUCTION OF SCIENTISTS IN THE UNITED STATES AND GREAT BRITAIN

The comparison of the existing numbers and the annual output of scientists in the United States and Great Britain is a hazardous undertaking for many reasons, but for two above all others:

(i) In Great Britain the only figures of existing stock relate to 'qualified' scientists. This includes university graduates together with the corporate and graduate members of certain professional institutions and the associates of certain educational institutions. But, generally speaking, the level is that of a university graduate. In the various surveys in the United States it appears that a somewhat lower standard than this has been normally adopted. Thus in the U.S. Census of Population, Occupational Tables, it appears that, in the past, a considerable proportion of 'chemists' have not had four years of College (*The Demand and Supply of Scientific Personnel*, D. M. Blank and G. J. Stigler, p. 11). In more recent surveys by the National Science Foundation a Scientist is defined as one 'engaged in scientific work ... at a level which requires a knowledge of ... physical, natural or mathematical sciences equivalent at least to that acquired through completion of a 4-year professional college course'. This clearly would make it possible to include those who were self-educated or had come up 'the hard way'.

(ii) In both countries there are, of course, statistics of the annual number of graduates in the important science groups. But is the first degree, the B.Sc. in Great Britain and the B.S. in the United States, of the same standard in the two countries? It seems impossible to be dogmatic about this. The level of achievement demanded for the first degree varies more widely between one educational institution and another in the United States than in Great Britain. Some observers have gone so far as to assert that the B.Sc. in Britain should be compared with the M.Sc. in the United States (*e.g. Universities and Industry*, Productivity Report: Angle-American Council on Productivity, pp. 11, 12). Without going so far as that, it seems reasonable to suggest that the British first degree is of a higher standard than that in the United States.

2. ANNUAL OUTPUT OF GRADUATES IN 1956

The figures for the two countries are shown in the tables below.

Great Britain

First Degrees Awarded in Pure Science Faculties, 1955–56

Honours	
Chemistry	1,027
Physics	624
Mathematics	465
Total degrees*	4,920

*Including pass degree
Source: University Grants Committee.

United States

Earned Degrees Conferred at First and Second Level, 1956

Field	*Bachelors' and first professional degrees*	*Second-level degrees*
Chemistry	6,178	1,164
Physics	2,335	742
Mathematical subjects	4,660	898
Total*	28,898	5,312

*I.e., Biological sciences, mathematical subjects, physical sciences.
Source: Statistical Abstract of the United States, 1958.

The conclusions which will be drawn from these tables will depend greatly upon one's judgement of the comparative standards of the first degrees. If the standards were the same then, taking together chemistry, physics and mathematics as the most clear-cut group, the United States, with a population three and a half times greater than that of Great Britain, would show an output of graduates six and a half times greater. If the British bachelor's degree corresponded to the U.S. master's degree, then the United States would show an output of graduates only about one-third greater than the British. If the truth lay somewhere midway between these two assumptions, it would suggest that, after allowing for the different size of population, the output of science graduates was about the same in the two countries.

3. THE EXISTING STOCK OF SCIENTISTS

Ideally, it would be desirable to compare in the two countries the total number of scientists employed in all tasks, the number employed in industry and, within the number employed in industry, the number employed in research and development where the scientist is engaged upon the tasks for which he has been scientifically trained. The nearest approach to this ideal is provided in Tables 1 and 2 below.

Table 1. Great Britain

Qualified Scientists Employed by All Authorities and in Industry, 1956

Qualified scientists	All authorities*	Industry
Chemists	20,692	13,195
Physicists	10,484	4,132
Mathematicians	11,482	1,387
Total	51,228	19,468

*Central Government; Local Authorities; Education and Industry.
Source: Scientific and Engineering Manpower in Great Britain, 1956.

Table 2. United States

Scientists Employed by All Authorities; in Industry and on Research and Development in Industry, 1954

	All authorities	Industry	Research and development in industry
Chemists	—	60,000	26,800
Physicists	—	7,500	4,800
Mathematicians	—	6,400	2,500
Total	290,000(?)	145,000	52,000

Source: Science and Engineering in American Industry: 1953–4 Survey, National Science Foundation.

Here again we reach the conclusion that with three and a half times the population the United States appears to have six times the number of scientists possessed by Great Britain. That margin would be reduced in proportion as the standard of 'scientist' were lower in the United States.

NOTES

1. The late Lord Cherwell, speaking in the House of Lords on 21 November 1956: 'Humanistic studies are agreeable, and were very valuable in their day. But they do not really help the country to survive today . . . The fact remains that the people of this country must be fed and clothed . . . the contribution of a man like Whittle was even more helpful to the people of this country than the efforts of any Regius Professors of History in our own Universities.'

   Also Sir Alexander Todd: 'To suggest that more than a modest number of those now studying, say, history or literature in our universities were being trained to the best advantage was not only nonsense but at the present time, dangerous nonsense' (*The Times*, 3 January 1957).

2. *Scientific and Engineering Man Power in Great Britain*, Office of the Lord President of the Council and the Ministry of Labour and National Service, 1956.

3. A new study along the same lines, *Scientific Engineering Man Power in Great Britain 1959*, Advisory Council on Scientific Policy, Committee on Scientific Manpower, came to hand too late to be examined in this article.

4. Royal Institute of Chemistry, Remuneration Survey, 1959.

5. Bulletin of the Institute of Physics, January 1957.

6. Thus the British Advisory Council of Scientific Policy, 1956–7, p. 4, says in one breath: 'It is not possible to lay down any proportion of the total national effort on research and development which should *a priori* be devoted to the civil sector' and in the next: 'But in our view, the resources devoted to civil research and development have been and still are far too small for a country whose competitive position in world trade is dependent upon economic development of new products and new processes and where the achievement of a rising standard of living must depend mainly on our success in increasing the productivity of the labour force.'

7. Thus the late Viscount Waverley, speaking in the House of Lords on 21 November 1956: 'So far as pure science is concerned, statistics appear to show that we are in no way behind Russia, the United States of America or any other country. It is in regard to technology or applied science that we are woefully behind.'

   And Lord Simon of Wythenshawe in the House of Lords on 21 November 1956: 'I want to make it as clear as I can that the crux of the position today is not scientists; it is engineers. A Nobel prize winner in physics has recently written: "The Science departments of our Universities are better and more vigorous than they have ever been in the history of this country . . . What is wrong in this country is that there are far too few engineers to develop our scientists' ideas as fast and as well as is done in some other countries".'

8. *Engineer*, October 1959.

9. *Scientific and Engineering Manpower in Great Britain*, Office of the Lord President of the Council and the Ministry of Labour and National Service, 1956.

10. The evidence given in support of this statement is very sketchy. In the United States, where a run of figures of industrial production and the number of engineers exists from 1890, there is no consistent relationship. Thus in the decade 1930–40 industrial output increased 0·15 per cent for each 1 per cent increase in the number of engineers; in the decade 1940–50

industrial output increased 1·2 per cent for each 1 per cent increase in the number of engineers.

11. See in particular J. K. Galbraith, *The Affluent Society*, p. 99, and the *British Annual Report of the Advisory Council on Scientific Policy*, 1956–7, p. 5.

12. Thus M. Abramovitz: 'It is not clear that there has been any significant trend in the rates of growth of total output and of output per head.' ('Resources and Output Trends in the United States since 1870', *National Bureau of Economic Research Occasional Paper No. 52*); and J. W. Kendrick, after suggesting that there was a significant acceleration of productivity advance from the end of the First World War as compared with the prior two decades, goes on 'there does not appear to have been either further acceleration, or retardation, in the primary trend rate of increase in total factor productivity since 1919.' ('Productivity Trends in Capital and Labor', *National Bureau of Economic Research Occasional Paper No. 53*.)

13. Lord Heyworth, in his annual speech in April 1959, spoke of these problems of the backward countries: 'There is no pattern of upbringing, no system of education, to develop the outlook and specialised skills which we must look for in countries like this. We cannot do a very great deal to improve matters because the development of patterns of society and ways of thought is part of a nation's historical development which no single firm could massively influence.'

The Sources of Invention*

I

It seems to be almost universally assumed that the launching of the space statellites was made possible only by employing vast teams of technicians working together in large research institutions under close central guidance and with unlimited resources and equipment. This may be true, although nobody in the western world can actually know that it is so. Any suggestion that the difference between failure and success might have resulted from a path-breaking discovery by some worker not in a large institution and perhaps not even interested primarily in high-altitude rockets would, nearly everywhere, be instantly dismissed as ludicrous. All this is indicative of the degree to which we are now dominated by the doctrine that technical progress can come only from mass attacks upon set problems.

In fact, a glance at the history of the high-altitude rocket hardly supports such a theory. Some of the more important early scientific writings on this subject, published in 1903, were those of a Russian schoolmaster, K. E. Ziolkowsky. He made many fundamental contributions to rocket technology. (Russia was probably further ahead of other countries in thought and work on rockets in 1903 than now.) Perhaps the most important scientific contribution to rocket theory, however, was made by Hermann Oberth, a teacher of mathematics in Transylvania, who in 1923 published his classic *By Rocket into Interplanetary Space*. Between the two world wars practical interest was maintained by a group of young German amateurs, some of whom were destined to become later outstanding figures in this field. During the war the German military authorities took up the development of the rocket and finally produced the V2, which covered a distance of 120 miles with a deflection of only $2\frac{1}{2}$ miles from the target, reached a speed of 3000 miles per hour and a height of nearly 60 miles. When Germany was finally overrun the Peenemünde experts were scattered. Some went to the United States and Britain, more finished up in Russia. Considering the rapid progress made by Germany in a relatively short period during the war, the development of high-alititude rocket since that time seems to have been fairly slow everywhere; for by 1945 there

Lloyds Bank Review, January 1958.

was no doubt that a satellite could be placed in the sky by the use of rockets and there was no great mystery about how, in general, this could be done. The fundamental discoveries in regard to high-altitude rocket propulsion, as distinct from the refinement and development of these ideas, were made by independent enthusiasts working with limited resources under discouraging conditions and for long ridiculed or ignored by the main bodies of organised science and technology.

II

Even, however, before atomic energy and the sputniks, new notions had been gaining ground about how inventions could best be stimulated and how scientists and technologists might be employed to the best effect. (These ideas began to be strongly advocated only during the 1930s. Before that time, it will be recalled, it was commonly believed that the problem of production was solved and that the distribution of wealth was the important task to be dealt with; that technical progress was perhaps going on too quickly and that scientists and technologists were probably doing more harm than good in the world.) The new doctrines really amount to a claim that the world has suddenly become a different kind of place, that the lessons of the past have largely become irrelevant and that we must all now adjust ourselves and our thinking accordingly. This 'modern' view can be summarised as follows. In the nineteenth century, most invention came from the individual inventor who had little or no scientific training and who worked largely with simple equipment and by empirical methods and unsystematic hunches. The link between science and technology was slight. In the twentieth century, the argument runs on, the characteristic features of the nineteenth century are rapidly passing away. The individual inventor is becoming rare; men with the power of originating are largely absorbed into research institutions of one kind or another, where they must have expensive equipment for their work. Useful invention, in particular, is to an ever increasing degree issuing from the research laboratories of large firms, which alone can afford to operate on an appropriate scale. There is increasingly close contact now between science and technology. The consequence is that invention has become more automatic, less the result of intuition of flashes of genius and more a matter of deliberate design. The growing power to invent, combined with the increased resources devoted to it, has produced a spurt of technical progress to which no obvious limit is to be seen.

In this article are set down some of the results of an enquiry, shortly to be published in full,[1] designed to test these opinions against the observable facts. It was hoped in this way to make some contribution to a better understanding of the dynamics of industrial societies. The study, it must be repeated, covered a period before atomic energy and space satellites. It may be that these latest spectacular discoveries, and the circumstances in which they have arisen, rob earlier experience of all pertinence for thinking about the future. I personally have doubts about this but I cannot enlarge upon them here. Further, the study was confined to *inventions* as contrasted with *development* of those inventions; it was concerned with the early crucial periods of radical innovation and not the later stages of improvement and exploitation of the original discoveries. It is, of course, impossible to draw a sharp dividing line between the two. On the other hand, it would be futile to deny that some new ideas are more revolutionary than others, that certain conceptions start a long chain of consequential improvements and that, unless the flow of these seminal ideas can be maintained, technical progress will finally come to a stop.

III

The first task was to pick out a group of twentieth-century inventions which might be regarded as a fair cross-section of the technical progress of the past 50 years; to make as detailed a study as possible of the conditions under which they had arisen and, in particular, to try to identify the respective parts played by individual inventors, the research activities of firms of varying size, of universities and of other institutions where research is conducted. A list of about 60 inventions was studied, ranging from acrylic fibres to the zip fastener, from air conditioning to xerography.[2]

The clearest conclusion emerging from the enquiry was that simple generalisations are not possible. The important twentieth-century inventions have arisen in all sorts of ways and through the activity of the different possible agencies. More than one-half of the cases can be ranked as individual invention in the sense that much of the pioneering work was carried through by men who were working on their own behalf without the backing of research institutions and often with limited resources and assistance or, where the inventors were employed in institutions, these institutions were, as in the case of universities, of such a kind that the individuals were autonomous.

The jet engine was invented and carried through the early stages of development almost simultaneously in Great Britain and Germany by men who were either individual inventors unconnected with the aircraft industry or who worked on the airframe side of the industry and were not specialists in engine design; the aircraft engine manufacturers came in only after much pioneering had been carried on. The gyro-compass was invented by a young man who was neither a scientist nor a sailor but had some scientific background and was interested in art and exploration. The process of transforming liquid fats by hardening them for use in soap, margarine and other foods was discovered by a chemist, working in the oil industry, who pursued his researches, and his efforts to get the process adopted, single-handed. The devices which made practicable the hydraulic power steering of motor vehicles were primarily the work of two men, one of whom worked strictly on his own, while the other was the head of a small engineering company. The foundations of the radio industry were laid by scientists; but the majority of the basic inventions came from individual inventors who had no connection with established firms in the communications industry or who worked for, or had themselves created, new small firms. In the case of magnetic recording, the early crucial invention came from an independent worker, as did a number of the major inventive improvements; the interest of the companies arose much later. The first successful system for the catalytic cracking of petroleum, which opened up the way for many later advances, was the product of a well-to-do engineer who was able to sell his ideas for development to the oil companies.

The history of the evolution of the cotton picker reveals two main lines of progress: in each case, individual inventors working with limited resources were able to take their ideas to the point where large firms were prepared to buy or license their patents for subsequent development. Bakelite, the first of the thermosetting plastics, was produced by a brilliant sole investigator. The first, and still the most important, commercially practicable method of producing ductile titanium was conceived of by a metallurgist working in his own laboratory. In the application of automatic transmissions to motor vehicles, the credit for mechanical novelty has to be shared between individual inventors and companies, but the former should probably rank above the latter; actually, the ideas of a shipbuilding engineer lie behind much of the modern progress, but both in Britain and the United States inventors working single-handed have contributed a great deal to the present-day mechanisms. Up to 1938, only one large aircraft manufacturer had taken much interest in the helicopter and even that only as the result of the personal interest of the head of the firm; the progress was made by the enthusiasm of individual inventors, usually with limited resources, obtaining backing in unlikely quarters in a manner which would parallel the many stories of 'heroic' invention in the nineteenth century. And, to mention one or two inventions from the field of consumer goods, the groundwork for the successful Kodachrome process was laid by two young collaborators, both musicians, whose ideas were taken up by a large photographic firm; the safety razor came from two individuals who struggled through financial and technical doldrums to great success; the zip fastener came from the minds of two engineers and was only taken up for large-scale production many years later; the self-winding wrist watch was invented by a British watch repairer.

The list next contains several important inventions emerging from firms which were small or of only moderate size. Terylene was discovered by a small research group in the laboratory of a firm which had no direct interest in the production of new fibres. The continuous hot strip rolling of steel sheets was conceived of by an inventor who might well be considered an individual inventor and perfected in one of the smaller American steel companies. The crease-resisting process emerged from a medium-sized firm in the Lancashire cotton industry. Cellophane tape was the product of what was virtually a one-man effort in a then small American firm. The virtues of DDT were founded by a Swiss chemical firm which, for that industry, was of modest dimensions.

Some outstanding successes arose out of the research of very large firms. Nylon was discovered by a small research group, headed by an outstanding chemist, in the laboratories of du Pont. Slightly later another very large firm, I.G. Farbenindustrie, produced and developed a similar fibre, Perlon. Several firms, all large, in Germany and the United States have devised methods of producing successful acrylic fibres. Freon refrigerants and tetraethyl lead were both produced in General Motors by small groups under Midgley and Kettering; the cases are interesting in that a motor engineering firm made these two important contributions in the chemical field and in that their discovery involved a strong element of chance. In the story of television, one outstanding figure was an employee of the Radio Corporation of America, but a number of the crucial inventions were made by a second American inventor who worked independently; and the first complete system for television broadcasting was created for the British Broadcasting Corporation by a British firm of modest size. The transistor was produced in the Bell Telephone Laboratories, a case which comes nearer than most to research directed towards a predetermined result. Polyethylene was discovered, in the course of some very broad scientific studies and as the immediate outcome of a fortunate accident, in the laboratories of Imperial Chemical Industries and developed by them; but methods of producing polyethylene at low pressures were later discovered at about the same time in one of the Max Planck Institutes in Germany and by American companies. Krilium was the discovery of research workers in the Monsanto Chemical Company, the result being attained by a combination of chance and a systematic search of a very wide field. In the discovery of the methyl methacrylate polymers, known variously as Perspex, Lucite and Plexiglas, two large firms were primarily involved: I.C.I. and Röhm & Haas; but an independent research student appears to have made an important contribution. The diesel-electric locomotive probably embodied less inventive effort than many of those mentioned above; it represented the development by European and American firms, and especially by General Motors in the United States, of nineteenth-century inventions. The recent remarkable growth in the use

of silicones represents the discovery of practical applications for com-
pounds produced by a British university scientist, the usefulness of
which was first realised by scientists in an American company. The discovery of Neoprene is a romantic story in which a priest, occupying a
chair in chemistry in an American university, was responsible for observations which were taken up by a large chemical firm and carried much
further by them to a successful conclusion.

Finally, some of the cases quite defied classification: where a research
worker in an industrial laboratory produced an invention outside his
own professional field; where an individual inventor and a company
reached much the same results at the same time; where a government
research station, an industrial company, scientists in the universities and
individual inventors all made important contributions to the final
result, and so on. Such cases, of course, heighten the impression of a
picture which admits of no simple explanation.

The cases taken as a whole reveal that no one country has a monopoly
of inventive power. The outstanding names and groups are widely
spread over many industrial countries. One significant exception is that,
in none of the 60 cases studied, had contributions been made by Russian
workers subsequent to the Revolution. Before that date, numerous
names of distinguished Russian contributors crop up: the early Russian
work in rockets has already been mentioned; in the early efforts linked
with television occurs the name of Rosing; Zworykin, who later on in the
United States was to make one of the vital contributions to the perfection of television, acquired his interests in this field in St Petersburg
before the First World War; Sikorsky, the great American helicopter
pioneer, had in fact built two helicopters in Russia as far back as 1909.
But, after the Revolution, it seems clear that Russia made no important
contributions in radar, television, the jet engine, the antibiotics, the
man-made fibres, the newer metals, the catalytic cracking of petroleum,
the continuous hot strip rolling of steel, silicones or detergents, until
others had shown the way and revealed what could be done.

IV

The twentieth century has, therefore, been much enriched by many inventions attributable to men who have worked under the kind of conditions associated, by long tradition, with the 'heroic age' of invention
in the nineteenth century. The next step in the enquiry was to look once
again at what happened during the last century. Was this an age when
uneducated inventors, ignorant of science, working in isolation in gar-
rets and cellars, blindly and unsystematically tried one thing after
another and occasionally stumbled by accident upon something worth
while but were invariably robbed of their due rewards by predatory

financiers? Such a picture seems to be a travesty of the facts. The links between science and inventive technology were often close. There were many distinguished scientists who were also important inventors: Kelvin, Joule, Davy, Dewar, Hofmann, Bunsen, Babbage and Playfair. It was frequently true that those inventors who were not formally trained in science showed a high respect for scientific knowledge and an anxiety to acquire it. James Watt spent much of his time with the most distinuished scientists of the day; Charles Parsons was a university graduate and the son of a President of the Royal Society; Trevithick, of the high pressure steam engine, consorted with members of the Royal Society; Cartwright was a Fellow of Magdalen College; Henry Maudsley was a close friend of Faraday; Wheatstone and Morse were professors; W. H. Perkin was a student at the Royal College of Chemistry; Edison made use of the Princeton University laboratories and worked closely with many scientists; C. F. Cross, the inventor of the viscose process, was a consulting chemist. This is to mention only some of the more famous names; the list could be greatly extended of nineteenth-century inventors with similar scientific contacts and interests.

Many of these men collaborated in ways which, in these days, would be dignified as team-work. Nor is it the whole truth that invention in the nineteenth century was merely empirical and accidental whilst that of the twentieth century has become scientific. It is far too large a subject to be argued in full here, but it is at least a tenable view that there has been just as much 'accidental' invention and discovery in the present century as in the last.

The evidence, therefore, suggests that much of the history of invention written up to the present day, by somewhat distorting the picture of what occurred in the nineteenth century and by then distorting it in the opposite sense for the twentieth century, has exaggerated the fundamental differences between the two periods and has understressed the continuity which runs through the whole story. Perhaps the world, in the matter of technical progress, is not such a new place as it is sometimes made out to be.

V

It was not the purpose of the enquiry to concern itself with policy; for what is needed, first and foremost, for a better understanding of the forces which influence the flow of innovations is more evidence in a field of study up to now sadly neglected. But the findings have some bearing upon major questions to which industrial societies ought properly to be addressing themselves.

We are in these days caught up in a great boom in industrial research and development which, in its present intensity, may be transient and in some ways artificial. It has been greatly stimulated by defence needs in the past year or two. It has been fostered by what are probably over-sanguine views about the value of science and technology in increasing the profits of individual firms or in raising general standards of living. But even when full allowance has been made for all this, there still remains a strong and newly-found belief that, by taking thought, it ought to be possible to increase the flow of new and useful technical and scientific ideas and to make fuller and more rapid use of them for material improvement. The policies which, in consequence, are being pressed have already been referred to. The maximum number of people should be given a basic training in technical matters; the different specialists must be encouraged or forced to share their knowledge and ideas in co-operative teams; scientists and technologists should be employed in large research institutions where, secure from the vicissitudes of the life of the independent inventor and provided with ample equipment, guidance can be given to the main lines of their in-terests. That, in fact, is what is happening in varying degrees everywhere. In Russia, we are informed, the whole body of scientists and technologists pursue their labours within a framework of purposes laid down by the central authority, benign but all-seeing. But, even in the western world, the institutionalisation of research and invention is going on apace. A steadily increasing proportion of those with scientific and technical training are now employed under conditions in which they are not free to follow their own bents and hunches, they are tied men. In some countries, even the autonomy of the universities is being threatened by their heavy dependence upon *ad hoc* grants for work on specified tasks.

Are these conditions most favourable to the flow of really new ideas? Or are they the conditions which, whilst perhaps increasing the number of minor improvements, will finally stifle originality? As John Stuart Mill once put it, the question is 'whether our march of intellect be not rather a march towards doing without intellect, and supplying our deficiency of giants by the united efforts of a constantly increasing multitude of dwarfs'. In trying to strike a balance here it is worth while looking at the side of the shield which in these days is so frequently ignored.

First, men with great powers of originality are in many ways a race apart. Like any other group, of course, they differ between themselves but on the whole they are constitutionally more averse to co-operation than the rest of us. 'I am a horse for single harness' wrote Einstein, 'and not cut out for landau or team-work'. This follows because their great gifts arise from the habit of calling everything, even the simplest assumptions, into question; because they are in the grip of inner compulsions which lead them to assume the right of deciding how their special powers should be employed and how best a task should be approached, to resent interference and to be thrown out of balance by it. Many of them are, by temperament, wholly unsuitable for work in any research institution which is formally organised. And, beyond that, it is even conceivable that, in many cases, their native powers of innovation might be weakened or destroyed by over-prolonged scientific or technical education.

Second, it seems to be possible to exaggerate the virtues of team-work. Of course, as knowledge grows and forces more specialisation upon scientists and technologists, systems of communication between the specialists must be progressively strengthened. And it is true that in some directions in recent years small teams are tending to replace the individual worker, although this is often because the man of original powers is given more assistance for his routine tasks. It is, however, a far cry from the useful, voluntary collaboration of a few like-minded people to the popular conception of serried ranks of Ph.Ds moving forward into the scientific unknown as an army guided by some common purpose. The working groups even in a large industrial research laboratory are normally small. The real moving spirits are few and the rest pedestrian, although of course useful, supporters. Quantity cannot make up for quality. The reasons for the limitation of team-work are obvious. Team-work is always a second best. There is no kind of organised, or even voluntary, co-ordination which approaches in effectiveness the synthesising which goes on in one human mind. Because of the growing specialisation, team-work undoubtedly is inescapable. But it carries with it a countervailing loss of power inevitable when several minds are groping towards mutual understanding. And the loss becomes the greater the larger the team and the less voluntary it is in character. Nor must it be overlooked that the members of a team must always go the same way; that the strength of a team may be determined by its weakest link; that friction even in small groups of men with original powers of mind is not uncommon; that all co-operation consumes time; and that a large team is essentially a committee and thereby suffers from the habit, common to all committees but especially harmful where research is concerned, of brushing aside hunches and intuitions in favour of ideas that can be more systematically articulated.

Third, it is erroneous to suppose that those techniques of large-scale operation and administration which have produced such remarkable results in some branches of industrial manufacture can be applied with equal success to efforts to foster new ideas. The two kinds of organisation are subject to quite different laws. In the one case the aim is to achieve smooth, routine and faultless repetition, in the other to break through the bonds of routine and of accepted ideas. Therefore large research organisations can perhaps more easily become self-stultifying than any other type of large organisation, since in a measure they are trying to organise what is least organisable. The director of a large research institution is confronted with what is perhaps the most subtle task to be found in the whole field of administration; a task which calls for a rare combination of qualities, scientific ability commanding the respect of colleagues and also an aptitude for organising a group. There are many cases to support the conclusion that a large research organisation may itself prove to be an obstacle to change. Ideas emanating from outside may be belittled or passed over. 'Is not every new discovery a slur upon the sagacity of those who overlooked it?' And it will always be seductive for an established organisation to take the smaller risks and more prudent routes when the rare and larger prizes are likely to be found in other directions.

VI

Here, then, is the dilemma which confronts any community trying to make the best of the native scientific and technical originality of its members. On the one side are the views of those, at the moment it seems in the majority, who conceive of the possibility of forcing the pace, as it was recently put by one research director:

We find the self-directed individual being largely replaced by highly organized team attack in which we employ many people who, if left entirely to their own devices, might not really be research-minded. In other words, we *hire* people to be curious as a group . . . we are undertaking to *create* research capability by the sheer pressure of money . . .

On the other hand are the fears of those, at present much in the minority, who suspect that such forcing tactics will mean that we may frustrate the awkward, lonely, enquiring, critical individuals who, to judge by past experience, have so much to give but can so easily be impeded. To pose the question in concrete form: the last time that a new form of propulsion, the jet engine, came to be conceived it was pressed forward by individual workers who had to meet frustrations and indifference, even resistance, on the part of established institutions. We are, presumably, not at the end of such innovations; there may be other new forms of motive power to come. And if, on some future occasion, the initiative comes in much the same way, do we resign ourselves to the idea that it must once again run the gauntlet of resistances from established interests? Are we further prepared to resign ourselves to the thought that, as research becomes more highly organised and the subject of institutional effort, any outside inventor will in the future have even less chance than in the past to force his ideas upon reluctant authority?

It may be that there are no clear-cut answers to such weighty questions. But the study of the inventions of the twentieth century would seem to support the following generalisations. Knowledge about innovation is so slender that it is almost an impertinence to speculate concerning the conditions and institutions which may foster or destroy it. But, in seeking to provide a social framework conductive to innovation, there would seem to be great virtues in eclecticism. If past experience is anything to judge by, crucial discoveries may spring up at practically any point and at any time. The only danger would seem to be in plumping for one method to the exclusion of others. In so far as society can usefully interfere, its task might well be to try to maintain the balance between the different sources of invention, to strive to prevent any one dominating to the exclusion of others. That country will, therefore, be happily placed which has a multiplicity of types of research agencies: the autonomous efforts of universities, government research organisations, industrial research associations, profit and non-profit seeking research institutes, the industrial research laboratories of firms of different size. And it would be well worth while to make efforts to guarantee that the independent inventor is not crowded out and that help and encouragement are available for him. As contrasted with the ideal ways of organizing effort in other fields, what is needed for maximising the flow of ideas is plenty of overlapping, healthy duplication of efforts, lots of the so-called wastes of competition and all the vigorous untidiness so foreign to the planners who like to be sure of the future.

NOTES

1. *The Sources of Invention* by J. Jewkes, D. Sawers and R. Stillerman, Macmillan, 1958.
2. Acrylic fibres, air conditioning, automatic transmissions, bakelite, ball-point pen, catalytic cracking of petroleum, cellophane, cellophane tape, chromium plating, cinerama, continuous casting of steel, continuous hot strip rolling, cotton picker, crease-resisting fabrics, Cyclotron, DDT, diesel-electric railway traction, domestic gas refrigeration, Duco lacquers, electric precipitation, electron microscope, fluorescent lighting, Freon refrigerants, gyro-compass, hardening of liquid fats, helicopter, insulin, jet engine, Kodachrome, krilium, long-playing record, magnetic recording, methyl methacrylate polymers, modern artificial lighting, Neoprene, nylon and Perlon, penicillin, 'Polaroid' land camera, polyethylene power steering, quick freezing, radar, radio, rockets, safety razor, self-winding wrist watch, shell moulding, silicones, stainless steels, streptomycin, Sulzer loom, synthetic detergents, synthetic light polariser, television, 'terylene' polyester fibre, tetraethyl lead, titanium, transistor, tungsten carbide, xerography, zip fastener.

Government and High Technology*

A QUESTION OF MOTIVES

Harold Wincott – the gentle, wise and shrewd Harold Wincott – whom
we remember tonight, once said to me that in matters of public policy
the primary function of the economist should be that of framing the
correct questions rather than that of providing cut-and-dried answers to
them. I think he was right. My question is this: why have successive
British governments spent such large sums on the encouragement of
high technology – which for practical purposes means nuclear energy,
aircraft – especially the Concorde and the Rolls-Royce RB-211 engine –
and computers?

The sums involved have been considerable even for these days of
casual public prodigality. The cost of the development of the several
reactor systems by the Atomic Energy Authority comes to well over £800
million. The development costs of the Concorde, shared between British
and French governments, have risen to about £1000 million. The cost to
government of the RB-211 has amounted to about £150 million.
Government has already made available for research and development
on computers some £28 million, and the final bill is expected to be four
or five times larger. So far the returns on these sums have been very disappointing, some would say derisory. We have built up no export
market in nuclear reactors. It is doubtful whether the price of electricity
is lower than it would have been without these reactors. We could have
purchased from other countries reactors more cheaply than those we
have built ourselves. Again it is generally accepted that the research and
development costs of the Concorde will not be recouped by sales. The
RB-211 engine still has to justify itself commercially. Our computer industry is not self-supporting.

Of course what the future holds, either in the increase of costs or the
emergence of some return upon costs, is anybody's guess. But clearly it
would be unwise to delay too long in striking a balance as to whether,
on the basis of experience and in the nature of things, this kind of

*Third Wincott Memorial Lecture, 31 October 1972.

activity on the part of the Government justifies itself. And, in the striking of such a balance, the recently published Sixth Report from the House of Commons Expenditure Committee,[1] Session 1971–2, on *Public Money in the Private Sector*, together with the Minutes of Evidence, offers a unique collection of documentary evidence upon which I intend to draw heavily in what I have to say.

Definition

It is important to recognise what is meant by the word 'high' in the term high technology. 'High' does not mean poised above sordid commercial considerations. Indeed successive British governments have always defended the money spent on the ground that it is likely to produce profits. Again 'high' does not mean that such branches of technology involve especially advanced levels of scientific study or technical achievement. The main centres of scientific excitement and progress in these days are surely to be found in biology, genetics and chemistry generally. And it is by no means obvious that what is called for in technical ingenuity is any less advanced in chemicals, pharmaceuticals or electronics than in any other field. 'High' does not mean those technical achievements which are comparatively free of the social irritations comprehensively described as pollution. On the contrary, the generation of nuclear energy carries with it quite terrifying problems for the disposal of lethal wastes and the booms of the supersonic aircraft everywhere endanger the chances of selling it. 'High' does not even imply the need for uniquely large capital expenditures. The sums I have quoted are, indeed, substantial. But they are no larger than, often not so large as, those which are devoted to exploration by the great oil companies and the great mining companies of the world.

High risk and high purpose?

No, high technology means exceptionally high-*risk* technology– projects to which companies, in close contact with realities, will not give their support because the chances of profit seem too small, problematical or remote, but where the Government, for one reason or another, feels that it knows better. Private enterprise will not jeopardise the requisite shareholders' capital but governments feel justified in risking the taxpayers' money.

It is here that the questions to the answers begin to pile up thick and fast. What has been the fundamental purpose of governments in taking this line? Why do they feel that their judgement should override that of others who might, on the surface, seem to be better qualified to judge? Why do they choose nuclear energy, supersonic aircraft or computers for this special treatment rather than any of the other numerous industries?

And, perhaps most important of all, how have governments assessed their success or failure and reacted to it?

Fear as the spur

Now, although the explanations and defence of this government strategy can be set down in more specific terms, some of which I will turn to in a moment, I suspect that all run back to one common central cause. That cause is *fear* – the fear on the part of an industrial country with a high standard of living that, with the steady spread of industrial expertise throughout the world, its own comfortable ways of living will be endangered by the competition of poorer countries. The fear is certainly not confined to Britain. America watches with alarm the encroachment of Japan and even of the European Community; Europe trembles at the evidence of the Japanese economic invasion; all the richer industrial countries shudder at the recent remarkable achievements of some smaller Far Eastern countries in the making of electrical goods and shipbuilding. Who is to say that, 20 years from now, many or most of the motor-cars or colour television sets will not be made in China or Taiwan or Korea, or that Birmingham or Detroit or Tokyo or Dusseldorf will not suffer the fate that fell upon the Lancashire cotton towns between the two World Wars? What will be left, it is asked, for the at-present rich countries to make and to sell to keep themselves going?

Such fears are understandable, highly contagious and largely without foundation. They become dangerous only if they are wrongly conceived of to be real and thereby produce panic reactions. It is indeed discouraging to have to record that such panic reactions are already evident. America, although still one of the freest trading areas in the world, seems to be moving towards protection for its most cherished industries. Europe is adding to its dislike of cheap imported food and equal distrust of cheap imported industrial products. Every country which makes ships or aircraft is busy subsidising so that inevitably the world is likely to have more aircraft and ships than it wants or is anxious to buy. Many countries that wish to expand and need capital which they cannot provide for themselves look askance at capital from abroad – the only place from which it can come – or insist upon accepting it only upon terms which render it unlikely that it will be offered.

It would take me too far afield this evening to explain why, in my opinion, these fears are dangerous in proportion as they are without basis. But briefly I would remind you that the economic theory of comparative advantage implies, except in some unlikely sets of circumstances, not only that richer and poorer countries can always continue to trade to their mutual advantage but also that, among the richer countries themselves, specialisation of production is so highly developed that the very richest and the not quite so rich will always be in a position to raise each other's standard of living. If you are suspicious of the truisms of economic science I can put it in this way: in the last quarter of a century the best customers of every industrial country have been the other industrial countries.

GOVERNMENT SPONSORSHIP OR MARKET DECISIONS?

I have digressed here because fundamentally I think the preoccupation of British governments with high technology is due to an almost neurotic reaction to the fear that other countries and governments are treading on our heels or have indeed actually surpassed us and that our only answer is to belt on even more rapidly with high technology to catch up with those in front or to escape from those who pursue.

Now, of course, any country will be better off if it becomes more lively and energetic in technical matters that have profitable commercial uses. But that is an answer to a question which is not relevant. The relevant questions here are two. Is it true that success in high technology industries is the widest and most open gateway to economic success – especially where it comes to ability to export? And even if it were, are governments, and government agencies, the bodies best fitted to pick their way to success among the infinite uncertainties and complexities in the world of high technology? Which is the best way of picking the winners, leaving it to governments or leaving it to private effort and the market?

Which horses to flog?

Some extremely interesting statistical investigations bearing upon the first of these questions have been carried out recently, some of the best by the National Economic Development Office.[2] Thus it can be asked, which products are growing most quickly in world trade? The answer is that they are not products found wholly or even mainly among the high-technology commodities. The front runners in fact are furs and fur clothing; watches and clocks; footwear; musical instruments and sound recorders; office machines; organic chemicals; scientific instruments and furniture. Similarly, the tentative efforts made to identify those products in which the UK has revealed its highest comparative advantages in world trading do not suggest that the high-technology goods have been the leaders. Of course these statistical exercises cannot be conclusive although they may well expose palpable mistatements of fact. In trying to interpret them it must always be remembered that what has happened in the past may not happen in the future. And also, that when a government sets out to tone up an industrial system it never really knows where to start. Should it try to stimulate the already progressive industries – which might turn out to be a policy of flogging to death horses already putting their best foot forward. Or should it set out to help the industries which are lagging behind – which might prove to be a policy of flogging horses virtually already dead. But the figures suggest that economic prosperity at least for Britain is more likely to come from producing the mundane rather than too much of the airy-fairy stuff.

Public policy, for better or worse, must be based on qualitative judgements. I do not think we are ever likely to find immutable laws here. It is easy enough to suggest that since governments tend to stand for control and uniformity and lack imagination they will suffer from a blind dread of innovation. Instances can be provided in support of this idea. It would be just as easy to spin the opposite theory that, possessed of the taxpayers' money and seeking for political kudos wherever it was to be found, governments will strike out recklessly along unknown paths. We must try to determine which is the more likely in our times and our surroundings.

Sources of innovation

It is worth while pointing out that the idea that governments have an increasingly important and effective part to play in stimulating the high innovating industries is somewhat paradoxical. For in the last 15 years a good deal of academic research has been carried out into innovation in private industry. Two conclusions, as a result, are by now I think widely accepted. One is the innovation does not flow wholly, or even mainly, from the largest corporations. The very size of a corporation may make it in some ways a centre of resistance to change. The other is that some of the largest corporations are themselves recognising that to force the pace too rapidly in the search for new things can be a business mistake, leading to losses and a lack of balance of effort among the many activities of a company. But if all this is established for private effort, why should it be taken for granted that governments, the largest of all institutions, should not suffer from the same inherent disabilities of size?

The obvious fears of statesmen in these days that technical advance in civil industries will not be fast enough without massive government intervention have many sources. Politicians personally often appear to be fascinated by the more dazzling technical devices which make the headlines in the newspapers. Lord Beeching has commented that:

I think [the British Government] has wasted an enormous amount of money on things justified by the pursuit of advanced technology – an almost childlike desire to play with toys.[3]

Beyond that it is often claimed that national independence and prestige

depend upon spectacular success in techology. This, of course, is not a
new story. Lenin once said that communism equals the political
preponderance of the proletariat plus electricity. This same kind of
argument has carried force in the western world. President de Gaulle,
who could always express in the noblest language even the dottiest of
economic ideas, spoke of the need

> to push relentlessly our technical and scientific research in order to
> avoid sinking into a bitter mediocrity or being colonised by the ac-
> tivities, inventions and capacities of other countries.

British statesmen have not been altogether immune. A former Prime
Minister once spoke of the 'white heat' of a scientific revolution. One
Minister of Technology became almost incandescent at the thought of
the technical miracles to come. It all adds substance to the unkind comment that high technology is 'the last refuge of the enthusiastic
nationalist'. This approach is really not good for sober commercial
calculations.

One result of all this is the ready way in which British governments in
recent years have fallen victim to what can be described as the hocus-
pocus of discussion on technology. Ministers, in the face of the evidence,
have clung to the ideas that innovation comes mainly from large
organisations; or that there is a correlation between expenditure on
research and development and national economic growth; or that the
country is confronted with a disastrous brain-drain. And it is still being
claimed that we live in a period of exceptionally rapid technical progress
and one in which the time elapsing between invention and application
tends to get shorter whereas it seems to be true that ours is really an
epoch of comparative technological sluggishness when there are not
very many authentically new things about and even these, for many
different reasons, are being developed rather slowly. (How much longer,
for example, will we have to wait for efficient battery-operated motor-
cars which will enable the pounding, smelly reciprocating engine to be
thrown on the scrap-heap; or the typewriter which will type as one dic-
tates, which will release hundreds of thousands of young women for
other more interesting tasks; or audio-visual cassettes which will enable
us to break away from the tyranny and the interminable boredom of
modern television; or a cure for the common cold; or much cheaper
and efficient ways of digging tunnels so that the surface of the earth
could be reoccupied by the people instead of being overrun by
machines; or really substantial cuts in costs of desalinisation rendering
it possible to turn deserts into gardens. This list could easily be
extended.)

So we find major decisions being made by statesmen because they feel
in their bones, or if you will pardon the vulgarity, they have a 'gut

feeling' that this or that course is correct. I do not wish to press this point too hard. After all, innovation mainly comes from discarding preconceived ideas. As Sir Denning Pearson has said, 'Anyone who undertakes the development of an engine like the RB-211 must be an optimist'.[4] But there is or should be this difference between private and public effort. With private effort the glitter of all things bright and beautiful is toned down by the shadow of the balance sheet and the possibility of bankruptcy. But with governments the sky gleams brighter longer.

Independent advice?

As main agents in innovation governments will always have difficulty in obtaining sound, independent advice. If the British Government, for example, is interested in the potentialities of a new British aero-engine, whom can it consult? Only Rolls-Royce, which can be expected to look upon the sunny side of doubt, or of its active competitors in other countries which can be expected to be biased in the other direction. If the Government is interested in a new British aircraft, there are now only two British companies; is the one to be consulted about the soundness of the views of the other? With nuclear energy, of course, the Government has been its own agent for research and development. The Atomic Energy Authority has been virtually the sole judge of progress and possibilities on matters where its own standing and existence have been at stake. It is, therefore, not surprising that so many mistakes in prognostication have been made, nearly all on the same side. The Atomic Energy Authority has provided for governments a series of predictions always overoptimistic, regarding the speed with which technical problems will be overcome, the costs of development programmes, the price at which electricity will be available and the extent to which nuclear energy would replace other forms of energy.[5] Its current calculations and predictions seem no less sanguine. As for the Concorde, the British Government entered into a binding agreement with the French Government with imprecise knowledge of the probable cost – which has in fact increased from £150 million to £1000 million.

Government, of course, may take the advice of outside consultants, but these can rarely if ever possess anything more than a limited knowledge of all the commercial and technical circumstances of the case. Or it may set up, in its own Departments, groups of technical experts. But this doubling up of staff must add to costs and sometimes leads, as I will try to show in a moment, to officials defending government schemes in which they can have very little confidence.

But what of the Treasury? Cannot these highly trained and experienced officials be regarded as a solid long-stop on these occasions? Fortunately we have, in the Report from the Expenditure

Committee, a most illuminating, although perhaps not surprising, account of the manner in which the Treasury operates in such cases, evidence indeed which deserves to be more widely and carefully read than has apparently been so up to now. As I interpret it, it amounts to a statement that Treasury controls can operate only within very wide margins. Officials can inject into deliberations and decisions what they regard as 'an appropriate degree of scepticism'. They know that in these affairs of high technology estimates always suffer from the same complaint – they are always too optimistic. But the limitation of Treasury control was well put in the evidence:

> ... over the years we have come to apply a discount factor, ... to all technical advice we are given. When any scientist tells us that such and such a thing can be done within x years, we probably say 2x; and if the technicians say the cost will be y millions, we probably say 5y millions. This is a sort of rule of thumb, pure experience ...[6]

This is all highly reminiscent of my own experience in wartime when I was concerned with the planning of the aircraft programme and when, in the exigencies of those times, we were forced to engage in wild guessing and often to rely upon our own judgements of the value of the estimates being set before us by aircraft manufacturers. But I cannot believe that in peacetime a viable economic system can be operated on the basis of this kind of guesswork, with margins of error of this magnitude.

Good money after bad

Another disability of government is this. With innovation at the high level we are discussing, skill and judgement in withdrawing from untenable situations are just as important as imagination and courage in pushing on under apparently unpromising circumstances. I always think that private industry, and especially the biggest companies within it, has in the past lost a great opportunity of teaching the world what is meant by business enterprise by not telling more openly and fully the stories of their big and costly failures in innovation. There is nothing to be ashamed of here. On the contrary, some of these losses constitute some of the most vivid illustrations of what is meant by risk-taking. But there are good reasons for supposing that governments which embark on high technology will always be in greater danger than private industry of being drawn further and further into fruitless expenditure and under less compulsion to cry off at the right time.

This is not merely because a government by a reversal of policy, and thereby a confession of failure, loses political face; or that it can put its hand into the deepest pocket of all – that of the taxpayers; or that it can often muzzle its critics with the charge that they are smirching the great achievements of their own country. Perhaps more important is the danger of the Government building up implied or expressed obligations difficult or impossible to discard or dishonour. Thus, although it is quite clear that the Government did *not* give an open-ended commitment to Rolls-Royce over the RB-211, yet there can be little doubt from the evidence that both Rolls-Royce and the Lockheed Aircraft Company were disagreeably surprised when, as it was put, the Government 'pulled the carpet from under their feet'. In the case of the Concorde, the fact that a British government had an agreement to collaborate with the French made any reversal of policy even more difficult and complicated. Sometimes the built-in obligations are inescapable. As the case for nuclear energy well illustrates, when Civil Service permanent establishments become too large for their tasks the line of least resistance will naturally be that of trying to make work for redundant staffs.

Problem of continuity

There are other secondary, although by no means minor, reasons why governments are perhaps not very effective agents for high technology enterprises. One is that such projects, by their very nature, can produce results only over a long period whereas the life of a government is normally short. Continuity may thus be endangered. Another is that when a government does finally reach a point at which a reversal of policy is decided upon, it often moves precipitately, as if to make up for lost time. Some day, I suppose, we will have the results of a full-scale inquest into the Rolls-Royce affair. But, on on the basis of the evidence now extant, it is possible to wonder whether Rolls-Royce would not have renegotiated its contracts more favourably than did the Government subsequently and whether, indeed, there was any real need to nationalise the company at all.[7]

DANGERS IN GOVERNMENT PROJECTS

I turn now to two disagreeable dangers, disagreeable in the political and constitutional sense, which may become associated with the kind of government projects I am discussing. The first is the possibility of secrecy in the handling of public funds; the second is that of thrusting upon the shoulders of public servants tasks which may change for the worse the character of the public service itself.

Secrecy

As for secrecy, a revealing case is that of the refusal of officials, of course under instructions from above, to provide a breakdown of the estimated cost of the Concorde which finally led the chairman of the Trade and Industry Sub-Committee of the Expenditure Committee to the sharp comment that:

> I realise the policy is not yours ... but I think it is the most outrageous example of Parliament being denied information about public expenditure since John Hampden refused to pay ship money ...

The curious must turn for details of this case to the Expenditure Report itself.[8] But the outline was this. The Government was in fact regularly informing parliament of its own estimated *total* cost of the Concorde. But it refused to disclose its own estimated costs of the main sections of the work – the airframes, the engines, etc. – carried out by the main contractors. The reason was that in reaching its own estimated total cost it had included estimated costs for the main sections of the work higher than those which had been submitted by the main contractors – that is to say the Government, doubtless embittered by past experiences, had allowed something for contingencies. But why this strategem? The officials explained that if they had provided the breakdown of their own costings this

> would have weakened the discipline and incentive imposed upon main contractors of trying to complete the programme within their estimates of costs.

Even so the practice, as the Expenditure Committee pointed out, was questionable in that it involved concealment on the part of the Government. The Committee might have added that the practice was probably unavailing. It could only have succeeded if the main contractors, already engaged in a highly co-operative task involving day-to-day contacts, could have been prevented from talking to each other about these costs. And as soon as the stratagem was suspected by the main contractors they would, of course, become quite happy to work to the Government's higher cost figures – and the so-called discipline effect would disappear.

Defending the indefensible

The second danger is, I think, more important. If Ministers are to reach important decisions in high technology by 'gut feelings' and if their civil servants are increasingly called upon to defend these policies by rational argument (which we all know they will do because of their strong traditions of loyalty and will do well because of the accumulation of experience and the high competence of the Service), is there not the danger that the whole character of the Service will be adversely affected by having thrust upon it the embarrassing task of defending what is rationally indefensible and known to be such. I certainly do not wish here to get involved with the question of who makes fundamental policy decisions – the Minister or his servants. But I would like to examine one story in some detail for a double purpose: to indicate how inherently weak was the Government's case and how thin and unsatisfying were the arguments to which its servants were forced to resort in defence of it.

ARGUMENTS FOR AND AGAINST GOVERNMENT INTERVENTION

The Expenditure Committee time and time again posed the question, why should Britain have a civil aircraft industry larger than that which would emerge through the activities of companies working with their own capital and operating independently or in collaboration with other companies here or abroad? Why government intervention at all? I will briefly summarise the answers that were given.

'National interest'

The first answer was that we *must* have such an industry because other countries have an aircraft industry. But the Government admitted that

> . . . there has been a clear understanding from the date of the Plowden Report onwards that there should be no attempt to keep the aircraft industry at a given size. Its size should be related to the projects which it can produce and successfully continue.[9]

This statement clearly implies that, should the economic forces decree, the aircraft industry would be allowed to die out altogether. If a thing must not be of any given size, it clearly may be of no size. Yet this statement was made as part of a plea that massive government aid should be available to keep the British aircraft industry in the forefront of technical achievement.

'Growth' industry

Another answer was that the aircraft industry is a 'growth' industry. The government spokesman suggested that, on a conservative basis, the amount of world business available in civil aircraft would over the next ten years amount to £30,000 million, of which he thought some 6 per cent would be the British share, i.e. £1800 million.[10] In the aircraft and air travel industries we know that practically every prediction of every type has been wide of the mark in the past quarter of a century. But with this particular estimate, what assumptions were being made about the scale of government subsidies in the guessing of future sales? Do figures of potential sales matter anyway; is it not potential profits that matter? The main query, however, surely is: if there is this enormous potential market, why do governments need to provide help at all?

Balance of payments

A third answer was that a substantial aircraft industry justified itself on balance-of-payment grounds; for not only have exports of aircraft been substantial but the industry has been an important 'import saver'. Here the reasoning got into a terrible tangle. There is no very useful distinction to be made between export industries and import-saving industries. Everything produced in Britain is either exported or consumed at home and thereby replaces an import. Everything produced therefore improves the balance of payments – hairpins as well as aircraft. In comparatively free markets, of course, every export of unsubsidised goods and every extension of the output of homespun goods at a lower cost than that at which the foreigner can supply is to be welcomed on balance-of-payments grounds. In this way the aircraft industry in the past has made its contribution and no doubt will be able to continue to do so. But to jump from that position to defending subsidised exports or subsidised home production is a complete *non-sequitur*. Exports can always be increased if they are given away; imports can always be reduced if they are forbidden and the article produced at a higher price at home. But the result will be a generally lower standard of living. What evidence is there to support the view that subsidised high-technology aircraft activities have improved the balance of payments in the last five years or are likely to do so in the future without diminishing the national income? I submit, so far, no evidence at all.

'Spin-off' effect

Another answer given, although recently with much less confidence than heretofore, was that high technology in civil aircraft brings a bonus in the form of 'spin-off'. The statement is, of course, technically correct. But it is just one illustration of what is generally true. The growth of science and technology is a continuous and ever-widening flow. One thing is always built upon, derived from, another. All research and development in each and every industry produces its 'spin-off'. I have not yet seen evidence that this is relatively large or more likely to arise in aircraft research and development than elsewhere.

Social benefits

Another answer given on behalf of the Government (and you will be relieved to know that this is the last I propose to deal with) is that certain broad social benefits can be expected to flow from the encouragement of high technology in aircraft. In recent years much play has been made by economists with the idea of possible divergencies between social and private costs, social and private benefits. I think we should be very cautious, not to say suspicious, in applying this idea to specific cases and building policy upon it.[11] Of course no one would deny that there are some straightforward cases where the principle can be applied and the necessary action is obvious. If a private factory belches out smoke or a nationalised industry pollutes local waterways then the obvious answer is to tell the responsible bodies to stop it and to meet the cost of stopping it. But to carry such calculus into more complicated and less certain cases is not defensible. It has to be remembered that these social costs and benefits cannot be measured with any accuracy. In many cases it is impossible to determine whether they are plus or minus. It is revealing that, nearly always, these divergencies are appealed to when advocating *extensions* of government activity and rarely when recommending the curbing of them. Only too often the attempts to quantify these divergencies constitute the rickety foundations upon which equally gimcrack cost-benefit analyses are erected, by which process practically anyone can advance practically any personal whim or prejudice in pseudo-scientific language.

So that when these divergencies are invoked to justify the heavy subsidising of high technology in aircraft on the score that this will increase employment, make the world a richer place, or foster the brotherhood of man, it is necessary to face other relevant questions. What would have been the effect on employment or the improvement in other forms of transport, or even in other types of aircraft, if these subsidies had been more widely spread or not granted at all, so that taxation, including taxation on profits, generally would have been lower? And if we cannot answer these questions with confidence then I think that most of these cost-benefit exercises should be confined to the academic halls where most of them really belong and where they provide much healthy intellectual excitement.

Civil Service standards

But I am not so much concerned with the particulars of these specific lines of defence of high-technology aircraft as with the more general point: that all these answers I have mentioned – with their internal inconsistencies and their appeal to vague and shifting economic concepts – are being put forward by government officials. This quality of argument on their part is all out of character. I am confident that if these same officials had been made judges in the case, and not been put up as the witness for the defence, they would not have shown much mercy on the evidence. It cannot be a good thing in our society if the art of advocacy is increasingly deployed in those quarters where we have the right to expect fair statements of facts and even confessions of reasonable doubt.

Planning the unplannable

In answer to what I have been saying it might be replied: if past failures are recognised and intelligently studied, and the proper lessons drawn from them, this must inevitably reduce the risk of future failures. This theme is found running through much of the evidence from government departments as given to the Expenditure Committee. Practice, after all, it is being suggested, makes perfect. This statement is seductive but may be erroneous. Its validity depends upon one critical assumption: the assumption that the analysis of past experience can provide a safe guide for the future. But there are many spheres of action in which this is not true for the simple reason that no past set of circumstances will recur or, if it should do so, will be recognisable as such at the time. After all, if the whole history of the world in the past century could be drawn together and accurately analysed it would not tell us what would happen over the next ten years or indeed what would happen tomorrow. If every past national central economic plan was studied in the greatest detail and the reasons for its failure laid bare, it would not prevent the next central economic plan from breaking down because of a new, wholly unpredictable set of errors. Nothing is sadder in the economic scene than the efforts of governments to plan the unplannable, to achieve simultaneously mutually incompatible ends. And we have to ask ourselves whether the efforts of governments to turn what is essentially high-risk technology into low-risk technology by taking thought is not a case of this kind.

In commenting on past experience Treasury officials have confirmed that '. . . most people would feel that the return the nation has had from its R and D expenditure has been disappointing'.[12] What has happened up to now and what seems likely to happen in the future suggest that that is the way it is going to stay.

Dangers of improved monitoring system

Certainly administrative changes would seem to offer no cure. For instance, it has been proposed that errors in the aviation world might have been avoided if the Government could have had the advice of a quite large group, including representatives of airlines, the industry itself, the fighting services and other industries – a kind of 'sorting-out body'. But might not a larger and less homogeneous body simply increase the conflicts of interest and outlook?

Or again, the Expenditure Committee has wondered whether it might itself take a useful hand in regularly examining witnesses from government departments in order to ensure that public money was being well spent. No one who has followed me so far will fail to appreciate the value I attach to the work of the Expenditure Committee. But it seems to me that its importance lies largely in the study of happenings after they have occurred in order to extract the benefits from being wise after the event. This Committee could not take part in formulating original decisions – that is the task of government. And it would probably be no help in watching expenditures day by day – that is an executive task.

The truth is that most of the administrative proposals relating to the need for improved government 'monitoring' (the latest magic word, which has replaced 'efficiency audits' and 'accountability') in high technology run the danger of throwing the baby away with the bathwater. As the Secretary of State for Trade and Industry himself said, when confronted with the suggestion of closer and more continuous surveillance by the Expenditure Committee: '. . . it is dangerous, to my mind, so to organise the monitoring system as virtually to emasculate the management activity itself'.[13]

CONCLUDING REMARKS

I warned you at the outset that my interest in raising questions is much greater than my ability in, or indeed my responsibility for, answering them. But perhaps you will bear with me in one speculation based upon what I have said so far. What I have been nibbling at is one tiny corner of that supreme question for society, for which we must always be making provisional, though we can never produce a final, answer: what should the State undertake and what should be left to private effort; how best can we combine the drive that comes from individual freedom in thinking and action with the force necessary to bind us together in a cohesive society?

There is one observation here that is so simple I am almost ashamed to mention it. It is that at any one time what a government *should* undertake ought to be determined by what it has already taken on and how well it is carrying out its earlier appointed tasks. Now, despite disagreements about where exactly the line should be drawn, there is universal consent that the primary obligations of government (without success in which all else must come to frustration) are, first, defence; second, the maintenance of law, order and justice; third, the maintenance of the vital central standards of measurement, including above all the value of money; and fourth, the prevention of fraud and misrepresentation. I think that few would disagree with my comment that in recent years British governments have not been performing these tasks as successfully as they used to perform them. That is not necessarily intended by way of criticism. It may be, personally I think it is indeed true, that the problems themselves have become more complicated and less tractable than they used to be. Government has had to run harder to stay where it is. But if a government finds that the performance of its primary tasks is tending to overwhelm it, is it not common sense for it to shed some of its less important commitments or delegate them to other institutions and agencies, among which agencies would be included free markets and private enterprise?

I am not suggesting that governments have no proper and inescapable functions in the wider field of science and technology. The Government must determine how much should be made available for pure science in universities and elsewhere. The Government must maintain research establishments for the provision of many beneficial services which can alone be provided by the central authority: public health, purity of products, safety of appliances, and so on. The *raison d'être* of such activities is to perform services which would not otherwise be carried out because a market price cannot be charged for them in the normal way.

But if our present-day governments would admit the falling standards of success in their primary jobs and decide that activities with lower priorities should be dropped, surely involvement in civil high technology should be regarded as one of the first for the discard. For here the aims of government seem uncertain, the charting of the original course a most baffling task, and the procedures for controlling the subsequent course highly obscure.

NOTES

1. Hereafter referred to as 'The Expenditure Committee'.
2. M. Panic and A. H. Rajan, *Product Changes in Industrial Countries' Trade: 1955–1968*, NEDO Monograph 2, 1971.
3. The Expenditure Committee, Vol. III, p. 457.
4. The Expenditure Committee, Vol. III, p. 493.
5. Duncan Burn, *The Political Economy of Nuclear Energy*, Research Monograph 9, IEA, 1967.
6. The Expenditure Committee, Vol. II, p. 66.
7. The Expenditure Committee, Vol. III, pp. 483–502: evidence of Sir Denning Pearson and Sir David Huddie.
8. The Expenditure Committee, Vol. III, pp. 588–91.
9. The Expenditure Committee, Vol. II, p. 127.
10. The Expenditure Committee, Vol. II, p. 124.

11. Sir Alec Cairncross summarised his views on this subject in reply to the question 'Can you sum up briefly why you think there is a justification for government aid to the private sector?' His answer was: 'The usual way in which economists give an answer to your question is in terms of divergencies between social and private costs. I could give an answer like that, but I feel that it is not usually much help to an administrator or to a Minister to enunciate the principle, because there are usually several different principles, and the question to be resolved is what weight you attach to each of them in a particular case. You can justify by reference to some principle help in almost any circumstances you like, and you can justify refraining from giving the help.' (The Expenditure Committee, Vol. III, p. 651.)
12. The Expenditure Committee, Vol. II, p. 71.
13. The Expenditure Committee, Vol. III, p. 674–5.

7 THE GOVERNMENT AND STATE INDUSTRIES

Introductory Note

Although, as is said in the General Introduction, the British seem to have been constantly mulling over the same economic problems since 1945 and apparently getting nowhere, this is so remarkably true of the nationalisation of industry that it merits special mention. The paper which follows 'The Nationalisation of Industry' was originally published in 1953, by which time we had had only a comparatively short experience of the consequences of the massive nationalisation schemes of the post-war Socialist Government. But an analysis of the grounds on which these schemes were advocated and their actual performance led me to conclude then that

> Nationalisation is peculiarly barren of anything fruitful or novel – there is something almost melancholy in its failure to introduce any fresh idea in the field of organisation or administration.

I based my conclusions on some simple propositions. First, that the idea that a nationalised industry can ever make itself 'accountable' to the public in any real sense is a chimera. Only a free price system and competition makes accounting a rational process. Second, that a government which first puts an industry 'into politics' by nationalising it and then, dissatisfied with the results, seeks to take the nationalised industry 'out of politics' is chasing its own tail. The only way of taking a nationalised industry out of politics is to denationalise it. Third, that with its nationalised industries, a government will always be tempted to court popularity by giving way to democratic pressures for the provision of goods and services on exceptionally favourable terms.[1] Fourth, that the nationalisation of an industry makes it a power in political squabbles which have little or nothing to do with efficiency of operation – for ministers wrestle for power with the executive heads of the nationalised industries; one nationalised industry struggles with another for supremacy in a given field; or one nationalised industry seeks to encroach further upon the territory of private firms. Fifth, neither theoretical reasoning nor practical experience suggests that a nationalised industry will set new standards in efficiency – on the contrary, because of the very size of the nationalised industry, its monopoly powers, the impossibility of devising a rational price structure and the absence of the pressure to make profits, it will tend to be clumsy and slow-moving, secure in the last resort in the knowledge that the taxpayers' pocket is there for the picking.

Such ideas as these commanded little respect when the following paper was written and the nationalised industries lumbered on like ageing mastodons in a world in which they were progressively unfit for survival. But a quarter of a century later the National Economic Development Office, after a 15-month long study of the subject, came out with a report which described the State industries in much the same terms.[2] Sir Ronald McIntosh, the Director General of NEDO, on the basis of the report, comprehensively condemned the machinery and operation of the State industries.

> There is a lack of trust and mutual understanding between those who run the nationalized industries and those in government. There is confusion about the respective roles of the boards of nationalized industries, Ministers and Parliament with the result that accountability is seriously blurred. There is no systematic framework for reaching agreement on long-term objectives. There is no effective system for measuring the performance of nationalized industries.

And so on. The curious reader will find other close parallels between the NEDO document and my own, written nearly a quarter of a century apart.

In its recommendations, however, NEDO provides us with just another example of the grim determination of Britain to hang on to exploded theories and to set out to patch up the irreparable. One might have expected NEDO, on the basis of its findings, to accept the simple proposition that 'the cure for the weaknesses of Nationalization is Denationalization'. Not so. For one of their main recommendations was that, in order to take the nationalised industries 'out of politics', a new 'Policy Council' should be inserted between Whitehall and the Boards of the State industries which would 'agree aims and the policies to reach them, provide criteria for judging efficiency and monitor performance'. In brief, it was being suggested that by further fiddling with the organising and control of the State industries which would certainly make them even more clumsy, what by all past experience had proved impossible would now miraculously become feasible.

NOTE

1. One almost comical feature of the thought of British governments, and especially socialist governments, is their somersaulting about profit-making by

A Return to Free Market Economics?

nationalised industries. It was originally intended that such industries must cover their costs by their proceeds 'taking good years with bad'. This was put forward as an improvement, both morally and economically, on the evils of the capitalistic system of profit-making. Over the years after 1948 the nationalised industries made heavy losses, most of which were written off by the government of the day. But after 1974 the Socialist Government altered its policy, abolished subsidies and instructed nationalised industries to charge appropriately higher prices. The result was that these industries began to make very large profits. But as Professor Charles Carter, the Chairman of an official committee set up to review the policies of the Post Office, pointed out, with the monopoly power of nationalised industries 'there is no point judging the service by the degree to which it makes profits. This is merely the power to overcharge'. In the case of the telephones the profits were so large that the Government finally ordered the Post Office to make refunds to subscribers. But Mr Denis Healey, the Chancellor of the Exchequer, defended the profit-making of the nationalised industries by claiming (see 'Newsweek'. 22 August 1977, p. 15): 'The nationalised industries have made profits of £m.500 which means they will be able to finance most of their new investment out of existing resources *like any ordinary business*' (my italics). In brief, what had been the evils of capitalism could now be regarded as the virtues of socialism.

2. National Economic Development Office: 'A Study of U.K. Nationalised Industries', November 1976.

The Nationalisation of Industry*

CLAIMS FOR NATIONALISATION

Nationalisation is a method of organising and administering industry whereby the community owns the means of production and the government is, at least in the last resort, responsible for its control. The crux of the idea is that the whole of one industry falling within the boundary of one nation should be subject to a unifying influence. Contemporary nationalisation, therefore, is a piecemeal and empirical approach to much wider ideas – such as that the whole of industry within one country should be brought under state operation or that the whole of the industry in the world might be usefully organised to work together under some supernational authority. This piecemeal approach, one industry at a time or one country at a time, is reflected in the view that certain industries are 'ripe' for nationalisation whilst others are not yet in fit form for the transfer from private to public hands.[1]

It is only recently that the claim has been made that nationalisation is a more efficient way of organising an industry than is possible while it remains in private hands. The socialist writers of the early part of the century were more disposed to claim other, broader social advantages – that nationalisation would abolish the evils inherent in competition, private profit-making and the private ownership of the means of production; or that it would open up the way for workers' control in industry; or that it would result in a more equal distribution of income or capital or that it would provide an answer to the manifold dangers of private monopoly. Since 1945, these broader arguments have not been absent. Thus it has been held that certain industries were 'basic' to the whole system and could, therefore, not be entrusted to private hands, or that the 'public services' should clearly be owned by the public; or that some industries, being 'strategic' to a system of central economic planning, must be under the control of the state or that others, such as the Bank of England or the iron and steel industry, represented citadels of

* The *University of Chicago Law Review*, Summer, 1953.

capitalism which must be reduced in order to establish the reality of socialism.[2]

But more and more in Great Britain it has come to be felt that nationalisation must stand or fall by the degree to which it replaces a relatively inefficient system of organisation by one relatively more efficient. The test must be whether it raises the standard of living. And it is not a little ironic that this switch to a new set of criteria has come just at a time when, as a result of experience of the operation of nationalised industries, grave doubts are widely felt as to whether they are, or can ever be, more efficient than the privately-owned industries they have replaced.

The claim that nationalisation represents a more efficient manner of running industry and of translating decisions regarding prices and investment into actions can best be examined in terms of the fundamental changes introduced in any industry subjected to nationalisation. They are:

1. The nationalised industry is a larger operating unit than those it replaced. From this arises the claim for the economies of scale.

2. The nationalised industry is monopolistic. Out of this arises the claim that it can adopt more complete integration and co-ordination of related functions.

3. The nationalised industry is not operated for private profit. From this it is asserted that price and investment policy can be made more rational and that the collaboration between different classes of workers in the industry can be made more willing, smoother and, thereby, fruitful.

TESTING THE CLAIMS FOR NATIONALISATION

In a period of relatively stable prices and costs, claims of this kind might usefully have been subjected to relatively simple tests. Comparisons of prices and costs and the scale of investment before and after nationalisation would have provided highly relevant evidence regarding net effects of changes in organisation. Actually, such tests are almost completely useless in Great Britain because of the gap in comparability created by the war and the economic instabilities of the post-war period. If, for example, it is observed that before the war coal in Great Britain was plentiful and relatively cheap, and that consumers could exercise choice in the qualities they purchased, while since nationalisation coal has been extremely scarce, relatively expensive, and consumers have had no control over the types of coal supplied to them, that may signify nothing. Too many other forces, in addition to the major change of organisation, were operating at the same time.

In the absence of anything better, attempts have been made to employ indices of physical efficiency, both for the purpose of assessing the consequences of nationalisation and for the purpose of rendering these industries 'accountable' to the public. But the emphasis placed upon such measurements and the determined conviction in many quarters that, provided the search is sufficiently prolonged and statisticians are sufficiently courageous and ingenious, some relatively simple physical measurements are to be found indicating whether an industry is becoming more or less efficient, are in themselves manifestations of much of the unsystematised thinking surrounding the whole of the subject.[3] Such indices as output of coal per head per shift, or units of electricity generated per ton of coal consumed or net ton miles hauled per total freight engine hour in service, simply indicate the effectiveness of the employment of one of the factors of production. They cannot provide an overall picture, they cannot measure the reactions which may thereby be produced upon the effectiveness of other factors of production. In consequence, they may give an extremely misleading picture of how economically coal is being produced, electricity generated, or freight hauled.

The idea that a nationalised industry can ever make itself accountable to the public, in the sense that the public can easily acquaint itself with changes in the efficiency of the industry by referring to figures of physical output in terms of physical input, so-called yardsticks, is a chimera. Once the test of prices, costs and profits is discarded, or is inapplicable, no other statistics have any great significance. It follows that the numerous institutional changes that have been suggested for improving the 'accountability' of nationalised industries are largely beating the air, for increased intelligence or energy on the part of those who are to employ the yardstick is of no account till the yardstick exists.

As an alternative it has been suggested that each nationalised industry should periodically be subject to a grand inquest by some outside body, consisting of Members of Parliament or of independent experts, which would examine the organisation in its entirety, scrutinise all the facts and communicate its general conclusions to the public. Now there are two, often associated but really quite distinct, duties which might be undertaken by such an outside investigating body. It might confine itself to declaring that the organisation was or was not being operated in a satisfactory fashion. Here we are back again at the question of what criteria could be imposed in reaching a decision and, in fact, nothing better could be expected than a set of rough and ready judgements made in non-defined terms. Or the investigators might strive to identify the precise weaknesses and mistakes of the organisation and to suggest ways of remedying them. The second duty is only likely to be carried out successfully if certain stringent conditions are satisfied. The investigators should be able, after a relatively quick look around, to attain a deeper understanding of the organisation than those who have long been in charge of it. The investigators should be prepared, after making their inquiries, to report that they have found nothing whatever amiss and not feel it incumbent upon them to make *some* recommendations because they have conducted an inquiry. And it must further be assumed that any good which the investigators can bring about will more than offset the real cost of the investigation, which will normally take the form of the time consumed by the investigators, the time consumed by the officials of the organisation in providing information for the investigators (or indeed in concealing facts which they believe will be misinterpreted) and any loss of confidence and drive in the running of the organisation which would follow from resentment on the part of officials at what they regarded as a misrepresentation or misunderstanding of their work. Indeed, the possibility that investigating bodies of this kind may do more harm than good leads many, even of those who favour nationalisation, to the conclusion that public accountability is undesirable, that the correct procedure is to choose the 'right' men, to trust them within very wide limits to conduct the affairs of the organisation and, in cases of palpable failure, to dismiss them and replace them by a fresh group of managers.

Two conclusions seem to follow, the one relating to the process of nationalisation, the other to the conduct of industries which have already been nationalised. It is a mistake to assume that the nationalisation of an industry can be carried out as a scientific experimental search for a more efficient way of organising industry.[4] An experiment implies a hypothesis which is capable of being proved true or false. There is no known way of establishing, from experience, the falsity or legitimacy of the hypothesis that nationalisation makes for economic efficiency. Nor is it possible with a monopolistic, nationalised industry to determine whether it is becoming more or less efficient in the economic sense. It might, therefore, be thought that decisions regarding nationalisation must be wholly political decisions in which the issue of economic efficiency, however much it is pushed into the forefront of public discussion, is irrelevant and in which, if indeed there is to be any rationality at all in the decisions made, broader social considerations of the kind emphasised by the early socialists must provide the guide to action.

It is not open to the student of industrial organisation to render final judgements as to whether nationalisation is good or bad; those judgements turn upon the standards of worthiness laid down. It is, however, possible for him to take the major changes brought about by nationalisation – larger operating units, monopolistic control and non-profit-seeking activities – inquire what claims have been made for them and examine, as far as facts allow, the validity of those claims.

SCALE OF OPERATION AND ADMINISTRATION

Nationalisation in Great Britain has produced industrial units which judged by any standard, are large. The National Coal Board employs about 700,000 persons and has fixed assets valued at about $840,000,000. The corresponding figures for the British Transport Commission are 900,000 and $3,920,000,000; for the British Electrical Authority, 175,000 and $1,820,000,000; for the Iron and Steel Corporation, 300,000 and $700,000,000. But, though large, they are not uniquely so. There are a number of companies which rival them in size. Thus the General Motors Corporation of America employs 400,000 workers and has written-down fixed assets of about $728,000,000.[5] Corresponding figures for du Pont are 75,000 and $756,000,000; for General Electric of America, 190,000 and $252,000,000. What is unique for the nationalised industries is the extent and the speed of the change in organisation to which they have been subject. The National Coal Board took over at short notice about 800 formerly independent colliery undertakings; the Transport Commission took over nearly 4000 formerly separate undertakings; the British Electrical Authority, over 600; the Iron and Steel Corporation, 92. These represented mergers on an unprecedented scale so that the nationalised industries have been confronted with a double problem of organisation, one temporary and one permanent: that associated with an extremely rapid *increase* in the scale of operation and that associated with a permanent *change* in that scale and, of course, in the early days, the two acted and reacted upon one another.

Three general observations would probably command very widespread assent. First, there seems to be no special reason why the whole of an industry which happens to fall within one national boundary should be the optimum unit for organisation in that industry. The proper scale would be determined not by the historical events which have determined political boundaries but by such factors as the character of the market for the product, the technical features of production, the rate of innovation in the industry and so on. If, therefore, a nationalised industry proved to be of the best size for operation the result must have been fortuitous. Second, even among the most ardent advocates of nationalisation, it is accepted that, whatever the future may hold, up to now the gains expected from operation on a large scale have not been fully realised.[6] Third, whatever may be said as regards the final aim of nationalisation, the process has been carried through, in some cases, at a speed too great for maintaining efficiency. Some of the public boards were compelled to act so precipitately that their immediate administrative problems were virtually insoluble.[7]

The effect of the new scale of operation brought about by nationalisation can be examined in two ways. It may be asked, what specific economies have been made possible by the existence of the larger organisation? Or again it may be asked, can the new organisation clearly be perceived as bringing about a *general* improvement in the operation of the unit in the way of speedier and wiser decisions, swifter executions and more sympathetic adjustments to changing conditions?

All the public boards make claims, in their annual reports, to economies directly made feasible by their size. The potential or achieved economies fall under five heads. Central purchasing of supplies and services in bulk can reduce prices and lessen the stocks which have to be held. The standardisation of equipment and appliances may again reduce the variety and volume of stocks needed for smooth working. Research can be centralised and otherwise improved. Costing systems can be made uniform and a basis established for comparison between one operating unit and another. Systems of staff training can be carried out on a more economical scale. And, at least in one case, that of road transport, a reduction in the number of administrative workers for a given volume of business has been claimed.[8] But, apart from transport, the economies claimed seem extremely modest. The possibilities of purchasing centrally and providing common services may be limited by the diversity of working conditions in different areas.[9] The British Electrical Authority has indicated that 'the advantages of utilising the specialised resources of existing research organisations . . . are such that the bulk of the research required will continue to be done through or by such organisations'. The Minister of Transport has pointed out that

> there comes a point when an increase in bulk purchase does not give a corresponding reduction in price but leads to a series of other problems – of storage and of local feeling – which have to be considered and which apply some qualifying marks to the advantages of bulk purchase. Turning to standardisation, undoubtedly certain good results to the railways have ensued, but I think hon. Members would be surprised if they knew the number of times I hear people say that British locomotives, for example, used to provide a most fruitful field for individual design which had reactions and repercussions all over the world, and standardisation can be carried so far that the desirable opening may be dried up.[10]

One specially interesting case is that of the organisation of long-distance road haulage by the Road Haulage Executive of the British Transport Commission. Road haulage had previously been carried on by a large group of firms of very varying size, most of them small. The Road Haulage Executive took over some 3800 of these undertakings with their 41,000 vehicles and organised them in eight geographical divisions controlling 29 districts and 225 groups. 'This process of grouping was essential to the creation of a national organisation with a network of services throughout the country and was also a necessary preliminary to the integration required by the Act.' This concentrated organisation fell under very serious criticism as being overcentralised. The Road Haulage Executive was certainly, by 1951, finding it difficult to compete with privately-owned vehicles. In that year the Executive was forced to admit the charge and to suggest a reorganisation whereby, in each of 50 districts, 'the manager would be responsible for the whole of his trading entity and for the successful operation of the activities within his sphere'.

It would be quite impossible to provide any simple estimate for the net gains arising from the large-scale operation of the nationalised industries. Perhaps the safest and the fairest deduction is that, in presenting the case for and against nationalisation, specific economies of scale could hardly be a crucial item one way or another.

When we turn to the *general* consequences of increased size more striking points emerge. In the widespread public discussion of the nationalised industries, far from their size being accepted as a virtue, it has come to be assumed that it constitutes their most persistent and troublesome problem.[11] The great debate has not been about the achievements made possible by the increased scale of operation but how best the public boards can overcome the defects and difficulties associated with their size, of how best they can circumvent just the kind of troubles long familiar to large organisations.

Criticisms of overcentralisation of the National Coal Board's activities have been made on all sides, the most common complaint being that delay and confusion arose from the fact that most of the members of the central National Board were responsible for executive functions running right down to the individual coal mines. For instance, the Chairman of the Yorkshire Miners' Trade Union declared: 'You cannot run the pits from London ... there is no more ridiculous fallacy than to believe that any industrial or political set-up in London can handle the perplexities of coal.'[12] As administrative delays became serious there was a strong public demand for an independent inquiry into the activities of the Coal Board. An independent committee was, in fact, set up in May 1948 to advise the Board on organisation after the publicity occasioned by the resignation of a prominent member of the original Board, whose lifetime interests had been in the technical development of the industry, and of several distinguished officials. The former gave as grounds for his resignation that he had 'no confidence either in the National Coal Board or in the organisation it has set up'. He described it as a cumbersome and uninspired organisation which could not deal with indiscipline in the mines, nor keep a check on production costs nor accomplish the vital technical reorganisation which the country expected to see carried out. He made proposals for complete decentralisation.

The recommendations of the independent committee were never

reproduced in full (the Coal Board deeming that 'it would not be in the best interests of the industry'), but from what information has been revealed it is clear that the committee recommended a large measure of devolution of authority. The Coal Board made certain changes, in consequence, but it is obvious that the problem has not yet been solved. In December 1950, there was a new demand in the House of Commons for a further inquiry into the working of the Coal Board but this was refused. And at the end of 1950, the *Economist* was still calling for 'drastic de-centralisation'.

When the British Transport Commission was established a large measure of decentralisation was introduced. The Commission itself was a small organisation engaged in major policy-making and direction. The executive functions were devolved upon a Railway Executive, a Docks and Inland Waterways Executive, a Road Transport Executive, a Road Passenger Executive, a London Transport Executive, and a Hotels Executive. This was undoubtedly due, in part, to the type of assets taken over but, in part, it also reflected current views – for the Transport Commission was set up at a time when criticism of overcentralisation by the Coal Board was particularly vociferous. The Commission itself commented thus:

> The Commission have divested themselves of responsibilities for the actual conduct of their various businesses, which nevertheless form one undertaking, although in certain limited directions the Commission's own organisation will provide a point of focus for the discharge of certain common services. The Members of the Commission are charged with no specialist or functional responsibilities. The Executives, on the other hand are, in the main, functional bodies and represent the higher management of the concerns whose operation and maintenance are entrusted to them as agents of the Commission.

Even so, there has subsequently been much outside adverse comment on overcentralisation by the Executives.[13] The White Paper on Transport Policy issued by the Conservative Government in May 1952, when they were making their case for partial denationalisation, commented:

> Experience has shown that the administration of the railways has become excessively centralised under the Act and that the Road Haulage Executive, with the elaborate system of depots working under its direction, cannot give trade and industry the speedy, individual and specialised services afforded by free hauliers before nationalisation.

The constant emphasis upon decentralisation in the nationalised industries is, in itself, proof that size is now normally to be considered a liability rather than an asset. This undoubtedly explains why each successive scheme for nationalisation has resulted in a less centralised, less formal system of organisation than the one before, culminating in the scheme for iron and steel in which 92 firms were to be owned by the State but, for operation, were to be only loosely linked by a small central organisation, and were to retain their own names, directors and specialised type of production. Whether, in fact, decentralisation is a universal cure-all for the obvious administrative weaknesses of the public boards is dubious. The more fervent advocates of decentralisation imply, by their very arguments, that the unification which was one of the basic aims of nationalisation is either impossible or undesirable, in which case denationalisation and not decentralisation would seem to be called for. More generally, decentralisation implies local autonomy, diversity of policy, competition between different methods, the absence or the severe restriction of central plans; most of the conditions for which nationalisation was supposed to provide a remedy. Indeed, a highly decentralised nationalised industry would hardly be a nationalised industry at all and it can well be imagined that, if decentralisation were pressed very far, then criticisms would arise that the industry in which it was introduced was failing to provide the uniformity of conditions, the homogeneity of policy, the central grip upon the whole organisation which are precisely the reasons for nationalising.

It is, therefore, conceivable that the nationalised industries are too large *ever* to be efficiently administered, that on their present scale they outstrip existing administrative technique, and that the see-saw between centralisation and decentralisation represents futile attempts to attain the unattainable.

Are there reasons for supposing that a nationalised industry may fail to cope with problems of administration which are handled with some measure of success by companies operating on a similar scale? Firms such as General Motors, Unilever, Imperial Chemical, and du Pont, despite their great size, manage to keep themselves going briskly and with profit. They do not appear to suffer from the same doubts and hesitations, the same palpable defects and changes in organisation, the same widespread public criticisms as have the British nationalised industries. Are there any fundamental reasons for this? Is it because the nationalised industries are more directly under the public eye so that their weaknesses are better known than the large companies? Or is it because the nationalised industries are still young and are passing through the pains of early growth?

There are good reasons for believing that the administration of a nationalised industry is, in important respects, more complex than that of a company. The nationalised industry is subject to political pressures of a disturbing kind. In the last resort, its actions will be determined by the Minister concerned and by contemporary public opinion. This remains true despite the attempts made in Great Britain to take the operation of the nationalised industries 'out of politics' altogether by placing them in the hands of public boards which were to be largely autonomous and subject to the overriding view of the Minister only on rare occasions and on matters of highest policy. There is, however, no way of taking the operation of an important nationalised industry out of politics. Nationalisation means that the industry will inevitably be pushed into the political arena, with all the consequent dangers of sudden and violent changes of policy. So long as the political parties are not agreed on nationalisation as a permanent arrangement, the industry may move between nationalisation and denationalisation with shifts in the balance of political power. In Great Britain, far from the nationalised industries having been taken out of politics, they are in danger of being torn into pieces in the course of the political struggle. So long as there are opponents of nationalisation, they will strive to bring to the forefront the weaknesses and failures of the nationalised industries; they can best do that by making such deficiencies the occasion for political attack. Where the nationalised industries are numerous, then conflicts may arise between them which, if serious, may become matters of public concern and ministerial intervention.[14] Differences of opinion may arise between the Minister and those in charge of the public board and, since both have the right to put their views to the public, such differences inevitably become the subject of public debate.[15] Finally, since these industries are providing important services and goods, ministers may be tempted to court popularity by giving way to democratic pressures for the provision of these goods and services on exceptionally favourable terms.[16]

The dilemma which arises when an industry has been placed firmly 'in politics' by being nationalised and then is organised in such a way as to take it 'out of politics' is very clearly shown in the efforts made to demarcate the functions of the Minister and those of the officials of the public board. In each one of the nationalisation statutes it was laid down that the Minister must hold responsibility for matters of 'national interest' or 'public interest'. The underlying idea was that the task of operating a nationalised industry could be broken into two parts: the handling of questions of national interest, which would be the function of the Minister, and the handling of 'day-to-day' policy which would be the responsibility of the officials of the public board. Thus, it was considered, the double purpose would be served: the main policies of the board would be directed towards the serving of the public interest but there would be no interference in the brisk daily dispatch of business by the boards; the virtues of public control and private enterprise would be combined. This splitting of responsibility was, further, to determine the extent to which Parliament could ask questions about, and interfere in the work of, the public boards.

But it has, in fact, proved impossible to give real meaning to this distinction between matters of national interest, of major policy on the one hand and matters of day-to-day importance on the other. The process of administration cannot be split up into parts in this way. Wise policy in major matters can only be built up by careful scrutiny of day-to-day matters. No event, in the first instance, can be labelled as a minor or a major matter. The manner in which a minor event is dealt with may determine whether it becomes a major one in the operation of the organisation. The administrator must constantly concern himself with the events which impinge upon his organisation in order to decide which are major (in the sense that they merit his attention because they are awkward, pregnant with danger or full of possibilities) and which minor. But the very choice of what is major and what is minor, which function would surely be regarded as a part of major policy,[17] can only be exercised through day-to-day attention to what would normally be regarded as detail.[18]

It would, therefore, appear that the public boards operate in an environment in which the administrative task of reaching decisions is more complex than those found in companies. The difference between the two cases will, indeed, depend upon how far companies are themselves subject to state controls and how the companies organise themselves (it is possible to conceive of cases where the company adopts a system of administration similar in kind to that of the public boards). Normally, however, even in conditions like those in Great Britain at present, it may be expected that the public board will encounter impediments to effective action and obstacles to systematic and consistent decision-making which do not hamper the company.

MONOPOLY

Nationalisation is generally looked upon as an act of exclusion: the state undertakes certain activities and, at the same time, legally debars private individuals from engaging in them. We must, therefore, consider what benefits are thought to arise from this extension of monopoly power. The matter is complicated in two ways: some of the nationalised industries provide services, such as rail transport, gas or electricity which have long been regarded as suitable for operation under monopoly conditions; some of the industries, such as iron and steel, have been nationalised on the grounds that they were already private monopolies. The purpose of the present section is to examine the virtues of those additions to monopoly power which can be attributed uniquely to the nationalisation experiment.

Each of the public boards has a tight grip upon one or a group of markets. The National Coal Board has virtually a complete monopoly of coal-getting in a country where nine-tenths of the heat and motive power is derived from coal. There is, of course, competition from gas, electricity and oil, but the costs of gas and electricity are partly made up of the cost of coal, and fuel oil still occupies a small place in the general market for heat and power. The British Transport Commission had conferred upon it a monopoly of the long-distance carriage of goods and persons. About four-fifths of the total sums spent by passengers are paid to the Commission. On the freight side the Commission owns the railways and the road vehicles engaged in long-distance transport, with the exception of goods carried in manufacturers' own vehicles. The British Electrical Authority has some competition from privately generated electricity but this does not seriously diminish its monopoly powers. The Gas Council produces nearly nine-tenths of the gas produced in the country. The Iron and Steel Corporation produces virtually the whole of the national steel output. Of course there is competition between some of the boards, such as that between gas and electricity. And in some of their ancillary activities the boards must meet private competition, particularly the Iron and Steel Corporation in its production outside iron ore, pig iron, steel, and hot-rolled products. But the purpose of nationalisation was to create monopolies and that purpose has been achieved.

Some technical claims are made for these monopolies. Thus the monopoly of the National Coal Board enables it to organise as one piece the whole of a coal-mining basin without being hampered by the claims of numerous landowners, but of course that justifies the unification of mining rights without necessarily justifying the unified operation of all the national coal mines. And the British Electrical Authority, by virtue of its control over all generation and distribution, can switch supplies from one area to another, although such economies are limited by the cost of transmission and the degree to which peak demands coincide in different parts of the country.[19]

In the early stages of nationalisation it was assumed, however, that the major gains of monopoly lay in a process which is variously described as integration, co-ordination or unification.[20] It is extremely difficult to discover what exactly is meant by the term integration and, therefore, even more difficult to ascertain whether integration has been achieved and what its benefits have been. The points to be made here can perhaps be illustrated by examining the British Transport Commission, for it is in terms of transport that the possibilities of integration have been thought to be greatest and most easy to realise. When the Transport Commission was set up in 1947 much was expected of integration.[21] In 1950, the Transport Commission was insisting that 'no opportunity has been lost to emphasise that integration is vital to the prosperity of the Commission's undertaking . . .'.[22] Yet time has simply led to growing disputes as to whether integration has brought any benefits and increasing perplexity as to what is integration. Each annual report of the Commission has spoken of the progress made in giving effect to, or preparing the way for, the policy of integration required by the Transport Act, culminating in the claim in 1952 that

> the way was prepared for many important steps in the process of integrating the different forms of transport, from which large economies would eventually result.[23]

Yet the Minister of Transport asserted, almost on the same day the report was issued, that

> it is the absolute failure in the realm of integration, despite all the effort put into it – and the very magnitude of the effort shows how impossible the task is to achieve – that is the justification for a new approach which forces upon the Government of the day the obligation to introduce a new Transport Bill.[24]

And while, in the course of the crucial debate in the House of Commons in July 1952, one party was holding that 'integration was a word that was used to mystify millions', the other was claiming that a real meaning could be given to it without, however, indicating what the meaning was.

The muddle over meanings can be clearly discerned in the aims and statements of the Transport Commission. They began with the widest possible interpretation of the idea:

> Rail, road and inland waterway services were to be developed as complementary to each other and were not to be regarded as rival forms of transport.[25]

This is understandable. It assumes that the customer is interested in having his goods (or himself) carried in the most effective way, that he has no interest in the methods of transport but simply in the result. Just as a consumer of electricity would have no direct interest in whether his light was provided by electricity generated by burning coal or by burning oil under boilers. Only one product is being provided; it is the function of the Commission from its specialised knowledge to fit together the different methods of providing transport, as one would fit together the different pieces of a jig-saw puzzle, in order to bring about the optimum physical fit. We may refer to this conception of integration as 'global physical integration'. For this kind of integration, monopoly is essential – all the pieces must be in one hand. The consumer has no choice over method.

The Commission is soon found, however, to be going back on its tracks when it declares that it

> had no intention of operating integration schemes which would impair freedom of choice where regular services of different kinds are available between the same points.[26]

If regular different transport services are provided, then, contrary to the first conception of integration, some choice is being left to the consumer over methods of transport. But why should that choice be offered? Why should the Commission not offer the best method of transport? Why the duplication? It must be either because the Commission finds it cannot carry through global physical integration or because, when it has done so, it finds two methods exist of carrying a particular load which are equally effective for its purpose. This second conception of integration may be named 'partial physical integration'.

In its 1951 report, however, the Commission goes far the other way:

> The Commission have made no attempt, and do not intend to attempt, to enforce arbitrary selections of their services upon the public. There is no question, for example, of forcing the customer away from road to rail. Suggestions to the contrary are not justified. *All the Commission ask is that the customer shall pay the real cost of the service he selects, and that he shall not receive one service at its bare cost if he insists at the same time on the maintenance of other services at less than cost.* Though in the present state of the country's financial and economic position it is difficult to establish what the true long-term costs of different forms of transport will be, it is of vital importance ultimately that the true costs of the various services shall be brought home to the customer. This will never be achieved by partial competition between services with different public obligations and with charges fixed on different principles. Only when co-ordinated charging arrangements for both Rail and Road are in operation can the true costs be made to 'compete' with each other, and thus bring into proper play those forces which will influence the customers as a whole to make use in the most economic ways of the services they desire.[27]

This implies that the different services shall be rival services, that the outcome of this rivalry shall be determined by the choice of the customer and 'integration' is whittled down to the function of guaranteeing that as far as possible, each service charge according to its costs. Clearly, with this conception of integration, it would not be necessary for the Commission to have a monopoly of operation of different methods of transport. All that would be necessary would be to make certain that each service was charging its 'real cost'. The consumer is then left perfectly free to choose the method of transport. This form of integration can be best called 'competition'.

At this point it might, therefore, be asked why the Commission requires a monopoly of operation at all. Why should it not be content with insisting that each service charge its 'real costs' and then providing the services called for by the consumer at those prices? Indeed, it may be asked why the Commission need intervene at all since no service is likely to continue in operation unless it covers its costs. Here the Commission would appear to make a further volte-face. It resists the idea of abolishing the monopoly on the grounds that 'fair competition' between road and rail is impossible. The argument is that, before nationalisation, there was a public system of transport – the railway system – and a private system – the road system. The public system had certain duties and responsibilities placed on it as a common carrier: it had to operate services regularly, to give all users equal treatment, to apply uniformly an approved tariff. Such responsibilities were not placed on the private system. Why, then, should not the public system be relieved of these obligations and then be allowed to compete with the private system? The answer the Commission gives is as follows:

> The public system, so long as it retains the essential characteristics of a public system and meets the public obligations laid upon it, cannot adequately deal with price competition which is casual, temporary or experimental in character. And to suggest that the public system should be freed from these disadvantages is really to turn it into a private system – something which the vast majority of the commercial and industrial community have never been willing to accept in practice. That a public system should carry only when it likes, or what it likes, and should carry at prices which differ according to season, or route, or user, or the particular circumstances of each 'job'; which fluctuate with the state of the 'markets' for each different type of traffic; and which are governed only by the competitive requirements of the system and its own search for profit, would be something novel and unlikely to be tried. How a true public system could meet private carriers on fair terms, unless the private carriers were made subject to suitable regulation of obligation and price in relation to real costs, is a problem for which no solution has yet been found.[28]

In brief, *if* there could be competition then there would be no need for the monopoly. Since there cannot be competition then there must be monopoly, and we are forced back again to the original idea of 'global physical integration'.

So far, integration has been discussed in terms of the transport industry, but the same principles emerge in the other nationalised industries, and the argument can now be widened to cover them. The main virtue of monopoly, the argument runs, is that it makes possible physical integration of resources. There appear, however, to be three serious drawbacks to such integration. First, that it logically calls for

more and more co-ordination, implying bigger and bigger units of control, and thereby outstrips the limits of administrative feasibility.
Second, that in the process of solving technical problems, it restricts or
extinguishes consumers' preferences and thus defeats its own end. Third,
that extensive integration will normally call for large-scale changes in
the duties and responsibilities of workers and thereby create new
problems in labour relations.

Integration without limit

Complete physical integration within one industry is, in itself, a most
formidable task to which there can hardly be an end. When the
Transport Commission was set up, individual manufacturers were still
left with the right, under so-called 'C licences', to use their own vehicles
to carry their own goods (although the original bill contemplated a
severe restriction of such rights). Since Nationalisation, the number of
these vehicles has increased enormously – from 490,000 in 1948 to
796,000 in 1951. There is no doubt that this increase is partly reaction to
the monopolising of public long-distance road haulage. But the growth
of the C licence is destructive of transport integration; it almost certainly
creates surplus capacity in road transport,[29] and logically it calls for the
withdrawal from all manufacturers of the right to carry their own
goods.[30] But if the Transport Commission were to take over all the C
licences, it would be called upon to operate more than ten times as
many vehicles as it now operates. In the case of electricity supply, there
is no law in Great Britain which debars individuals or firms from
generating their own electricity. But the British Electrical Authority has
always looked with a somewhat jaundiced eye upon private generation.
The Authority has, indeed, declared that they 'are not opposed to the
installation of private generating plants where economically justified'.[31]
But they go on to argue that private generation cannot be in the national
interest unless (a) the efficiency of the private generators is equal to that
of the public, (b) the load factor of the private generators is equal to that
of the public, (c) all new schemes for private generation should be
examined in consultation with the Electricity Boards, and (d) firms using
private generators should not expect a 'stand-by service' from public
generators except on terms which fully cover the costs involved. In brief,
freedom for private generation will normally be an embarrassment to
optimum integration.

The anxiety to place all the relevant pieces within one hand has led,
indeed, to friction among the public boards themselves. Hence the dispute between the National Coal Board and the Gas Council as to
whether the former should be permitted to operate coal carbonisation
plants[32] and the dispute between the Coal Board and the British Electrical Authority as to how rapidly coal mines should be electrified and as

to whether the Coal Board should be allowed to generate electricity.³³

If, however, there is virtue in integration, there can be no reason why it should be confined to some arbitrarily delimited industry. There is already a demand in Great Britain that the three boards for coal, gas and electricity should, in turn, be subject to centralised control and integration because the industries are now 'following separate paths'.³⁴ Given time, it would make itself apparent to the integrators that all industries follow separate paths and should be integrated by the imposition of a unified monopoly control. For example, the oil industry would certainly have to be co-ordinated with the fuel and power industries. Fuel is carried by railways in the form of coal, it is also carried by gas companies and electricity companies in the form of gas and electricity: transport and power and fuel should be integrated. The fuel industries seek to provide warmth in houses; the building industry, by improving insulation, is trying to achieve the same end: building and fuel and power should be integrated. There is no limit to integration short of a unified control over all economic activity. The paradox here is that while more and more co-ordination is being called for *between* nationalised industries, where presumably it would be relatively difficult, less and less co-ordination (i.e., more and more decentralisation) is being demanded *within* those industries, where presumably it would be relatively easy to achieve.

The place of the consumer in integration

Every business is concerned with what it will produce for itself and what it will buy from outside, that is to say, with the extent to which it will integrate its activities. The limits within which it must operate will normally be narrowly determined by the discrimination of the consumer, for should the integration result in the offer of inferior choices, the non-integrated firms will take the market and the experiment in integration will be at an end. But where physical integration is attempted by a producer holding a statutory monopoly, then the consumer's satisfaction will depend upon the power of the producer to understand completely the consumer's preferences and to respect them. The danger is that the producer, while seeking for integration which eliminates physical waste, may believe that he is leaving the position of the consumer unaffected, whereas he is really undermining it. For example, a transport monopoly may believe that, although it has replaced road by rail traffic in a particular case, the consumer will have his goods delivered exactly the same way. But the monopolist is never in a position to be sure of that. While the new and the old form of service might *generally* be the same, only the consumer can know the significance of apparently minor differences between them. For example, the new service might be slightly more reliable in the winter than in the summer, the old slightly more reliable in the summer than in the winter; only the consumer would know the importance of summer and winter regularity for the transport of his goods. The producer, either through his inevitable ignorance or by reason of his preoccupation with the obvious technical gains from integration, may normally be expected to underestimate the importance of consumers' preferences.

Two illustrations, drawn from the relations of the public boards themselves, may be given. In 1952, the National Coal Board, greatly concerned about the future supply of coal and power, recommended that any further growth in the heating load of electricity should be prevented and that, in order further to reduce this load, domestic consumers should apparently be forced to desist from the use of electric fires and be compelled to use gas fires.[35] Calculations were given purporting to show that in terms of physical integration, fuel would be saved. The British Electrical Authority, while seeking to controvert these calculations, concluded:

> The Authority feels strongly that the consumers are in the best position to balance the various factors which determine the most economic and efficient means of meeting their individual requirements, and therefore that the freedom of each individual to choose the fuel and fuel-saving appliances most suited to his needs should be preserved.

In the second case the roles were reversed. The British Electrical Authority argued that the National Coal Board should electrify its coal mines more rapidly.[36] But the Coal Board properly pointed out that the decision in the case of each coal mine was to be arrived at by the consideration of many factors, most of which were outside the knowledge of the British Electrical Authority.[37]

Integration and labour relations

All good administrative arrangements must take into account the fact that human as well as physical resources are involved and that any arrangement which fails to evoke co-operation by the worker thereby condemns itself. All organisations are confronted with this problem but the large monopolistic organisation may be in greater difficulties than most. First, because it is large, the maintenance of personal relations which bring understanding is more difficult. Second, the fact that the worker is employed in a monopoly, and therefore has no other obvious source of employment, may make him more determined to safeguard his interests. Third, the fact that one organisation must deal with all the labour in the industry calls for uniformity of treatment difficult to establish when operating conditions may vary greatly. Fourth, the schemes for physical integration possible under monopoly will naturally cause upsets to established expectations.[38]

To sum up: the only general case that can be made for monopoly in the nationalised industries is that, without it, the physical integration of assets will be impossible. To the extent that the pursuit of full integration is disclaimed, then the need for monopoly is reduced. The virtue of monopoly is, therefore, dependent upon the merits of complete co-ordination. But such co-ordination is a technical conception, its achievement is likely to frustrate the preferences of consumers, reduce the freedom of the worker. If that conception is carried forward logically it calls for the co-ordination not of an industry but of all industry. At that stage the problems of administration, already acute in the lumps of the economic system now nationalised, would become an overriding obstacle to efficiency.

The integration actually achieved

An examination of the detailed claims made by the boards to economies arising through integration suggests that most of these economies are, in fact, not dependent upon an operating monopoly and sometimes are not even dependent upon public ownership. To take, again, the British Transport Commission, which has provided, in its annual reports, the most systematic description of progress in integration and co-ordination, the Commission makes some claims which are really economies of scale as, for instance, when the responsibility for maintenance of the road vehicles of the Road Haulage Executive and those of the Railway Executive is placed in a common organisation. Some of the economies might well be brought about by competition. Thus the closing down of the redundant railway branch lines and stations does not call for monopoly: it was going on before nationalisation. Some of the economies partake of the nature of merchanting centralisation long familiar in competitive systems. For example, the Commission, in its 1951 report, is at pains to describe a system in which, in the transport of small consignments between London and Manchester, the Road Haulage Executive takes the responsibility for gathering together such consignments, sorting them, handing them over packed in large containers for transport in trainloads by railway between the cities, and then distributing them to their final destination.[39] But of course there is no reason why a private road organisation could not have used the railway facilities in this way or why a dispatching agency could not have provided such services for the consumer and simply employed existing road and rail facilities, or why independent rail and road companies could not have organised those inter-connections without being under common ownership. The same argument would apply where the Commission submits as improvements of integration 'late omnibus services from stations after return rail excursions' or 'portable stands at agricultrual shows displaying both Railway and Road Haulage literature'.

The experience of the British nationalised industries as regards monopoly, leaves us confronted, therefore, with a series of *non sequiturs*. Monopoly can only be defended if the aim is complete physical integration. But the case for integration of this kind has never been made satisfactorily. The various industries have not, in fact, made any attempt at establishing complete physical integration. Indeed they claim that they wish to leave the consumer with his preferences. Meanwhile, the economies of integration which have actually been introduced are economies which do not really depend upon possession of monopoly powers.

THE ABSENCE OF PROFIT-MAKING

By their statutes, the nationalised industries are instructed that they must cover their costs by their proceeds 'taking good years with bad'. That means they must not make losses but it also means that, after allowing for capital increases, they must not make profits. The proscribing of profit-making derives directly from the underlying philosophy of nationalisation, which is that profit-making is improper. Can the economic consequences of this notion be traced? The question leads directly into the most complicated issues regarding price and investment policy.

The older arguments do not appear to take us very far. It used to be said that, if profits had not to be made, then prices would be that much lower, the consumer would benefit. Against this, it was said that to aim at the making of a surplus was itself an incentive for the maximum drive and energy, that the absence of this incentive would lead to general economic debility. But I know of no method by which one can test the validity of either of these ideas.

An indirect approach to this question can, however, be made along two lines. First, a monopolist who is instructed not to make profits must find some way of fixing his prices so that he obeys the rule. It can, therefore, be asked whether the *pricing policies* of the nationalised industries are such as to give results superior to those obtained in a free market. Second, if profits are not to be made, decisions regarding investments must be reached in ways different from those pursued in a free market economy. It can, therefore, be asked whether *investment policies* of the nationalised industries have anything to commend them as against the investment mechanisms of a free economic system.

Pricing policy

There are two branches of pricing policy, the fixing of the general level of prices and the determination of price differentials. In both cases the monopolised industries have run into formidable difficulties. The first case is well illustrated by events in the coal-mining industry. At present the National Coal Board is paying its way, proceeds are covering costs. But at the general level of prices being charged by the Coal Board, the demand for coal is greater than the supply. The rationing of coal is, therefore, necessary with all the crudities which go with rationing – absence of choice of quality for the consumer, expense of government administration, and so on. The obvious way out would, of course, be to allow the price of coal to rise until demand and supply were equalled. But if the price of coal were to rise to that point, then the Coal Board would make very large profits. This is an example of the general case, familiar to economists, that where the marginal cost curve is rising, prices based on average cost and not on marginal cost may mean a demand greater than supply. The knots into which British policy has tied itself are revealed in a recent official report on fuel and power policy.[40] One half of the committee was in favour of raising the general price of coal so that there was a closer approximation between price and marginal cost. The other half objected on the ground that it was foolish deliberately to raise the price of coal at a time when it was vital for Great Britain to keep down prices and costs. But even the first group, which favoured an increase in price, was not prepared to allow the Coal Board to make profits. This group suggested that the increase in price should be brought about by imposing an excise duty on coal.[41] Such a policy of taxing coal raises, however, more questions than it answers. Is such a tax a good tax? What guarantee is there that the resources thereby placed in the hands of the State will be as well employed as if these resources were left in the hands of the industry?

The general point is, therefore, that a policy designed to avoid profits means prices related to average costs. With a rising marginal cost curve this means a demand greater than supply. This means rationing. One of the important functions of the price system is jammed. And rationing of a raw material widely used in industry will almost certainly contribute to industrial inefficiency.

What next of differential prices? What policies have the boards been following in drawing up their detailed price schedules? It is claimed that since the nationalised industries have these price schedules completely within their control and since they need not aim at a maximum profit, they are in a position to provide favourable prices to specially deserving groups. In effect, they can grant socially desirable subsidies. For example, the Coal Board has deliberately kept high-cost mines in operation, partly because the coal was needed, partly because employment was thereby provided in isolated areas. The Central Electricity Authority has a statutory obligation to encourage the extension of supplies to rural areas. The Transport Commission has inherited the obligation to provide special privilege fares, workmen's tickets, and the like. This is the well-known principle of 'pooling-costs'. The obvious objection to the pooling principle is that, should there be a case for subsidising special groups, the cost of doing that is surely best spread over the community as a whole. There is no particular case for placing the burden of, say, a subsidy to some users of electricity upon the other users of electricity.

Leaving on one side the so-called social obligations of nationalised industries, the public boards from their inception have regarded it as one of their first duties to produce what they describe as a 'rational price structure'. Indeed, in the case of the Transport Commission, that responsibility was placed upon it by its statute. What progress has been made in producing rational price-structures? Two points are very clear here. First, the task of creating, in the absence of a free market, 'rational price structure' is proving much more difficult, and the time taken for this purpose is proving to be greater than was originally envisaged. The experience of the National Coal Board is striking: in 1946, with its first annual report, the Board indicated that: 'for the time being . . . sales would continue to be made at existing prices.' In 1947, with its second annual report, the Board states that: 'the present price structure of coal is unrealistic and the Board intend to bring in a new and rational price structure as soon as possible.' In 1948, the Board reported that: 'at first, the Board intended to leave things as they were until they could introduce a new price structure for the industry. . . . After going more fully into the matter, however, they have come to the conclusion that this cannot be done all at once or done soon.' In 1949, we find in the Board's annual report: 'The Board are convinced that, in the interests of consumers, testing and proving exercises are necessary before a long term price structure can be established.' In 1950, we find the Board saying: 'The Board made no important price adjustments in 1950. But by the end of the year they had prepared for further moves to be made in 1951 towards a rational price structure.'[42] Only in 1951 did the Board record that it was nearing the end of its labours in this matter. To what end shall be shown later.

Similarly with the British Transport Commisson. By the Act of 1947, the Commission was charged with the duty of preparing 'a Charges Scheme, relating to all the services provided by the Commission for the carriage of passengers and goods' before August 1949. It was given two years to carry out this function. In 1949, the Commission was forced to ask for an extension of this period until 1951. In 1951, the Commission was forced to ask for a further extension until 1953. So that the charges schemes are not yet complete.

For four or five years, therefore, the major public boards have been searching, without finality, for rational price structures. A simple deduction from this is that, for four or five years, these industries have each been operating with a price structure which is believed to have been irrational; which cannot have been particularly good for British industry.

It is the Coal Board which has gone the furthest in establishing a new price system. The principles which they have apparently decided upon hardly seem novel and are not very reassuring. Briefly, these principles are:

(a) The relative prices of different kinds of coal should be based upon a detailed technical assessment of the different types of coal. The aim seems to be that the price differentials should be those which 'a rational consumer' would pay. The obvious objection to that principle is that the only way to find out what a 'rational consumer' would choose would be to provide him, of course, with whatever information and advice was possible and then leave the market free. It is difficult to see how scientists can ever tell us what the correct price for a commodity is. It is, however, only fair to point out that, by applying this principle, the Coal Board has probably gone some way towards the restoration of those basic differentials, ironed out during the war, which would probably emerge in a free market. That the Board has not fully succeeded is shown by the complaints that have been made both by the British Electricity Authority and the Gas Council.[43]

(b) There should be a zone system of uniform delivered prices for coal. That is to say any consumer will pay the same prices for coal whatever coal mine it comes from; all customers in the same zone will pay the same price; all prices will be delivered prices. Put briefly, this system is similar to that pursued by an industry employing a basing-point system. It carries with it the same objections as a basing-point price system – that it makes for an inefficient location of industry and it slows down the elimination of weak units in the industry.

The search, in the absence of a free market, for these rational price structures, has, undoubtedly, led to a good deal of muddle and frustration, and it would appear that this is now being recognised even by the Boards themselves. For in very recent months a new principle seems to have been gaining ground – the principle that prices should be equalled to 'relevant' costs. The Ridley Committee reported in favour of this. The Transport Commission has reached the conclusion that 'the consumer should pay the real cost of the service he selects', and it has argued that if privilege tickets at low prices are to be provided the cost of the subsidy should not fall upon the other passengers but should be met by a tax upon the whole community.[44] The Gas Council 'accepts in principle the contention that the price of a product or service should as nearly as possible equal the cost of providing that product or service'.

And, of course, this movement is reflected in the actions of the present government which, in its scheme for denationalising transport, is aiming at competition between road and rail and, to that end, intends to try to make the competition fairer by leaving railways much greater latitude in fixing charges in relation to actual cost.

It is not difficult to discern the inconsistencies between present practices and the new principle of linking costs and prices. There is no agreement as to what are 'relevant' costs – are they average or marginal costs? A system of uniform delivered prices, such as is now practised by the Coal Board, clearly implies a pooling of transport costs. The Central Electricity Authority is certainly not enthusiastic for measures which would enable it to impose upon its customers, at peak load, prices related to cost. But it would appear that the present movement of opinion and of practice is away from the notion that the public boards have social responsibilities to special sections of the community, away from the idea that some scientific assessment of the technical qualities of a commodity enables a proper price to be fixed for it, away from the pooling of costs and towards a closer linking of costs and prices. That, at least, seems a step in the right direction. But the principle is hardly a new one.

INVESTMENT POLICY

In the pre-war period, British critics of private enterprise argued in two quite different ways. On the one hand, it was said that, since private enterprise would inevitably degenerate into monopoly, the restrictionist policy of the monopolist would lead to too little investment in some important industries. On the other hand, it was said that private enterprise, because of its unco-ordinated nature, would result in entrepreneurs overinvesting in good times and thus creating problems of surplus capacity later. The grounds upon which nationalisation was advocated in Great Britain reflected both these notions. The steel industry was nationalised because, so it was alleged, it had starved the community of steel-making capacity. The coal-mining industry was nationalised because, among other reasons, it seemed powerless to handle the conditions of overcapacity to which it was especially subject. Has capital investment in Great Britain been more rationally distributed since nationalisation?

There is no technique by which economists can examine a table recording the details of the national industrial investment and thereby decide whether the distribution of investment has been about correct or, if incorrect, in what ways. Where vast errors are made, of course, they cannot be overlooked. (Nobody doubts, for instance, that the very large investment made by the British government in the African ground-nuts scheme was an error, because the return was nil.) But where the question is that of more or less, there may be as many different individual judgements as there are different observers. Criticisms have, in fact, been advanced of British post-war investment policy on three grounds: that the nationalised industries have been able to obtain too large a proportion of total savings, to the detriment of private industry; that, within the public sector, the electricity industry has obtained more than its due share of investment;[45] and that the distribution of capital has been used to maintain the existing location of coal and steel production to the disadvantage of other, low-cost, centres.[46] These are personal opinions. But it is reasonable to assume that, where the party in power favours nationalisation, it is likely to be sympathetic to the demands of the nationalised industries. And British experience suggests that the struggle between the various public boards over the distribution of capital has a militant quality by comparison with which the normal competitive processes of a free market seem mild. There is certainly no reason to suppose that a period of nationalisation ushers in a kind of millennium by which each individual, informed by some inner light, unerringly recognises what is the national interest and spontaneously moderates his own demands in accordance with it.

One point, however, is clear. The essence of an investment decision is prediction of future conditions. And the success of investment will turn upon skill in forecasting the future and the rapid recognition and remedying of investment errors. Now there appears to be no reason why nationalised industries should be more likely to predict the future successfully than others. Indeed, the pressures, political and other, which fall upon them may easily accentuate errors. This can be illustrated by current discussions in Great Britain about the probable future demand for coal.[47] The National Coal Board prepared a long-distance plan in which it reached the conclusion that the best estimate it could give, and work to, was that demand in 1961–5 would be 230–50 million tons of coal. That estimate has been challenged. The Ridley Committee suggested that this was about 20 million tons too low. The Federation of British Industries estimated that it was 50 million tons too low. Both the Electricity and the Gas Authorities complained that this estimate did not allow sufficiently for the probable increases in electricity and gas requirements. The Coal Board, supported by the Gas Council, sought to defend its figures by declaring that the policy of the British Electricity Authority in pushing the use of electricity for heating purposes, and thus enlarging its estimates of its future demand for coal, was 'incompatible with the national interest'; in effect, the Coal Board queried the need for coal as embodied in the programme for expansion of the Central Electricity Authority. It further pointed out that if it had to plan to produce more coal it could only do this with sharply increasing costs of production. Nobody, apparently, has yet tried to work out whether, if costs and prices rise this way, anybody will be able to afford to buy any coal at all. So these public boards, each naturally putting its own interests in the forefront of its thinking, throw in conflicting calculations upon which, sooner or later, some kind of action must be taken. It is conflicts of this kind which have recently led to the suggestion that a kind of super public board should be created, the task of which would be to co-ordinate the activities of the existing public boards, although why a super public board should be able to guess more accurately than a public board has not been made clear.

All investment decisions, whether they are made by private enterprise or by public bodies, involve the taking of action upon the basis of incomplete evidence. That is what risk-taking means. But no reason has yet been advanced for believing that major investment decisions made by private firms are more likely to go wrong than such decisions taken by public boards in the kind of atmosphere in which Great Britain now proceeds to determine the probable future demand for coal as a preliminary to investment decisions by the National Coal Board.

CONCLUSIONS

For the student of industrial organisation, the right question to ask about nationalisation is whether it has added to our stock of knowledge concerning the best way to organise industry in order to raise the standard of living. Since no institution is perfect, no suggestion for change should be dismissed summarily. But, judging from the British experience, the major impression left is that nationalisation is peculiarly barren of anything fruitful or novel. When it is remembered what hopes have in the past been placed upon it, what emotions it has aroused, what upsets have been suffered to bring it about, there is something almost melancholy in its failure to introduce any fresh idea in the field of organisation or administration. It has long been known that there were economies to be gained, within limits and in appropriate circumstances, from an increased scale of operation. Within limits and in appropriate circumstances – but the nationalisers have perverted this subtle doctrine into a crude rule of 'the bigger the better' and have done nothing to match improved devices of management against the crowding problems to which size gives birth. It is natural that the search should be uninterrupted for ways of so co-ordinating groups of men working with capital equipment that no movement will be made, no effort expended, no equipment provided superfluously. The nationalisers held out to us this promised land of perfect co-ordination, provided only they were first granted monopoly – the exclusive rights in perpetuity to cater for certain needs, freedom from outside competition, and the power to accept technical innovation at rates convenient to themselves. But what has Great Britain, having somewhat lightheartedly given hostages to fortune in this way, received in return? Nothing but promises of bounties from co-ordination for the future, complaints that the monopoly powers were not extensive enough, suggestions for even more grandiose schemes of co-ordination. And, finally, in very recent days, the discovery of the merits of the principle that prices should be related to 'relevant' costs – a notion which is not very new.

All of which suggests that the early advocates of the nationalisation of the means of production, distribution and exchange were on much firmer ground in appealing to its social virtues than the later advocates in claiming that they had discovered a secret for rendering industry more productive. If a community really comes to believe that profit-making and the private ownership of industrial capital are so repugnant to its ethical standards that it must replace them, then there is nothing remaining for the economist, as economist, to say. But if, as is the practice more generally these days, it is assumed that the search for what is considered morally right will also lead to a pot of gold, that doing good will also bring an economic bonus, then it would seem that the economist may well register a protest.

NOTES

1. The tests for 'ripeness' as set forth by different writers are confusing and not always consistent. Kautsky, *The Social Revolution 144* (1902), argued that the big industries should be nationalised first: 'Without a developed great industry socialism is impossible. Where, however, a great industry exists to a considerable degree it is easy for a socialist society to concentrate production and to quickly rid itself of the little industries.' J. R. Macdonald thought that the rule should be the easiest first: 'The harvest which is ripe and most easily reaped will be gathered first and the experience gained in reaping it will be used when more difficult harvests have to be brought in. Thus we will begin the process of nationalizing capital with services like the railways or with the exploitation of national resources like mines.' Jay, *The Socialist Case 224* (2nd ed., 1947), regarded the national ownership of land as having the highest priority: 'There is no form of socialism more desirable than the ownership of land, factories and houses. . . . The public ownership of land should therefore be one of the first duties of a socialist State.' More recently, however, the view seems to be gaining ground that some industries will only very slowly, or perhaps never, reach the stage of ripeness, or indeed that nationalisation is not an essential part of socialism at all. Thus, Mr Harold Wilson has declared that 'the cotton industry . . . did not fall into the list of basic industries whose position or organisation called for nationalisation'.; Mr Strachey that 'Nationalization is one of the means to the attainment of Socialism, not the thing itself'. And in two volumes emanating from socialist sources, Crossman, *New Fabian Essays* (1952), and *Socialism: A New Statement of Principles* (1952), the idea of nationalising all industries is regarded as obsolete.

2. There is, however, as perhaps there has always been, a mystical element in nationalisation. Thus Robson, Problems of Nationalised Industry 367 (1952), states:

    Nationalisation . . . *must* succeed for the simple reason that failure would be a national disaster of staggering dimensions. There is every reason why it should succeed. It has sprung from a great popular revolt against the ethics, the incentives, and the results of capitalist enterprise. It represents an attempt to substitute higher moral values, superior human incentives, and a wider conception of economic benefit than those which are implicit in private enterprise. It has behind it the hopes and aspirations of many millions of plain men and women. . . .

    It is, however, hard to reconcile these sentiments with the views of the same author in the same book: 'The attitude of the voters in the General Election of 1950 was strongly noncommittal. A conspicuous feature of that electoral contest was the comparatively small part played by the nationalization issue. . . . Nationalization played an equally small part in the General Election of 1951.' Ibid., 352–3. Again, Davies, 'Problems of Public Ownership' (Labour Party Pamphlet, 1952), suggests that, in addition to industries which might be ripe for nationalisation because they were 'basic', or monopolistic, or inefficient, some industries might have to be nationalised 'to enable Labour to carry through further stages of its Socialist programme'.

3. There is something almost poignant in the pursuit of the unattainable here. Thus Robson, op. cit., p. 7, says, 'I made prolonged efforts to obtain an essay on this topic [of 'statistical yardsticks' of efficiency] from a number of eminent statisticians engaged in university teaching and research, in public corporations, and in the Civil Service. The tenor of their replies was to the effect that their studies in this field are not sufficiently advanced to enable them to produce an essay on the subject. This lack of statistical knowledge is a matter of serious consequence to the public. I hope it will not endure for long'.

4. The failure to understand this point leads some writers to claim that nationalisation is the natural outcome of a newer, more effective form of organisation replacing one which could no longer compete with it. Thus, Robson, op. cit. p. 366, regards the emergence of the public corporation in the twentieth century as a parallel to that of the joint stock company in the nineteenth. But there is a world of difference between them, in the sense that the former was voluntarily taken up in all cases where its advantages were palpable, could be discarded as freely as it was adopted, and still left room for other forms of business association; the latter was compulsorily imposed, cannot be discarded without serious dislocation, and leaves no room for other forms of organisation within its field.

5. These large firms also own considerable assets in other forms, such as marketable securities and investments in other firms. The total assets of General Motors, for example, are in the neighbourhood of $2,520,000,000.

6. Davies, op. cit. states that 'the full advantages which the community, including the workers in the public industries, were led to expect from public ownership have not yet, in every case, been fully realized'.

7. These difficulties varied from case to case. They were probably greatest with the National Coal Board and with the Road Haulage branch of the British

Transport Commission. See National Coal Board 2d Ann. Rep. 5–10 (1947); British Transport Comm'n 4th Ann. Rep. 123–24 (1951).

8. British Transport Comm'n 4th Ann. Rep. 49 (1951).

9. Thus, the British Electrical Authority: 'The examination of the extent to which certain services were common to Area Boards and the corresponding Generations Divisions . . . [showed] that the degree of possible joint working varied considerably from Area to Area because of varying local circumstances, and that the major activities of the Boards and Divisions were so different as to offer only a limited scope for joint services.' British Electrical Authority Rep. and Acc'ts 67 (1949–50).

10. House of Commons (22 July 1952).

11. Davies, op. cit., p. 7: 'Some of the administrative problems of the nationalized industries arise from the very size of the industries taken over. Bigness is perhaps their greatest drawback.'

12. Quoted in House of Commons (February 1951).

13. And, indeed, within the organisation itself. The London *Times*, p. 5, col. 3 (12 July, 1952), reported: 'There are tensions and disagreements which do not appear in the annual report between the Transport Commission and the Railway Executive. There is conflict as to where the line should be drawn between general policy making and management, and strife between centralizers and decentralizers.'

14. Thus, the British Electrical Authority has pointed out that it, like all other consumers, 'has no freedom in the purchase of coal and cannot, therefore, select the qualities which would give the highest degree of efficiency'. British Electrical Authority Rep. and Acc'ts 51 (1947–9). It has complained of the unfavourable position in which the electricity supply industry has been placed by the adjustments of prices by flat rate increases irrespective of the grade of coal. Ibid., p. 37 (1949–50). It resisted the proposed increased railway freight charges in November 1949. Ibid., p. 38 (1949–50). The British Transport Commission has pointed out that the 'unsuitable qualities of coal now available' have increased the fuel consumption. British Transport Comm'n 1st Ann. Rep. 61 (1948). The National Coal Board opposed the suggested increase in railway freight charges in 1949. National Coal Board 5th Ann. Rep. 25 (1950). The most striking case of disputes between boards, however, is to be found in the evidence presented before the Ridley Committee on National Fuel Policy in 1952. The Gas Council accuses the British Electrical Authority of adopting a price policy which unfairly hampers the Council. The BEA accuses the Gas Council of not charging consumers the full cost of their capital equipment. The Coal Board attacks the BEA for its attempts to spread its load and declares that space heating by electricity is uneconomical. The BEA rejoins that the Coal Board has failed to supply coal in adequate quantities and suitable qualities.

15. Two important instances have occurred where the public board and the government differed as to what was 'in the best national interest'. The British Electrical Authority has pressed for a larger proportion of the total capital investment. British Electrical Authority Rep. and Acc'ts 13 (1950–1). And, in 1952, the British Transport Commission and the government clearly disagreed about the possibilities of integration in road transport.

16. Perhaps the most striking case occurred when the government stepped in, in June 1952, and prevented proposed fare increases in the London region. At

least one writer, Lewis, 'The Price Policy of Public Corporations', in Robson, *Problems of Nationalized Industry 192* (1952), has argued that the public boards should be subject to more day-to-day control than they are at present. Thus, he argues, that the Minister, and not the management of the public board, should decide in each case whether a profit or loss should be made; and that all prices of a public board should be made subject to the scrutiny of a price tribunal. This, of course, would push the working of the public boards even more definitely into the political arena.

17. The story is told that when Sydney and Beatrice Webb were married, they agreed that he should make decisions in the big matters and she in the small matters, but that one of the small matters was deciding, in each case, what was a small and what was a large matter.

18. Thus, the head of one of the largest businesses in the world regards it as one of his most important functions to examine each day a classified list of all the complaints made regarding the firm's products.

19. The British Electrical Authority claims that, through the 275,000-volt transmission grid which it proposes to build, the total generating capacity otherwise required will be reduced by about 5 per cent.

20. Whether these words are exactly synonymous is difficult to determine. The British Transport Commission uses the phrase, 'integration and co-ordination'. Unless the Commission has failed to integrate its own language, this suggests that 'integration' and 'co-ordination' are different things. 'Unification' has tended to become unpopular, since it seems to connote 'centralization' and 'centralization' has recently come to carry unpleasant associations.

21. The Minister of Transport, in the House of Commons (16 December 1946), said, 'Give this Labour Government five years of power in this field of transport services, and the people of this country will see more progress than would be made in 500 years of Tory Rule'.

22. British Transport Comm'n 3d Ann. Rep. 22 (1950).

23. British Transport Comm'n 4th Ann. Rep. iii (1951).

24. House of Commons (22 July 1952).

25. This was the theme of their 'Statement of policy on the Integration of Freight Services by Road and Rail'.

26. British Transport Comm'n 3d Ann. Rep. 22 (1950).

27. British Transport Comm'n 4th Ann. Rep. 16 (1951'.

28. Ibid., p. 42.

29. This is all the more certain since, under the existing law, a C licence vehicle cannot carry the goods of anyone save its owner. It follows that the C licence vehicle will often return empty, i.e., waste is created of just the kind which nationalisation is supposed to eliminate.

30. It has often been suggested by supporters of nationalisation that C licences should be restricted on the familiar ground that they are 'creaming off' the traffic. The attitude of the Transport Commission has been to minimise the importance of the growth of C licences, to suggest that the growth may be temporary, but at the same time to deprecate it. See British Transport Comm'n 4th Ann. Rep. 30–31 (1951).

31. Report of the Committee on National Policy for the Use of Fuel and Power Resources 130 (1952) (hereinafter referred to as the 'Ridley Committee Report').

32. Ibid., p. 179.
33. Ibid., p. 147–8.
34. Evidence of Trades Union Congress, ibid., p. 219.
35. Ibid., p. 122.
36. Ibid., p. 149.
37. Ibid., p. 178.
38. Such labour problems have undoubtedly complicated the schemes of integration of the British Transport Commission. British Transport Comm'n 4th Ann. Rep. 4 (1951).
39. Ibid.
40. Ridley Committee Report, op. cit.
41. Ibid., at c. IV.
42. The Board in this year continued to explain the grounds upon which it was seeking for a rational price structure. The following (¶108) deserves to be preserved as an exhibit in any museum of economic obscurantism: 'A rational price structure is needed both to promote the efficient use of coal and to help the Board in deciding upon their production plans. If there were no scarcity of coal there might have been no need for an elaborate exercise to work out a rational price structure: the "market" would indicate what prices were too low or too high and so point the way to what prices should be. But in time of scarcity the indications of the market are not clear. Nearly all coals are scarce, whether they are correctly priced or not, and degrees of scarcity are not easily determined. A faulty price structure does not leave the over-priced coals unsold; it means dissatisfaction among consumers. So the Board had no choice; they had to work out a new price structure as a starting point. In the long run, the indications of the market will not be ignored.'
43. Thus, the British Electrical Authority complained: 'Even after the latest price revision, the average pit head price of fuel to the Authority per therm is still somewhat higher than the price per therm paid by many other users, although the quality is so much lower. . . . The Authority have, therefore, been called upon to subsidise other coal consumers such as the Gas Boards.' Ridley Committee Report, op. cit. p. 152. The Gas Council reported: 'The National Coal Board prepared in March 1951, a scheme for giving price reductions to domestic and industrial coal users by increasing the price of coal for carbonisation. . . . The gas industry believes that the principle of this scheme was applied in a discriminating fashion against the gas industry when coal prices were revised on Dec. 31st, 1951.' Ibid., p. 169.
44. British Transport Comm'n 4th Ann. Rep. 29 (1951).
45. In the period 1948–57, gross capital investment in the public corporations was slightly more than one-half the investment in private companies. Of the gross capital investment in the nationalised industries, about one-half has gone into electricity supply and distribution.
46. See Allen, 'The Outlook for British Industry', *Westminster Bank Rev.*, August 1952.
47. Ridley Committee Report, op. cit., pp. 12, 121, 136, 148, 211.

8 ENTREPRENEURS ON THE DEFENSIVE

The Industrial Policy Group: The Failure of an Experiment*

I

The setting up of the Industrial Policy Group in 1968 and its ultimate demise in 1974 may be only a minor event in the economic upheavals of the period, yet the life story of what was in some ways a unique experiment has some light to throw upon the fundamental causes of our economic troubles. The Group was created through the initiative of Sir Paul Chambers who became the first Chairman with Mr Arthur Shenfield acting as its Director. Its constitution was of the simplest. The Group was a club, necessarily limited in size by the manner in which it was to operate. It was to consist of 20 to 25 members each of whom was the head of a large corporation.[1] The members made no special effort to create a balanced representation of the British economy. Most of their companies were manufacturing, although building, distribution and finance were represented. Many of the companies were multinational; a number of them long before detractors had even recognised that there were such things in the world. It was intended that the membership of the Group should change from time to time. In one sense this was inevitable – for the heads of large companies normally serve in that capacity only for a spell before retirement. In any case, in a group of limited size it was recognised that some rotation of experience and interest was an advantage.

 But the members had certain things in common. All were engaged in the administrative leadership of very large organisations; such a task in its fundamentals must remain the same whatever the company is making or selling. They knew that, collectively, they possessed, through their

*The early part of this paper is based largely upon an article I wrote for the National Westminster Bank *Quarterly Review*, November 1970: 'The Industrial Policy Group—An Experiment in Communication'.

own experience and that of their immediate colleagues in their own companies, an intimate knowledge of many industrial matters certainly not surpassed and hardly equalled elsewhere. And they were not unconscious of the peculiar mixture of feelings – running from misrepresentation through suspicion to respect and admiration – with which the public thought of Big Business.

The most important thing they had in common was their hope that the Group would be able to raise the level of public debate by first clarifying, through discussion, their own views on subjects where they certainly had the right to speak and then publishing these views in short papers. The papers were to represent nothing but their personal opinions. Although, by the very nature of the reasons which had brought them together, the members expected to share common views on many things, they did not necessarily seek unanimity. They recognised there would be occasions and subjects upon which they might disagree and where the most useful contribution they could make to the forming of wise public policy was to set down, frankly and in full, the grounds for their disagreement. They were addressing, in their papers, no single or uniform audience. There would be times when their experience and suggestions might be of immediate and direct interest to ministers, and other occasions on which a wider public audience and even students in universities could gain most from the information they could provide. They sought to be a pressure group only in the sense that facts and ideas presented by those who knew most about what they were discussing should, and it could be hoped would, exercise pressure.

At any time and under any conditions, therefore, such a Group, representing a significant proportion of the industry of the nation and exercising upon the national income by their decisions perhaps as great an influence, one way or another, as any similar number of men in any other walk of life, might have been expected to hold collective views which merited careful examination by the whole community. But in the peculiar conditions of the time there seemed to be special reasons why such a body might serve a useful purpose.

First, Britain was in a sorry economic tangle. It was becoming increasingly evident that one of the great enigmas of the post-war world was that Britain, with such great natural advantages – a stable political system, highly developed science and technology, accumulated industrial skills and habits – should show such a depressing performance in productivity. A vast literature had appeared upon this subject but no explanation had been persuasive or was generally accepted. It was, therefore, not altogether surprising that Britain had another unenviable record: she had, more than other industrial countries, persistently and, some would say recklessly, experimented with 'economic gimmicks' – short and easy cuts to prosperity – in a desperate attempt to restore her fortunes. Nationalisation, denationalisation, renationalisation, central economic planning, the 'restructuring' of industry, economic dashes for freedom, extensive and detailed price and income controls, detailed control of the location of industry; one after another these panaceas had been introduced with exaggerated hopes and, since there are no such things as economic miracles, each in turn had left behind its disillusion-ment. Confusion as to facts and causes had led to a plethora of bogus prescriptions and remedies. Unless it was fatalistically supposed that there was really no rhyme or reason for what happens in the economic system, there must have been good causes for the British economic dis-temper. It was not fanciful to suppose that, in the identification of those causes a useful part might be played by a group of businessmen with an intimate knowledge of industrial conditions and methods in many other countries, and a first-hand acquaintance with the fundamental problems involved in administering large bodies.

Second, there seemed to be an urgent need in 1968 to challenge and try to reverse the distorted public image prevailing about Big Business. Widespread suspicion and hostility to private enterprise were to be found nearly everywhere. Industrial profits were regarded as virtually immoral and the fall in those profits, the mainspring of economic progress, was light-heartedly ignored. Quite extraordinary mis-representations about the higher management echelons in industry were rampant. Thus, when the Group was first set up, Mr Callaghan, at that time Chancellor of the Exchequer and ham-handedly running down the economy to the final devaluation of the currency, spoke of the members of the Group as 'rather dubious people' with 'potentially sinister' pur-poses. And no one protested. A leading British journalist was able to describe British industry as 'presenting such a picture of anaemic malnutrition that the idea of its being able to stand on its own feet appears almost risibly unreal. Industrialists scarcely believe in themselves'. And no one, so far as I know, protested. Academics were wasting their time discussing the motives of businessmen, and what it was they were trying to 'maximise', without even mentioning that perhaps businessmen were trying to maximise the satisfaction to be derived from doing a better job in feeding, housing and clothing people. Given this kind of lead from the current creators of opinion it was not surprising that in turn the more able young people began to look with distaste upon the prospect of taking any part in business or that young scientists clung to their research in the universities and belittled what they might be doing in industry to raise standards of living, abolish back-breaking toil and reduce pain throughout the world.

Third, the setting up of the Industrial Policy Group was an experi-ment in improving communications. It was thought that it might assist the professional economist to become more knowledgeable about in-dustry and thus reduce the risks of his doing damage by spreading faulty ideas among the young. In the field of industrial organisation and policy, certain economists, those indeed who had been most successful in getting their views accepted, such as Professor Galbraith, had frequently been wrong both about what was actually happening and about what should happen, and these mistakes went far to explain the curious confusion which had long surrounded this branch of descriptive economics.

To illustrate: for almost the whole of the first half of this century it was widely accepted, on the authority of economists, that the concentration of industry was on the increase, that big firms were rapidly replacing small and that, in future, industry would inevitably consist of a few giant industrial empires. It was not until 1950 that more careful and detailed work proved that this idea was incorrect; that there was no evidence of such changes. But ideas are powerful things and this particular idea had fostered the belief that nothing could be manufactured economically except on a very large scale and that innovations and technical progress would come only from the large organisations able to conduct research on a massive scale. It had led one group of people, who feared the future as it was being portrayed, to recommend powerful counter-measures on the part of the State to prevent the growth of firms and particularly the growth of monopoly. It had led another group, who liked what was supposed to be happening, to recommend governments to hurry on the prevalent trends so that the day would more quickly arrive when industries could conveniently be nationalised. Yet throughout this period the distribution curves of the sizes of businesses in manufacturing industries, for example, in American and British industry were changing hardly at all.

Could the Industrial Policy Group, given the limited amount of time and effort its members could afford to devote to the task, do anything to raise the level of debate and even reverse the trend of thought? Given the enormous power of the underswell of thought and emotion, mainly the latter, which controls popular feelings on economic matters, the hopes of the Group for prompt results may have appeared highly ambitious, even quixotic. That view, at least in the short run, proved correct.

In its first two years the Group published three papers. In Paper No. 2 in 1968 on 'Government Expenditure' the Group concluded:

Government expenditure is both excessive in total and wrongly distributed. . . . We find disturbing in the extreme the surge upwards of Government expenditure in the past three years. . . . We see industry hobbled by high taxation and shortage of the savings from which risk capital can come; and we find the prime cause of these obstacles to industrial enterprise in the attempt to direct too high a proportion of the nation's resources into channels determined by the Government.

It continued:

> We do not pretend to be competent to produce uniquely correct solutions for all the practical problems presented under each main head of Government expenditure.

It pointed out that the results of greatly increased government welfare services had over the years resulted in less, not more, real welfare and that

> Reform is needed as much for the improvement in welfare as for the release of the taxpayer from an intolerable fiscal burden.

This paper was followed up six months later by a companion paper on taxation which concluded

> We believe that our taxes are both excessive in total and wrongly balanced. . . . We have reviewed the taxation system in the light of the canons of equity and efficiency, and also of their adjunct, simplicity, and we have found it wanting under each head. . . . The reform of the system and the reduction of the burden upon taxpayers are inescapable conditions for the recovery of the economy and the achievement of rapid economic growth on stable foundations.

If those views had not been so stubbornly and perversely ignored, our present economic plight would not be so grave as it is.

III

In the middle of 1969 Mr (later Sir) David Barran become Chairman of the Group and I was invited to become its Director. I gladly accepted because I sympathised with the aims of the Group and because my academic studies had always led me towards conclusions, concerning the sure foundation of a vigorous system of private enterprise, similar to those held by the members of the Group with their greater practical experience.

I confess to an added minor reason why I was happy to receive the invitation. I was anxious to inform myself more fully about one aspect of the working of a highly developed and complex industrial system which has for long intrigued right-wing economists and sometimes created a sharp difference of opinion between them. Did a system of private enterprise contain the seeds of its own decay in the sense that if wide freedoms were left to producers to follow their own ways this would leave open to them the possibility of cornering markets and thus stifling competition? One group of economists has always belittled this danger, arguing that, in practice, competition can never be repressed, that if it is curbed at one point it will spontaneously appear or regenerate itself at another. Another group of economists, however, has always thought that the dangers of monopoly growing out of private enterprise were real and serious enough to call for continuous government action to watch developments and provide administrative and legal restraints where competition was clearly being eroded. My own doubts on this point had been formulated earlier:

> I cannot believe that, in the last resort, a thoroughly effective competitive system stands much chance of survival or that anti-monopoly legislation is likely to be worth the candle unless businessmen themselves believe in and accept the rules of the competitive game, however sharp may be its barbs and arrows. It may seem to be a small matter to expect of the businessman that he should sincerely favour private enterprise. It is in fact not so. He is being asked to do much more than make speeches which claim virtues for 'free enterprise' and are critical of Government operation of industry. He is being expected deliberately to refrain from agreements to fix prices or output; to recognise, however galling it may appear to him at the time, that when his organisation reaches a certain size or commands a certain proportion of the market, then the public has a direct interest in what he and his Company are doing; to co-operate positively with the Government in accepting (and even, dare one say it, in devising and improving) rules for keeping industry lively and resilient through the perpetual rivalry of competitors. . . . This is a lot to accept. But, in the long run, sufficient imagination and courage on the part of the businessman to do so is probably a condition of his survival.
>
> ('No Industry Without Enterprise'
IEA Paper 'Growth Through Industry', p. 13.)

Under the Chairmanship of Sir David Barran six papers were published by the Group. In Paper No. 4, 'The Case for Overseas Direct Investment', stress was laid upon the value of such investment to the economy and to the balance of payments and a case was made for loosening the restrictions upon direct investment overseas. The arguments were given full support, but not until seven years later, by the British Treasury.[2] In these days Paper No. 4 might be read with great benefit by those left-wingers who recommend the restriction of new and even the repatriation of existing foreign investment as a measure for helping to create the Utopia of a siege economy.

Paper No. 5, 'The Case against the Selective Employment Tax', challenged the elementary fallacy that if manufacturing industry in the narrow sense was declining relative to the service industries, such as transport, distribution and finance, then that in itself was evidence that the economy as a whole was weakening and needed remedial action

from the Government. It was shown that this view ran counter to what
in fact was happening in the more prosperous industrial economies and
that the attempt, through the introduction of this particular tax, to
remedy a non-existent trouble was irrational and was creating
numerous anomalies. The Selective Employment Tax was, of course,
subsequently repealed.[3] But the argument upon which it was based, that
a prosperous economy can be built only upon the relative expansion of
the manufacturing sector, is still reflected in present day 'strategies' for
creating prosperity.

The next four papers, taken together, were an attempt to portray the
main features to which an industrial economy would have to conform if
it were still to be regarded as a 'mixed' but viable system of private
enterprise, the extent to which the British industrial system could still be
so regarded, and the main threats to its continued virility. In order to do
this, it was necessary first to challenge some alleged facts as to what was
really happening within the structure of British industry (a comparatively simple task) and next (but more difficult) to try to disentangle the confusing and misleading theories which had over the years been developed
by economists about 'competition' and the conditions it must satisfy if
the social and economic case for it were to be regarded as established.

It is useful to recall here the dogma which confronted the Group at
the time of this attempt to present what they considered as the correct
picture. It was widely assumed that large firms were everywhere rapidly
replacing small; this apparently was a fact of life which just had to be
accepted. These changes in structure were, it was thought, not wholly
disadvantageous; they were, after all, in the main occurring because big
firms were more efficient than small, and there was virtually no limit to
the economies of scale. So there was a case for government intervention
even to hurry on the formation of large corporations – by what was
called a policy of 'restructuring industry'. But, of course, if giant companies were thus to dominate, then the problems of size and monopoly
would arise and the Government would have to intervene more actively
and intimately to guard against the dangers inherent in this situation. So
the distorted picture which gradually became imprinted upon the minds
of our rulers and of the public at the time was that there had to be a
'mixed economy' but that this would by normal processes come to consist of a few giant nationalised industries and a few giant public companies and that these public companies would increasingly and conveniently fall under the control and guidance of the Government.[4]

Paper No. 6, 'The Structure and Efficiency of British Industry', concluded that there was

> no satisfactory evidence to support the view that the relatively slow
> progress of British industrial productivity in recent years is at-
> tributable to major deficiencies in the structure of British industry.

The idea that great companies were sweeping away all others was misrepresentation. It was asserted by academic statisticians that the share of the largest 100 firms in the net output of manufacturing in Britain in 1970 was around 52 per cent. In fact recent official figures show that the correct percentage for 1971 was 38.6 per cent and this percentage had hardly changed between 1963 and 1971.[5]

More important, Paper No. 6 showed that, in comparing the industrial structure in the United States with that in Britain, there were many more similarities than differences. The average manufacturing company employed about the same number of workers in the two countries and the size distribution was much the same. In America it was true there were a small number of companies larger than anything found elsewhere, but it was far from established that those American companies were an outstanding source of strength.

The central doctrine of Paper No. 6 was that undue emphasis was being placed upon the idea of the 'optimum size of firm'. What was needed for industrial efficiency was an 'optimum distribution' of sizes of firms. In anything like a competitive system, very varying sizes of firms would spontaneously emerge and the system would be so complex and dynamic, so continually in process of change that interference by governments was more likely to do harm than good – which apparently was what had in fact happened.

In Paper No. 7, 'The Growth of Competition', the question was posed: what truth was there in the view widely held by politicians, academics and journalists that, for one reason or another, competition was steadily on the decline? If that indeed were the case then the defence of private enterprise falls to the ground, since the essence of this system is the operation of competition in all its forms; choice by consumers and emulation, rivalry and substitution among producers. Examining the factual evidence, and speaking from experience, the Group argued that: 'Competition has never been as intense or more extensive than it now is' and that this largely accounted for the steady long-period improvements in the standard of living of the western world. Competition took the form of the widening range of goods and services available to the consumer; of extended rivalry between different materials and processes; between firms of different sizes; between the industries of one country and those of other countries; between older and newer technical processes. Competition, indeed, was most likely to be stifled by the direct intervention of governments, through the creation of monopolies within their own borders by measures such as nationalisation, or through the blocking of international trading through import controls. Paper No. 7 also went to some pains to point out that, on this subject, formal economic theorising had done a great deal to cloud understanding and confuse the issues of the practical world. Everything turned on what is meant by 'competition'. Formal economic theory can provide a

cast-iron case in favour of competition so long as the reasoning begins
from a strict definition of 'perfect competition'. But, in fact, 'perfect
competition' as thus defined does not exist and never has existed. Does
it then follow that the case for competition falls to the ground? Not so,
it was argued in the paper. For real competition (the competition that
matters, that generates the beneficial choices, the emulation and the
rivalry), can be fully active and effective even under conditions much less
stringent than those called for by 'perfect competition'. So that what
economists had come to regard as imperfect competition (or oligopoly)
did not really undermine the case for the competition that mattered.
This was really an illustration of the propensity of economists at times to
be lured into the belief that when they had modified their theories they
had really changed the world.

Nevertheless, despite its contention that normally competition was a
powerful, pervasive and continuing influence in the industrial systems of
the western world, the Group recognised that, as a further safety device,
governments would be wise to watch over the trends in industry and act
where monopolies would seem to be being formed. They developed
their views on this subject in Papers No. 8, 'The Control of Monopoly',
and No. 9, 'Merger Policy'. It was argued that the first line of defence
against monopoly was to restrain and even reverse the activities of post-
war governments which had run counter to competition. Freedom of international trade was one important safety measure. It was pointed out
that public corporations had been steadily growing in importance in
Britain and were accounting for 10 per cent of the national labour force
and 20 per cent of the annual capital accumulation; that these
nationalised industries had had monopoly rights conferred upon them
by law. It was argued that these legal monopolies should as far as possible be swept away and nationalised industries and private enterprise
equally exposed to the test of the market. Suggestions were made for
speeding up, largely by simplifying, the activities of the Monopolies
Commission and for distinguishing, in the supervision of mergers,
between those which were simply another form of the growth of a company directed towards increased efficiency and those which aimed at an
undue control of the market.

My impression was that in the preparation of Papers No. 8 and No. 9
at least some of the members of the Group were, from time to time, inclined to ask themselves whether the complexities of their tasks might
not be reduced and more of their time and energy thereby made
available for the improvement of the efficiency of their own companies,
if they could have been allowed to escape from some of the thorns of
direct and never-ending competition. But I cannot think that any fair-
minded reader, going back to Papers No. 8 and 9, could deny that these
documents came out heavily in favour of competition and the duties
which it was necessary for governments to undertake to help to maintain

it. I certainly do not know of any formal statement made by any similar body of top business executives anywhere (and certainly not in the United States) which so plainly and clearly acknowledged what was implied by the maintenance of competition at the intensity which gave full support for the case for private enterprise.

IV

Under the normal arrangements for rotation, Sir Arnold Hall succeeded Sir David Barran as Chairman in the middle of 1971.[6] Under Sir Arnold's guidance the Group published in February 1972 Paper No. 10, 'Economic Growth, Profits and Investment'. This paper was, for several reasons, probably the most important published by the Group. It produced a wide sweeping survey of the causes of the growing signs of debility in British industry and of the possible cures for this. It attracted wider public attention than most of the earlier papers. In its forthright approach, the Group found itself in contention with some of the main economic policies of the then Conservative Government, and its analysis and findings diverged in important ways from the current views of the C.B.I. and, in consequence, resulted for the first time in the publication of a paper to which reservations were attached by two Members – Sir John Partridge, the President, and Mr Campbell Adamson, the Director General of the C.B.I.

Paper No. 10 was one of the first, if not the first, document from such a high level, to warn that British industrial weakness was attributable to a decline in 'real' profits which had already resulted in a severe deterioration in the financial position of many companies; that if this decline were not checked the end could only be disaster; that while the returns on existing capital were so low, to talk of the need for further investment was to treat the symptoms as if they were the cause; that other countries with whom we were in competition were not suffering in the same way from the slide in profitability; that while industry was bleeding to death internally in this way, general, direct investment incentives offered by the Government, in favour of which there had never been much to say, were almost irrelevant.

Why governments and informed public opinion had remained so apathetic to what was perhaps the most general and dangerous situation which had ever confronted British industry would in itself be a fascinating subject for study. Undoubtedly the mood of the public at that time, which rendered it almost heresy to suggest that profits served any useful purpose whatever, and the failure of businessmen themselves to recognise the need, in a period of inflation, to calculate their real profits correctly, were two important factors. But the detailed statistical work which has since been carried out makes clear that even Paper No. 10 was not painting in dark enough colours the immediate past and the probable future of profitability.

The article, 'Trends in Company Profitability', in the March 1976 number of the Bank of England *Quarterly Bulletin*, largely the work of J. S. Flemming, enables us now to see what was really happening among British industrial and commercial companies between 1968 and 1974.

	Pre-tax rates of return per cent per annum		Post-tax real rates of return per cent per annum	
	'Historic cost' return	'Real' rate of return[a]	'Forward'[b] looking	After allowance for tax relief on stocks
1968	14.7	10.0	5.4	
1969	13.3	8.5	3.9	
1970	12.8	7.3	3.1	
1971	13.1	7.3	3.5	
1972	14.3	7.5	4.3	
1973	16.5	6.6	3.4	(6.3)
1974	16.8	4.0	−0.3	(4.1)

[a] Return after revaluation of the capital stock and of capital consumption less stock appreciation.
[b] 'Forward'-looking return is the calculation of real rates of return as they would appear to a firm considering new investment in relation to current investment incentive.

The figures above of course collected retrospectively, confirm that the fears of the Group, based on the experience of the day and what they foresaw, were only too well-founded. For by 1974 post-tax real rates of return, for a 'forward-looking' entrepreneur, would have actually become negative but for the fact that even Mr Healey, despite his ambitions to make the pips squeak through heavy taxation, had become alarmed at the fall in profitability and had granted tax reliefs which at least arrested the downward slide.

In Paper No. 10, however, the Group did not confine itself to this grave warning regarding declining profits; it attacked the misunderstandings and fallacies associated with what can only be described as the current 'obsession with investment' – the blind belief that the one sure way to bring about industrial expansion, however unpromising might be the outlook, was to invest and to continue to invest. The Group, in opposition, insisted that there could be both profitable and unprofitable investment; that under private enterprise capital should be steered at the appropriate times to the potentially growing points of the economy and that the decisions here could only be made rationally by individual entrepreneurs assessing the peculiar circumstances and conditions of their own companies. And in Paper No. 10 they declared that

> We do not accept the view that there is any general tendency for businessmen to under-invest. On the whole and *given the economic circumstances*, we are not under the impression that the Companies we represent would be in a healthier, more competitive, more profitable state now had we invested more over the last ten years.

They further argued that the history over the past 30 years of the attempts of government to stimulate the level of investment by the granting of *general* investment incentives had been a failure. Government policies in these matters had changed so frequently that they had positively added to the uncertainties of business, had probably not increased investment in total and had bred a number of other anomolies. And it was concluded that if the calculation of profits were correctly made to allow for inflation and if taxes on 'real' profits were reduced then the way 'would be open for the gradual phasing out of general investment incentives'.

The doctrine of the Group was, therefore, that given a promising rate of current and prospective profits, investment, in proper time and place, would follow through the spontaneous decisions of numerous entrepreneurs in the best position to judge of possibilities.

This broad-based attack on the 'obsession with investment' was badly needed at the time. For this obsession was the parent of quite extraordinary misconceptions. The C.B.I. was claiming that 'investment is the key to competitiveness' even at a time when it was widely recognised in the business community that there was already a surplus of capacity generally in industry and when the big difference between this country and other countries lay not in difference of investment but in the low output per worker, the low output per machine actually installed and the difficulty in bringing about economy in the numbers employed on new machines introduced for cutting costs. There was even more remarkable sophistry abroad. I refer to the attitude of Mr Heath and his Government in later paragraphs. But even as late as 1 April 1974 Mr Healey, in the House of Commons, delivered himself of this sententious maxim: 'Historically the level of profits in Britain has very little to do with the level of investment'. And a month later he developed his ideas:

> There is a wide degree of agreement . . . first, that shortage of funds is not likely to be an obstacle to investment this year and secondly, that the future rate of return on capital determines investment rather than the level of profits in the past.

Fortunately for all of us, faced with facts, he changed his mind within the following few weeks and declared that 'Our firm intention is to take action if we judge it necessary to see that investment is not endangered by the undue restriction of profits'.

V

Although it was not formally disbanded until the middle of 1974, Paper No. 10 was the last to be published by the Group. Of the reasons which led to this decision one can only speculate. There was certainly a general feeling that their papers had not apparently gained the attention or produced the impact that had been hoped for. The members must have recognised that they were still operating in a suspicious, where not actually hostile, atmosphere. It is easy to forget that up to 1974 there was hardly one important newspaper that robustly defended private enterprise, while radio and television programmes were giving little or no time to anything but socialist doctrines. (Admittedly this has changed since.) Attention and respect the Group could hardly expect from the Labour side. But for the greater part of its life a Conservative Government was in power which seemed dedicated to broad economic policies running counter to those being enunciated by the Group. The difference of opinion between the Group and the C.B.I. which had appeared most clearly in Paper No. 10 must have been discouraging. In all the circumstances it is perhaps not surprising that the members, loaded down as they were with the problems of their own companies, concluded that they might better devote their time to their own bailiwicks.

It would not be right to assume that from February 1972 to the middle of 1974 the Group was idle. Indeed, strenuous but unsuccessful efforts were made to reach, on vital economic issues, agreement sufficient to justify the publication of further papers. Perhaps the failure here reflected a weakening consensus on what was best to do in the confusion of the times; perhaps it was due to the belief that the Group was not likely to be listened to very intently.

In the light of after events it seems particularly a pity that the Group did not make known its views on inflation – a pity because the members were of one mind about some basic aspects of the subject which came to be understood only slowly by governments and the public at large.

The Group realised that statutory controls over prices, incomes and profits, even if defensible as emergency measures in the very short period, would rapidly pile up anomalies which would make things worse and not better. A majority were also of one mind in thinking that unless a proper control were placed by the Government on the supply of money then nothing else would avail and that excessive government expenditure was a prime obstacle to the setting of safe levels to money supply. They were, for the most part, agreed that the 'monetarists' were misguided when they argued that the increase in trade union power and militancy could not contribute to inflation. They were convinced that recorded unemployment was being unduly swollen by the more generous provisions of unemployment and other social benefits from the public coffers; that trade unions in Britain could properly be expected, as in most other countries, to carry a greater degree of the financial responsibility for the maintenance of their members and their families during strikes; that picketing should be restricted firmly to its legal limits; that there was an urgent need for the public to be fully informed about the facts and issues in any important industrial dispute; that to discuss wages and wage adjustments in terms of 'take-home' pay – thus ignoring the social service benefits that flowed from taxation – was an evasion of the real situation. And many of the members felt that the inflationary settlement of miners' wages which had followed from the Wilberforce Report was a lesson of how such decisions should not be made.

Since 1973, of course, all these contentions have been widely discussed and more generally accepted. Perhaps the Government and the public might have faced up to reality more quickly if the Group had found it possible to publish its views.

VI

To sum up, I suspect that the efforts of the Group fell upon stony ground for two main reasons: the attitudes and policies of the Conservative Government, and especially its leader, in the crucial period 1970–74 and the association of the Industrial Policy Group with the C.B.I.

The return to power of the Conservatives in 1970 did not, as might have been expected, create a continuing environment favourable to private enterprise. After a very brief interlude, the Government engaged in widespread forms of intervention which must at first have surprised and then disheartened those who foresaw the recovery of British industry coming through greater freedom for the industrial decision-makers. The rise in the number of registered unemployed produced something of a panic and led to a policy of supporting weak industrial units under legislation which succeeding Labour Governments were only too happy to inherit and use. Rising prices led to detailed and elaborate controls over prices, incomes and profits, controls which were introduced as immediate ambulance work but which kept the patient tied down on a stretcher.[7]

The British political system puts into the hands of the Prime Minister enormous power, if he so cares to use it, over economic policy in all its aspects. From 1970 onwards it is not to be doubted that Mr Heath, because of his prestige within his own party after the famous electoral victory of that year, his widely recognised integrity, his patriotism and the confidence he felt in his own economic doctrines, was the maker and the maintainer of Conservative policy. In practice, his doctrines proved to be a puzzling mixture. In earlier times he had on occasions staunchly defended the market economy. His determined attack on resale price maintenance and his emphasis on the benefits of free trade within a European Common Market were well known. And it is possible to pick out from his speeches quotations which picture him as wholly convinced of the virtues of the market economy. In important ways and actions, however, he proved to be something of an interventionist, with views certainly different from those being advanced by the Industrial Policy Group.

He often spoke of the more senior British businessmen with impatience as if he felt that they were not the best that industry might have found or that, if they were, they had to be kept up to scratch by exhortations from above. (He would quote Disraeli that 'England is a very difficult country to move)'. He suspected that at least some businessmen were collectivist: 'They were punch drunk because they had been knocked about so much by taxation and Government controls since 1939'. He expressed grave doubts about 'the good old-fashioned and straightforward market economy' as 'hopelessly irrelevant because of the shift in the balance of power within the community'. He frequently protested that he had no time for 'laissez-faire' or a 'free-for-all system' without specifying what he understood by these terms. He could be caustic about 'the simple form of mechanistic economics' and, although he placed little trust in the works of any economist, he seemed most suspicious of those who defended the free market economy. And, of course, although he so rarely resorted to rhetoric, yet he did on one famous occasion speak of 'the unacceptable face of capitalism', a gift which his political opponents gratefully accepted and later employed to great effect.[8]

The rift between Mr Heath and the entrepreneurs, however, was more than a matter of personal misunderstandings. Mr Heath had a concept of a 'new capitalism' which would be markedly different in method from the 'old capitalism' found, for instance, in the United States or Germany, in four respects. First, he argued that British industry was not investing enough, in other words the businessman did not understand what was in the best interests of his company or his country and that Mr Heath knew better. He complained that industry did not invest far enough ahead of demand:

The curse of British industry is that it has never anticipated demand. When we came in we were told there weren't sufficient inducements to invest. So we provided the inducements. Then we were told people were scared of balance of payments difficulties leading to stop-go. So we floated the pound. Then we were told of fears of inflation: and now we are dealing with that. And still you aren't investing enough.

(The *Director*, June 1973)

There is not much virtue in a private enterprise system if its practitioners are always trying to find clouds in the sky as an excuse for
staying indoors.

(The *Daily Telegraph*, 5 February 1973)

Second, Mr Heath clearly believed that the economy could be
operated with the very low rate of unemployment to which we had
become accustomed after 1950 without creating a serious danger of inflation. In this sense, although he constantly pointed to the fundamental
changes in our economic society and the need for adjusting policies in
the light of them, he was very much an old-fashioned Keynesian. In
1973 he had complained that 'We still have half a million unemployed,
with all that that means in terms of home resources which we ought to
be using', and, contrary to the opposite views which were supported by
much evidence, he argued that our unemployment statistics underestimated the scale of the problem.

Third, and this presumably went along with his views that we could
spend our way out of anything but a very low rate of unemployment, he
disputed the contention that the money supply must be the prime determinant of the general price level and he consistently argued against the
reasoning which the monetarists, British and American, were pressing
upon him.

Fourth, he never appeared to lose faith in direct intervention in the
way of control over prices, incomes and profits. Until the defeat of
the Conservatives in the early part of 1974 the control mechanisms were
becoming more complicated as new devices were hopefully introduced
to correct the distortions of the old.

Mr Peter Walker seems to have been in closest rapport with Mr Heath
in these broad attitudes to economic problems. The manner in which he
was then and later to press his views can hardly have helped any possible
understanding between a Conservative Government and entrepreneurs.

Mr Walker was, and indeed continues to be, very downright in his
formulation of the ideals of the Conservative Party. The party should
not 'retreat into the bunkers and bolt holes of narrow middle class
politics. . . . We must avoid a retreat to the primitive idols of the Conservative Party'. In 1972, feeling that businessmen were not active enough
in preparing for entry to the Common Market, he recommended that
businessmen should be 'chivvied up' by shop stewards, trade union
leaders, mayors and local councillors. In the world of ideas, his main
target seems to have been the American Professor Milton Friedman
whom, he thought, 'preached the simple solution, such as controlling
the money supply according to some specific formula' and 'based his

defence of capitalism upon the supremacy of laissez-faire'. (Professor Friedman must have been astonished to have his views so interpreted.) Mr Walker clearly looked upon Lord Keynes as one of 'the intellectual progenitors of the modern mixed economy capitalist society'. But he appeals to Keynes in support of ideas regarding public expenditure, unemployment and inflation which Keynes himself had almost certainly discarded before his death.

The attempts of the Industrial Policy Group to change the general course of thinking on industrial policy were further complicated and frustrated by its close association with the C.B.I. This was trouble of its own making. At the founding of the Group it had been agreed that the President and the Director General of the C.B.I. should be ex officio members. These two members, with the best will in the world, could hardly be expected to support reasoning which ran counter to their very much larger and more representative organisation. This is certainly not the place nor the occasion (even if I were competent to carry out the task) to pass judgement on the work of the C.B.I. over the years. But it can hardly be disputed that, from the inter-war period to the present day it has accepted the idea that the interests of the business community and of the country would be best served if the Government, organised business and the trade unions could consort together and agree on policies. The expansion of the earlier Federation of British Industries into the C.B.I., through the inclusion of the nationalised industries, and the further attempts, only partially successful, to widen the influence of the C.B.I. by absorbing financial and distribution organisations, was further action logical enough in the light of its aims and purposes. For if it wished to be associated with and regularly consulted by the Government it was not unreasonable, and certainly not impolitic, for it on occasions to give ground to the Government, to accept schemes about which it had serious doubts, to offer to make sacrifices, to propose compromises as the price to be paid for the achieving of wider ends over longer periods.

Certainly the Conservative Government between 1970 and 1974 could not complain that the C.B.I. had not been helpful and co-operative even when the Government was engaged in some rather surprising U-turns. On a number of occasions, where the pull might be described as that between politics and the principles of a market economy, the C.B.I. proved to be accommodating. In 1971, in its concern about the threat of inflation, it introduced a system of price control among a sector of its members, doubtless hoping that this voluntary example would lead to matching action from the trade unions on wage restraint. This move was both foolish and futile. It helped to launch the idea that prices and incomes could be usefully controlled directly, it reduced industrial profits at a time when they were unduly low and it brought no response from the trade unions. But the C.B.I. continued to defend the idea of pay restraints and price controls. It made no protest over the disastrously inflationary wage settlements, arising out of the Wilberforce Report, during the coal-mining dispute. The fact that the National Coal Board was a member of the C.B.I. would have made such a protest invidious. It was very much a late comer in recognising the dangers of swollen public expenditure through the extension of the welfare society. It was awakened to the dangers of the growing militancy of trade unions only at a late stage. And, as has been explained above, it defended industrial investment inducements despite the fact that in accepting these subsidies companies were placing themselves dangerously under the thumb of the State. Sir Campbell Adamson, the Director General of the C.B.I. for seven years, has indeed suggested that during his term of office 'his contribution must be counted negative in economic terms'. In saying this he may well have been more than generous in defence of the organisation and the businessmen whom he served. For it is almost in the nature of things that the C.B.I. will inevitably come to support a corporative type of economy. In any case, given the number of businessmen, running into many hundreds, who spend so much time, which otherwise might be devoted to their own businesses, on so many committees at the headquarters of the C.B.I. any failure in its general strategy should surely be attributed to the businessmen and not their officials. Be that as it may, the association between the C.B.I. and the I.P.G. in four crucial years did not help to further the aims which the Group had originally set itself.

VII

The major lesson I draw from this episode is that a system of free markets, however great may be its potential benefits, will always have its determined and single-minded detractors and its defenders and well-wishers who will often be less than whole-hearted because of their divided loyalties and disposition to compromise. Indeed the free market, like freedom and democracy itself, must at times appear to be such a fragile plant that its continued survival seems little short of a miracle.

The enemies fall into different classes. Some abhor the very idea of free exchanges and reward for individual enterprise and perhaps see a chance of improving their own condition even if only as agents of power centred on the State. Some, at least in their honest moments, confess to the enjoyment of the flesh pots but salve their consciences by asserting that they are ready to be stripped clean, provided only that someone else takes the initiative in organising the dispossession.[9] And there are finally the more saintly who subscribe to a communism based upon perfect equality and who so frequently and sadly become the pawns or dupes of the more earthy-minded.

As for the defenders, it would be naive, and indeed unfair, to fail to recognise the dilemmas which can often leave them in two minds and thus enfeeble their efforts. At first glance it might be supposed that businessmen, the main agents of a free economy, would put up such an overriding case, by word and action, for this system that their opponents would be wholly discredited. But take some actual situations in which the entrepreneur may find himself. Suppose his domestic market is being flooded by cheap foreign goods. Suppose, in choosing a site for a new factory, Site A is marginally inferior on his calculations to Site B, but that if Site A is chosen he will be offered a large government grant. What right has he to ignore the interests of the shareholders and nevertheless choose Site B? Suppose that he is faced with a partial close-down of the factory which he could avoid if he accepts a subsidy which the government is pressing upon him. Under such conditions it would need an entrepreneur taking a very long and wide view, supported by his employees and the shareholders, to refuse to touch the State aid which inevitably carries with it the increasing likelihood of State intervention. Suppose the entrepreneur is convinced that if only he were allowed to create a monopoly he could reduce prices and increase demand, employment and profits. It will be tempting to him to set on one side the long-period, hypothetical consequences of persistent competition and to accept the more certain short-period results of having the market to himself.

Similarly with the right-wing politician who comes to power prejudiced in favour of the free economy. What does he do about a nationalised industry, which may already have suffered denationalisation and renationalisation? How does he balance the advantages of stability, of leaving things alone, against the upset of once again reorganising an industry in the form which, in the long run, he believes to be more efficient? All politicians are men of power and self-confidence. They will always be noticing things which are obviously going wrong. They will often correctly perceive the immediate advantages of the steps which they and their colleagues in government could undertake to correct matters. They will tend to underrate the salutary effects of the threat of bankruptcy to incompetent executives or of unemployment to negligent workers. They are likely to forget that by interfering unnecessarily with economic operations which could safely be left to the spontaneous control of free markets, their performance in the proper spheres of State action will become the poorer.

I am, therefore, driven to the conclusion that the conflict between private and public economic action is one of ideas and the outcome of it will depend upon a struggle between scholars, who are or ought to be free to speak their minds. Put simply, it is a struggle between Karl Marx and Adam Smith – and the very fact that, despite the passage of the years and the intervention of secondary voices, this is the form it continues to take, is a proof of this contention.

Those who wish to see the powers of the State constantly augmented will, of course, seek out and stress the deficiencies of the free market system and argue that any and every divergence from a theoretical state of perfection can be wholly corrected. They are Utopians.

Those who oppose such a doctrine will recognise the inevitable imperfections of a real world, record what nevertheless has already been the high measure of success of market economies, constantly search for ways of improving and widening the scope of price mechanisms. And, above all, they will never allow the public to forget a simple idea which their opponents always try to forget: that the evil that collectivists do will be visited upon our children and their grandchildren; for each form of collectivism breeds another and the evils of one form of collectivism can never be remedied by another.

NOTES

1. At the outset the Members were: Sir Paul Chambers, Mr D. H. Barran, Sir George Bolton, The Viscount Boyd, Sir Stephen Brown, Sir Nicholas Cayzer, The Lord Cole, Sir Reay Geddes, Sir Cyril Harrison, Sir Maurice Laing, Mr H. G. Lazell, Sir Joseph Lockwood, Mr A. F. McDonald, The Lord Netherthorpe, Sir John Nicholson, Mr E. J. Partridge, The Lord Pilkington, Sir Peter Runge, The Lord Sieff, Mr R. G. Soothill, Sir William McEwan Younger, and ex officio Members: Mr A. G. Norman, President, Confederation of British Industry and Mr John Davies, Director General, Confederation of British Industry.
2. 'For many years now there has persisted an undercurrent of public concern about the effect of United Kingdom investment overseas on the balance of payments. Despite the Exchange Controls at present in force, some critics continue to argue that the U.K. is 'exporting capital' on a massive scale, to the detriment of the official reserves, the balance of payments generally or the exchange rate, with the result that the Government is forced to run the economy at a lower pressure of demand, and a higher level of unemployment, than would otherwise be necessary. In fact, criticisms on these lines are usually based on misunderstanding.'
   > Economic Progress Report, Information Division of
   > the Treasury, September 1976.
3. This, fortunately, in spite of the almost lyrical defence of the tax by a number of economists and journalists. Thus Mr Peter Jay spoke of 'the seemingly miraculous ability of the Tax to square the circles of political economy'. (*The Times*, 6 March 1970)
4. Nobody got into a bigger muddle on these matters than Mrs Barbara Castle (then First Secretary of State and Secretary of State for Employment and Productivity) who, speaking in the House on 8 April 1970 said: 'The Government have pursued two complementary strategies. On the one hand, with the help of the Industrial Reconstruction Corporation, they have stimulated the most far-reaching restructuring of industry since the Industrial Revolution.

On the other, they have recognised that the concentration of industry into a smaller number of hands has created a situation of market power which can lead to less efficiency, not more, and which will call for public scrutiny.' She clearly did not understand the difference between 'complementary' and 'conflicting'.

5. It may be true, although we cannot yet know, that since 1971 government intervention, in the form of price and profit control, higher taxation and the intricacies and cost of extended welfare services, has given the quietus to many small companies. If so, that is simply a case for less government intervention.

6. At this time the membership of the Group was: Sir David Barran, Mr R. M. Bateman, Sir Raymond Brookes, Mr E. J. Callard, Sir Val Duncan, Sir Reay Geddes, Sir Arnold Hall, Sir Cyril Kleinwort, Sir Maurice Laing, Sir William Mather, Sir Alexander McDonald, Mr R. A. McNeile, The Rt. Hon. Lord Netherthorpe, Sir John Partridge, The Lord Plowden, The Rt. Hon. Lord Poole, The Rt. Hon. Viscount Watkinson and Dr E. G. Woodroofe, and ex officio: Mr W. O. Campbell Adamson, General Director, Confederation of British Industry.

7. It is not without point to speculate upon what might have happened in the way of further detailed intervention in incomes policy if the Conservatives had not been defeated in early 1974. But the Pay Board, set up by the Conservative Government and under the Chairmanship of Sir Frank Figgures, had been invited to report upon the problems of pay relativities. The Report on this subject, published in January 1974, consisted both in its analysis and its recommendations of a long string of almost meaningless ramblings which would have produced chaos if any attempt had been made to use them as a basis for action. Thus the Pay Board in its Report, after parading such glimpses of the obvious as: 'A wide range of meanings is attached to fairness in the context of relative pay', or 'The difficulty (in wage relativities) of moving ahead and staying ahead is a common feature whether the change is made on fairness or labour supply grounds', or 'The feelings of unfairness become especially acute where there has been a sustained period of falling further behind some comparable group.'

The Pay Board went on to confess: 'Collective bargaining as it is practised in this country has no mechanism for making enduring changes in the relative pay of groups in separate negotiating units' and 'When it comes to relativity issues between negotiating units at industry level, there is no existing forum in which the opinions of those at both ends of comparisons can be reconciled', and 'There is at present no technique to hand of general application, no single formula or criterion for determining whether pay relativities are right in terms of economic or social factors, and no ready means of diagnosing trouble in advance.'

All this, however, did not deter the Pay Board from pressing on. It is true that it declared that 'We counsel caution' and 'We stress the need for consensus'. But the Board seemed to feel it was making an advance when it divided its problems into two groups, the first that of making a preliminary selection of the cases to be examined and the second the procedures to be followed in carrying out such examinations. But neither in selection nor examination did it suggest what criteria should be followed. As for selection it asserted: 'The essence of a claim under the heading of relativities is that one group should move in relation to others.' And that 'Those exercising judgment would need to have and to make public broad criteria defining those eligible for special consideration.' They then suggested, doubtless in despair, that the best way of handling the whole problem of selection would be to bring in the C.B.I. and the T.U.C. since 'The procedures would be much better worked out between them and the Government' although the Pay Board itself declared that 'We refrain from suggesting the actual criteria that might be used in the selection'.

Having firmly placed the whole problem into the hands of other bodies, the Pay Board then went on to give advice about the examination of the selected cases. 'The examination will involve not only the group which has applied for special treatment but also the related groups who will be affected if special treatment is allowed.' And 'Certain relativity problems cannot be solved in isolation because the group which claims special treatment is enmeshed with other groups'.

Whatever may have been the other benefits or penalties which followed from the defeat of the Conservatives in early 1974, at least we may congratulate ourselves upon the fact that they were thus prevented from attempting to establish a code of wage relativities based upon the humbug of the Pay Board.

8. Mr Peter Walker later put a different interpretation on the rift between Mr Heath and the entrepreneurs: 'Where he (Mr Heath) made enemies was at those dinner parties, frequently with businessmen and men of the City, where he argued fiercely. Such men do not expect the Prime Minister and Leaders of Parties to question the conduct of their activities. They expect them to be grateful recipients of advice. Nor do they expect advice to be tendered to them. Whereas Ted Heath considered that the objective at such dinners was to debate current problems, debating was neither their objective nor their skill, and the next day they would retail their resentment on the failure of the Prime Minister to listen, when an outside observer would perhaps recognise that it was he who had listened and it was they who had not.'

9. Thus Richard Crossman, *The Diaries of a Cabinet Minister*, Vol. 2, p. 190: 'Prescote is magnificent now the grey skies have blown off. I'm sitting here in comfort and am therefore bound to wonder whether that fierce old Tory, my brother Geoffrey, is reasonable when he says that I can't be a socialist and have a farm which makes good profits. I tell him that the two are compatible provided that, as a member of the Government, I'm ready to vote for a socialist policy to take these profits away and even, in the last resort, to confiscate the property. Nevertheless that isn't a complete answer.'

9 MONOPOLY AND ECONOMIC PROGRESS*

I

In no branch of economics are there at present greater obscurities than in that which treats of monopoly. Differences of opinion are not confined to topics where judgement must always be exercised – as for example whether a monopolistically organised system is good or bad; whether monopoly is inevitable or avoidable;[1] or whether the State can play an effective part in restraining monopoly. The controversies extend into fields where systematic analysis and measurement might have been expected to lead to fairly objective conclusions – whether monopoly has been increasing or decreasing in the western countries,[2] and whether certain practices such as resale price maintenance,[3] basing point price systems[4] or price leadership are consistent with the operation of a competitive system.

It would probably be agreed that a full-scale policy of preventing monopoly and maintaining competition necessarily involves extensive government intervention in industrial organisation and operation and it is obvious that whether the State *should* try to constrict monopoly largely turns upon whether it *can* do so effectively. This article, however, is wholly concerned with a prior question. On what economic grounds should the State concern itself with the extent of industrial monopoly and seek methods to limit it?[5]

II

It is, of course, not possible to reach final conclusions for or against monopoly in industry by examining the issues in strictly economic terms since those issues run far beyond the purely economic. In the traditional liberal view of society, for instance, the assumption is made that there should not be any undue concentration of power in the community – even in the hands of the State itself. Only through a wide diffusion of power, it is thought, arising out of the existence of property rights and

*Economica, August 1953.

expressing itself through the rich and varied forms of voluntary co-
operation, can the social dangers of concentration be avoided. For if
power coagulates then we are confronted either with collectivism, in
which the State may be forced to take enormous powers to suppress the
threat of rival groups, or syndicalism, in which powerful pressure
groups struggle for supremacy with the State standing helplessly by.[6]
This view of society carries with it the implication that, even if there were
real economic losses in preventing the kind of industrial concentration
that is associated with monopoly, the losses should be accepted in order
to safeguard other more important social values.

Even when the subject is approached from the economic angle the
conclusion can never be cut and dried. For there are certain circumstances and conditions in which there would be general agreement
that goods or services can best be supplied under monopolistic control.
Few would now suggest that competing supplies of gas, of water or of
electricity should be available in any one district although a strong case
for competition between gas and electricity for heating and power can
be made. Many of those who accept the liberal conception of the
organisation of industry might argue for a monopoly in the control of
railways whilst at the same time advocating the virtues of competition
between railways and other forms of transport by road, sea or air. In the
spectacular case of the development of atomic energy a monopoly by the
State would be considered the only possibility for much of the most important work, although private enterprise may in future play a large role
in the peacetime uses of the fundamental discoveries. These are all fairly
straightforward cases; there is also a marginal group of cases where
doubts might well arise as to the virtues of monopoly, such as large-
scale schemes of economic development of the Tennessee Valley
Authority type.

The grounds upon which monopoly is almost universally accepted in
some cases have been much examined and are familiar. In one group of
cases there is a public need which obviously will not be met by private
enterprise because it would not yield a profit since the individual
beneficiaries are not prepared to offer a sufficiently high price. An illustration is that of the Tennessee Valley Authority, the fundamental
aim of which was to control floods over a wide area by methods which
would not have been adopted under normal market operations. In a second group of cases a service may well be able to pay its way, a
profitable price may be exacted for it, but for any one of a number of
reasons monopoly supply will probably be more efficient than competitive and, the virtues of monopoly once accepted, the State has
special responsibilities for safeguarding the consumer against monopoly
power. This is true of the supply of gas or electricity. A third group of
cases occurs where an industry or service would not, at least in the short
period, yield a profit in the commercial sense but where it is considered,

on grounds of national security, that the industry should exist. An illustration is the development of atomic energy. Another group is found where some new technique would appear to hold out prospects of fruitful exploitation but only over such a long period that the private investor and entrepreneur cannot be expected to take the risks. Although other elements are found here, civil aviation would appear to provide an illustration. Civil aviation has always appeared to contain the potentialities of vast general economic benefits but it has rarely, if ever, in the past proved profitable. Governments have, therefore, been disposed to subsidise it heavily and to impose monopoly control along with financial support, presumably on the grounds that there are some long-period risks which private enterprise will not handle but in which public risk-taking is legitimate.[7]

All these instances, however, are peripheral to the present topic; they still leave the greater part of industrial activity untouched. Is monopoly or competition the best system under which to produce the vast range of goods and services where either monopoly *or* competition is clearly feasible?

III

The older writings on the subject of monopoly do not take us very far. These commonly attributed standard evils to monopolies: high prices, extortionate profits, predatory activities designed to destroy or frighten away weaker competitors, the suppression of existing patents or of improvements which would upset current practices and capital values, the use of political power to influence the legislature. Now, whatever may have been true of the past, it would be extremely difficult to prove that these are necessarily the defects of present-day monopolists. Those who hold monopoly power are as conscious as anyone else of the charges normally brought against them and they may be at pains to avoid anything which would justify suspicions and arouse public disapproval. It may, for instance, be true that monopolists charge too low prices rather than too high – indeed, the allegation that the monopolist introduces rigidity into prices is, in part, an assertion that in periods of boom he does not charge high enough prices. It would not be easy to prove that monopolists earn unreasonable profits, for, apart from the fact that they are extremely sensitive to the danger of incurring public odium in this way, the definition of what constitutes reasonable profits is itself a matter of judgement. Many monopolists, far from engaging in predatory activities, might more properly be charged with the very opposite – that they are too prone to apply the rule of 'live and let live'; that they too easily accept the doctrine of providing fair shares in the market for all; that they do not press their advantages vigorously enough. And certainly at the present time when any businessman, who is alleged to be a monopolist, instinctively appears to take the defensive not by claiming that monopoly is a superior form of organisation but by denying that monopoly exists, it appears highly doubtful whether he would regard it as wise to use his powers to influence or corrupt legislative bodies, most of whom in the Western world have declared themselves opposed to monopoly.[8]

One instance of the kind of defence which an organisation, undoubtedly exercising a substantial control of the market, may offer when confronted with the traditional charges is provided in one of the reports of the British Monopolies Commission.[9] In the British electric lamp industry the Commission reached conclusions which were not substantially in dispute. A group of firms in the Electric Lamp Manufacturers' Association controlled, directly or through other companies owned by them, 73 per cent of the total output of filament lamps and 62 per cent of discharge lamps. The group fixed prices, so that there was no price competition between them; they fixed output percentages and any firm exceeding its percentage paid a fine. Most of the important patents in the industry were controlled by the group. Most of the bulbs and caps for the whole industry were produced by two members of the group. The group maintained a system of retail price maintenance and a system of exclusive agreements with wholesalers and of discounts to those retailers agreeing not to sell the lamps of independent manufacturers. Such was the actual position as the Commission found it. The earlier activities of the Association had been even more restrictive. Until the war the group operated under an agreement designed to force independents into the ring by controlling materials and by patent litigation; their patent licensing system was extremely restrictive; there were no provisions for the amendment of sales quotas; upper limits were fixed to the life of some lamps; fighting companies were created to attack independent manufacturers. In brief, practically all the methods and institutions of monopoly could be found in this case.

Now the defence, and it was formidable, made of this organisation was simply that none of the alleged evils of monopoly had arisen from it.[10] Its prices were reasonable – reasonable in the sense of being lower than before the war and lower than in any other country outside the United States. Its profits could not be considered excessive. It had shown itself to be technically efficient and highly alive to the importance of research. A good deal of competition had, in fact, made itself evident in the industry, particularly in the manufacture of discharge lamps. Finally, the pre-war predatory activities of running fighting companies, restricting the licensing of patents and forcing independents into the ring had been discontinued.

Doubtless other cases could be found where serious restrictive practices were deliberately and persistently pursued. The Monopolies Commission appears to have turned up one such case in the match industry.[11] But the evidence tendered to us so far by the Commission suggests such cases are not likely to be numerous. If, then, monopoly can usually be shown not to produce the evils traditionally associated with it, on what grounds can it be challenged?

IV

The formal, analytical grounds upon which monopoly has up to now been criticised or condemned have little relevance for practical policy. To show that, in static conditions, prices will be higher or output lower under monopoly of one degree or another, than under an idealised state of perfect competition, does not help in exercising judgements about a dynamic economy. For this scheme of thought is not related to the real world, it misses out 'the kind of competition that matters'. It achieves finality of conclusion only at the expense of practical content.

The analytical treatment of dynamic conditions may, perhaps, some day be created. But in the meantime, mainly as a result of recent writings[12] putting the case for monopoly in a more favourable light, one question has become more sharply formulated. Can monopoly be regarded as favourable to technical and economic progress? The clash between such writings and the more traditional views on the subject of monopoly can be illustrated by short quotations. At the one extreme is the opinion expressed by the Courts[13] in a recent important case in the United States, an opinion embodying the philosophy of anti-trust legislation of that country:

> Possession of unchallenged economic power deadens initiative, discourages thrift and depresses energy; immunity from competition is a narcotic, and rivalry a stimulant to industrial progress; the spur of constant stress is necessary to counteract an inevitable disposition to let well alone.

At the other extreme we have Schumpeter (who, whether he finally proves to be right or wrong in these matters, was clearly the pioneer in asking the right questions):

> enterprise would in most cases be impossible if it were not known from the outset that exceptionally favourable situations are likely to arise which if exploited by price, quality and quantity manipulation will produce profits adequate to tide over exceptionally unfavourable situations provided these are similarly managed . . . restraints of trade of the cartel type as well as those which merely consist in tacit understandings about price competition may be effective remedites under conditions of depression.

And Galbraith has concluded that 'there must be some element of monopoly in an industry if it is to be progressive'.

Dame Alix Kilroy, after describing how the British Monopolies Commission has in some cases been prepared to find virtue in monopoly arrangements, concludes that the Commission's criteria are 'empirical and not ideological', i.e. are not based on any general presuppositions of the merits or defects of monopoly. And Sir Henry Clay in his article considers that there is little ground for the assumption that what regulation of output and prices there has been in British manufacturing industry is responsible for any large part of the post-war economic difficulties of the United Kingdom.

The issue might, therefore, appear to be fairly clear cut: which brings about the swifter cost reductions and the more numerous new goods and services, competition or monopoly? Actually it is not so simple as that. In the first place, even if it were held that industrial monopoly were undesirable in an otherwise competitive world, does it make a difference if industry must perforce operate among monopolistic organisations of wage earners, farmers and the professions? Both Sir Henry Clay and Professor Galbraith appear to think so, the former holding that industrial monopoly may be justified *because* of the existence of monopoly elsewhere, the latter that industrial monopoly is acceptable *provided* that monopoly exists, or can be encouraged, elsewhere. In the second place, account would clearly have to be taken of the *smoothness* and *continuity* as well as the actual *speed* of progress. At least three of the writers quoted above are prepared to argue that, when an industry falls into depression, organised control of prices and output may be necessary in order to prevent an uncontrolled spiral of losses which might be fatal to new investment and technical progress. Conversely, Schumpeter argues that, in a period of very rapid discovery, the uncontrolled introduction of innovations might become so rapid, with one wave of improvements swiftly sweeping away another, that innovation would be stifled because it would yield no return. Monopoly, according to this argument, might well increase the average rate of progress by regulating its pace from time to time. In the third place, those who are disposed to favour the case for competition seem strangely reluctant to fit into their scheme of thinking, or even to do much thinking about, the patents system. After all, a patent is a monopoly conferred by law and, among other reasons, it is conferred in the hope of encouraging invention and innovation. But if patents do encourage innovation why should not other forms of monopoly? And if, in their present form, they do not, why should someone not say so?[14] And in the fourth place, the issue is confused because the apologists for monopoly do not speak with one voice; their arguments, indeed, sometimes seem to be mutually exclusive. Lack of space forbids reference to more than one of these differences between them but it is an important one – the difference of approach of

Schumpeter and Professor Galbraith. Schumpeter was impressed by the continuing power of competition in dynamic conditions,[15] the reality of capitalism, he argued, lay in the 'perennial gale of creative destruction' of old methods by new. The process of replacement would normally be so powerful that, unless checked periodically, it would frustrate its own purposes, creative destruction might become too destructive. The innovator must be provided with a breathing space. But Schumpeter was thinking all the time of a highly fluid economy, he takes for granted that 'the competition that matters' will be there anyway. Rapid innovation requires monopoly, he claimed, but monopoly will be ephemeral, and therefore innocuous if not positively desirable, because it will be torn down by the next wave of discovery.[16] Professor Galbraith, on the other hand, considers that most industries have moved, or are moving, towards a position in which a few large firms inevitably dominate total output. This, he thinks, is all to the good for only firms of considerable size will possess the resources to carry on technical research on an adequate scale. But there is no gale of creative destruction in Professor Galbraith's conception of things. Once providence[17] has brought about an industry consisting of a few large firms, progress becomes automatic and, apparently, painless. There can be no effective competition from smaller firms; technically they are out of the race. And the three or four pillars of the industry will not engage in any tactics which will hurt themselves or others. 'Like advertising and salesmanship – and unlike price competition which is unique in this respect – technical development is a safe rather than a reciprocally destructive method by which any one firm can advance itself against its few powerful rivals'. So that whereas Schumpeter thought in terms of creative destruction which should be kept on the rein, Galbraith seems to think in terms of indestructible creation which should be given its head.

V

In seeking to establish a presumption (and it probably can never be more than a presumption) in favour of or against monopoly as an accelerator of technical progress, the evidence must either be drawn from history or from speculations as to the inherent nature of different kinds of economic institutions. Studies of those periods in history when monopolies and monopolists were numerous and important are specially relevant here. There is some convincing evidence, for example, that the Industrial Revolution in Great Britain was retarded by the presence of monopoly[18] and that when it did come the growth took place in those parts of the country where industrial legislation was least restrictive.[19] These views have not, however, gone unchallenged.[20] Or comparisons might be made between the progress of different countries which have taken up dissimilar attitudes towards monopoly. Full play has been made, for example, of the fact that although German industry has been monopolistically organised during the whole of this century, technical progress has been more than ordinarily swift. But here the outstanding fact which must be explained, or explained away, is the unparalleled technical advances in the United States, where competition is always considered to be more vigorous than elsewhere.[21] Comparisons might be made between monopolistic and non-monopolistic industries in the same country. Professor Galbraith has employed this method to great effect for the United States, claiming that 'the foreign visitor, brought to the United States by the Economic Co-operation Administration, visits the same firms as do attorneys of the Department of Justice in their search for monopoly'.[22] The small-scale competitive industries have bad records, he thinks, the oligopolistic industries have good records of technical advance. What is needed here is a more thorough testing of this conclusion in terms of more industries and more countries. It may be true in the United States that the competitive coalmining industry is less progressive than the oligopolist oil industry. But in Great Britain the monopolistic coalmining industry is clearly less progressive than the relatively competitive oil industry. And even in the United States the uninformed visitor might well think that the American women's clothing industry was more progressive than the American Post Office or the American machine tool industry than the subway companies. In any case a comparison of the technical advance made by different industries is a very tricky one. Ideally what is required is the degree to which different industries have in fact taken advantage of the technical progress which, given the state of scientific knowledge, is theoretically possible.

Or comparisons might be made within one industry, of firms which occupy a dominating share of the market with those of much more modest dimensions. Must we expect in the future that the greater part of technical progress will come from costly research organisations, only to be afforded by very large firms, that 'most of the cheap and simple inventions have been made'? There is already a large literature on this subject but it is compounded with a good deal of ballyhoo[23] and it is not easy to arrive at firm conclusions. A number of simple points seem frequently to be overlooked. In the past the major technical improvements have not come from the large industrial research organisations. Now, it *may* be true that, quite recently, fundamental and permanent changes have taken place in the nature of technical problems and in methods of research which render past experience inapplicable and which will, for the future, deprive the lone inventor, the small firm, the chance discovery, of their former importance. But in an age which has seen the successful emergence of the ideas of many independent inventors, including very recently Baird and Whittle, one may well remain sceptical about the sweeping assumptions of a sudden and discontinuous break between the conditions of the past and the probable conditions in the future. Again, it is easy to be carried away by the figures of the large sums *spent* on industrial research by the bigger firms. Expenditure is simply a cost and what we are interested in is returns, particularly in research where the overwhelming proportion of the expenditure will normally be abortive. There is not, in fact, any evidence that the larger Armerican firms spend more, as a proportion of their sales, than do smaller firms.[24] Further, there are good reasons for believing that the economies of large-scale operation in industrial research are not always easy to attain. In all research organisations, and especially in big organisations, a fundamental conflict exists between administrators and researchers: increasing size calls for increased control over personnel, increased control will normally be repugnant to the type of mind best capable of research.[25]

VI

Nevertheless, all such empirical studies are clearly worth pursuing much further. What seems to have been unduly ignored in discussions of the consequences of monopoly are the deductions which it seems reasonable to make about the inherent nature of established authorities, of which the industrial monopoly is one example. Experience of all types of institutions suggests that established authority tends to inertia. Those who have once come into command of a situation or an institution gradually come to think of their task and their responsibilities in a set way. Working rules gradually stiffen into tradition, the purpose may remain but it narrows or fails to widen with changing circumstances. Vested interests look askance at revolutionary ideas.

The resistance to change thereby created will tend to be the stronger when an institution is hierarchical and monopolistic in form. That is why military organisations provide some striking cases of innate conservatism. Naval authorities put up a formidable fight against the steel ship equipped with propellers and a compound engine.[26] There was sturdy resistance by the high officials in the American Navy to the introduction of continuous-aim gun firing.[27] There was much opposition, in the development of aircraft, to the introduction of the monoplane, the retractable undercarriage, the feathering propeller and to some of the fighting aircraft which subsequently proved supreme. Whittle, who at the time was actually in the Air Force, applied for his first patent on the jet engine in January 1930, 'and submitted the idea to the Air Ministry, who declined it on the ground that practical difficulties in the way of development were too great'.[28] When T. E. Lawrence was engaged upon the design and development of new types of speed boat, subsequently proved to be highly successful, he found that 'the pundits met them with a fierce hostility: all the R.A.F. sailors and all the Navy said that they would break, sink, wear out, be unmanageable'.[29] Numerous similar illustrations could be provided from the history of the professions.[30]

It is no great jump in logic to suppose that industrial monopolies, which if they are of any size will be hierarchically organised, will be subject to much the same laws. Indeed, the history of industrial innovation would strongly suggest that organisations, like men, can, through the exercise of the peculiar energies called for in the process of innovation, exhaust their power of generating such energy again. New ideas and new methods have so often called for new men and new institutions. 'It was not the stage coach owners who built the railroads, nor the owners of fleets of clippers who developed the steamer. . . . Nor did the railroad magnates promote the automobile . . . the automobile magnates did not become airplane pioneers.'[31]

Whether, in fact, large industrial organisations with a dominating position in a market, have ultimately proved, through ignorance, lack of imagination or indifference, to be blocks to progress must clearly be finally decided by the economic historian and much more relevant economic history would need to be written before that point was reached. Some recent works seem to support the view that monopolies, even when vigorous enough in developing the more traditional methods, in pursuing what lies beneath their noses, can be sluggish or even resistant as regards ideas which lie a way off from their main interests. In the manufacture and development of electric lamps, the General Electric Company of America, which held a dominating position in the industry for over half a century and had a good record in improving lamp design and production methods, was not the leader in introducing new forms of lighting, the discharge lamp and fluorescent lighting.[32] In the British electric lamp industry it is clear that it was one of the independent manufacturers and not the Electric Lamp Manufacturers' Association which set the pace in the spread of fluorescent lighting.[33]

Here, the history of the development of radio and television is perhaps of more than ordinary significance, partly because it has been studied in some detail, partly because it is a very recent case and cannot be dismissed as belonging to a period when conditions were quite different from those of the present or probable future, partly because the discoveries involved were very spectacular.

The early introduction of wireless telegraphy for common use was due to the imagination, obstinacy and resolution of Marconi, who furthermore had considerable private funds to be devoted to the purpose. Although there were already, particularly in the United States, large industries containing very large firms, concerned with electrical communications and the manufacture of electrical equipment, they showed little or no interest in the dazzling possibilities of communication without wires. Neither in the telegraph and cable industry, where

Western Union was the dominating company, nor in the telephone industry, where the American Bell Telephone Company had already by the beginning of the century attained great size, nor in the electrical manufacturing industry, was it recognised that new ideas of vital concern to them were extant. It is true that after the turn of the century, when the possibilities were there for all to see, the most important research was conducted by the large corporations but, even between the wars, the big corporations were apathetic towards one of the most fruitful discoveries, frequency modulation, which was forced to the front only by the persistence of Armstrong, an independent inventor.[34]

With television it might have been expected that, because of its close relation to radio, established interests would seize more promptly upon the commercial and social possibilities. That has proved to be the case. In the United States Maclaurin believes that monopoly shortened the time lag in the practical application of new ideas, the driving force being the Radio Corporation of America, which between 1930 and 1939 spent $9 million on experiment and development. By 1930 the British Broadcasting Corporation was providing facilities for televising to Baird, and the Derby was actually televised in June 1931. But it is well to recall the doubts which went before this and the frustrations which confronted the early pioneers. The three outstanding names are perhaps Zworykin and Farnsworth in the United States and Baird in Great Britain. Zworykin joined the Westinghouse staff in 1920, at which time no research was being undertaken on television by any of the important laboratories. For a time he was refused permission to work on television and it was not until 1928, with the discovery of the ionescope, that real importance was attached to his work or any substantial assistance provided for him. Farnsworth was a lone and largely untrained inventor who lacked business acumen and was for a long period chronically short of resources for his experiments. It was only after 1926 that he found adequate financial backing and, although never at ease in the stage of business development, it is significant that by 1938 Farnsworth had been responsible for three-quarters of the patents granted and applications lodged in television. Baird was, from all accounts, a strange and erratic person with whom it must have been difficult to co-operate and who, it subsequently proved, was on the wrong track with his mechanical scanning method, but no one would doubt that he possessed exceptional technical ingenuity and was responsible for the first substantial television service in the world.[35] But in 1925 his ideas were widely regarded with extreme scepticism by those in the related branches of technology and, until 1930, whatever may be the truth of the matter, he always spoke most bitterly of the impediments placed in his way by the British Broadcasting Corporation.[36]

The practical applications of technical advances were always slow to reveal themselves. Even Marconi missed the significance of wireless telephony[37] and Baird that of the cathode ray tube.[38] No one foresaw the value of wireless communication for the broadcasting of public programmes of speech and music.[39] Wireless was until 1920 regarded as a new kind of telephone or even of a system by which electrical energy could be distributed in bulk.

Established authorities in many ways obstructed the full and rapid exploitation of the new ideas. Apart from the attitude of some of the bigger commercial companies already referred to, the British Post Office, in the early stages of development, checked Marconi, looking upon him as a potential competitor of State telegraphs, by refusing to connect the Marconi Overseas Service with the Post Office telegraph lines.[40] In 1920 the British Post Office stopped experimental broadcasts of concerts being made by the Marconi Company on the grounds that these were interfering with what the Post Office described as 'genuine work'.[41] Broadcasting had to be resuscitated by amateurs. There seems little doubt that it was the suspicions and timidity of the British Post Office which was largely responsible for the initial setting up of British broadcasting as a monopoly.[42]

The story may be continued a little further by examining some of the consequences of the State monopoly of broadcasting in Great Britain. This is a subject which arouses the most extraordinary emotions in the British breast[43] and it is not intended here to examine all its manifold aspects. The historian of the future however, will, in my opinion, surely find it surprising that this new medium of communication – with its great potential for creating mass opinion, where monopoly was therefore dangerous, and obviously destined to be most commonly employed in providing light entertainment, where monopoly would seem to be unnecessary – should have been regarded as a proper subject for a complete monopoly of programmes, of studios and of transmitting agencies.

There are, however, three conclusions bearing directly upon the subject of this paper which seem supported by the evidence. First, for many years the monopoly was utilised to give the consumer what it was thought he ought to have and not what it was supposed he himself wanted. Lord Reith[44] has made that clear:

without monopoly many things might not have been so easily done that were done. The Christian religion and the Sabbath might not have had the place and protection they had; the place and protection which it was right to give them; the giving of which seemed to be approved. The Christian religion, not just as a sectional activity among others, but as a fundamental. And as to the Sabbath, one day in the week clear of jazz and variety and such like; an effort to preserve the inestimable benefit of a day different from other days. Less persistent transmission of good music, of good things in every line. School broadcasting – initiated, urged, developed, financed by the B.B.C. with rather negative and timid approval from authority – might not have been essayed. Almost everything might have been different. The B.B.C. might have had to play for safety; prosecute the obviously popular lines; count its clients; study and meet their reactions; curry favour; subordinate itself to the vote. *Might* have had to; it probably would not; but its rc.d would have been far harder.

The B.B.C. was not even interested in knowing what people listened to. For the first fifteen years of its life no systematic listener research was carried out. And, after that, the results were treated as confidential and were not communicated to the General Advisory Council or the Regional Advisory Council, or made available to Parliament or the public.[45] As late as 1949 the B.B.C. was claiming that competition in broadcasting would drag down all listening to the 'lower forms of mass appetite'.[46]

Second, the B.B.C. has sought to extend its monopoly powers in several directions. It has made a number of attempts to prevent foreign stations, particularly Luxembourg, from broadcasting in English programmes which contained advertising material of highly reputable British businesses. There has been, and still is, a real demand for these broadcasts. In 1938, we are told, the total British audience listening to commercial programmes from foreign stations on Sundays was comparable to the total audience listening to the B.B.C.[47] In 1949 the Sunday Luxembourg audience was about half the size of the audience for the British Home Service (the advertising agencies actually claimed it as larger than this).[48] Before the war the British Post Office sought to hinder these foreign broadcasts by refusing to grant telephone facilities for the relaying of programmes from Great Britain.[49] In 1946, in a White Paper on Broadcasting, the British Government declared their intention of taking 'all steps within their power, and to use their influence with the authorities concerned, to prevent the direction of commercial broadcasts to this country from abroad'. The Advertising Company responsible for the broadcasts from Luxembourg complained in 1949 that B.B.C. artists were placed under restrictions aimed at the commercial broadcasts.[50]

Third, the B.B.C. has either sought to impede or has been slow in the adoption of innovations. The story of the resistance of the B.B.C. and the Post Office to wire broadcasting has been told by Coase,[51] who concludes:

there can be little doubt that the development of wire broadcasting in Great Britain has been seriously restricted as a result of the existence of a monopoly of broadcasting.

Subsequent to this the B.B.C. suggested, before the Broadcasting Committee, still further restrictions on wire broadcasting, most of which the Committee found itself unable to accept.[52]

Considering that the early inventions in television were made in Great Britain and that before the war the British television programmes were superior to all others (in the United States, for example, no American station was running a regular 'commercial' service until 1941), the postwar developments were slow. Undoubtedly, this was partly due to the shortage of capital in post-war Britain and some of the leeway has since been made up. But it also seems clear that the delay could, in part, be attributed to a disposition on the part of the B.B.C. to attempt to keep the new medium too closely under the wing of the old monopoly of sound. The first two Controllers of Television after the war resigned because they felt they were being unduly cramped.[53] And the Broadcasting Committee[54] felt constrained to report that 'within the general framework of the B.B.C. television should enjoy greater autonomy than it has had hitherto'. The Committee also seemed to believe that the B.B.C. had been unnecessarily unco-operative in meeting the plans of the film industry for television services direct to cinemas.[55]

Great Britain has also fallen considerably behind the United States in the exploitation of V.H.F. broadcasting.[56] The new technique is highly lethal to monopoly. It opens up possibilities, largely seized upon already in the United States, for the establishment of a new form of communication between the members of relatively small groups with common interests based on locality, occupation or forms of leisure. These have so far been denied to the British public. One of the more important manufacturers has, indeed, claimed that 'the technique exists, but present monopolistic policy prevents the benefits from being obtained'.[57]

VII

The history of broadcasting and of the way in which it came to be organised in Great Britain is but one case. But it is an extremely important case in that the defects of monopoly made their appearance here under circumstances highly unfavourable to the creation and maintenance of monopoly. The new system of communication was so novel, spectacular and useful that its claims could not, in the long run, be gainsaid. The advantages of a long string of inventions could not finally be denied. Broadcasting, as the very word implies, cannot ultimately be channelled and confined; national boundaries become meaningless in the ether. The successes and progress of one country cannot be cloaked from those living in other countries, unless the final brutal monopolistic method of jamming is employed. We have here a set of ideas, techniques and services capable of sweeping away vested interests which would stand in their way. Yet short-sighted obstinacy and restriction have all played their part in resisting the tide.

If all these things are to be discerned in this case, what is likely to happen in others where new ideas, though substantially useful, have not the same inherently overwhelming power to assert themselves? How much has the world lost where the established authorities have been more powerful in their resistance or more sluggish than in the case of radio and television; where the men obsessed with the new ideas were not as obstinate as Marconi, or not in possession of private fortunes, as Armstrong, not as blindly indifferent to adverse odds as a whole chain of inventors in this field; where sources of outside capital were not so plentiful; or where competition between one country and another could be blocked by tariff and regulation?

In conditions so rapidly changing as those of the dynamic economies to which we have become accustomed in the past two centuries, the prime defects of monopoly may well have been not that they were wicked or extortionate, deliberately restrictive or blindly predatory, but simply that they were there, blocking the ground and finding it impossible to generate sufficient energy to do continually, or even to do more than once, what they had originally performed in breaking new ground, in pursuing innovations. In that sense the waste of monopoly would lie, not in depriving the community of what it now has or what it might have in the immediate future, but of what it might have in the longer future.

NOTES

1. Compare J. K. Galbraith, *A Survey of Contemporary Economics*, p. 118, 'anti-trust laws cannot positively alter the basic structure of a capitalist economy ... or make satisfactory contact with oligopoly,' with W. Eucken, *This Un-successful Age*, p. 47, who speaks of 'the marked competitive tendency un-leashed by modern technology which is taking increasing effect the more it develops'.

2. Compare A. R. Burns, *Decline of Competition*, p. 3, 'elements of monopoly have always been interwoven with competition but the monopoly elements have increased in importance. They can no longer be regarded as occasional and relatively unimportant aberrations from competition. They are such an organic part of the industrial system that it is useless to hope that they can be remedied by law and the industrial system brought into conformity with the idea of perfect competition,' with the conclusions of G. J. Stigler. *Five Lectures on Economic Problems*, p. 54, when speaking of American industry, 'it is my present judgment that competition declined moderately from the Civil War to the end of the nineteenth century and thereafter increased moderately'. G. W. Nutter also throws doubt upon the view that there has been any significant increase in industrial monopoly in the United States since the beginning of the century (*The Extent of Enterprise Monopoly in the United States 1899–1939*).

3. Compare the findings on resale price maintenance of the *Report of the Committee on Resale Price Maintenance*, 1949, and *A Statement on Resale Price Maintenance*, Board of Trade, 1951, with the findings of the Sub-Committee ... [on] the Principle of Fixed Retail Prices, 1920, and of the Committee on Restraint of Trade, 1930.
4. On the differences of opinion among economists on the basing point price system see F. Machlup, *The Basing Point System*, pp. 49–51.
5. In the White Paper, *Employment Policy*, of 1944, which is usually taken as recording an important change in the attitude of the British Government towards monopoly, stress was laid upon the value of monopoly control as an integral part of a policy of maintaining a high and stable level of employment (paragraph 41). But, unless it is argued that the British economy after 1945 was a competitive system, experience since the end of the war suggests that full employment and extensive industrial monopoly can exist together. It is, however, open for anyone to argue that, because of the monopolist elements in British industry after the war, a higher degree of inflation was required to maintain full employment than would otherwise have been needed.
6. M. Oakshott, 'Political Economy of Freedom', *Cambridge Journal*, 1949.
7. It should not be overlooked that activities which have traditionally been turned over to monopoly control may subsequently become proper subjects for competitive operation. An interesting case is the appearance of the new turn-pike roads in the United States.
8. It is interesting to notice that in the defence put up by the Electric Lamp Manufacturers' Association before the monopolies Commission they had 'never contemplated any kind of closed shop,' partly for 'political reasons'.
9. The Monopolies and Restrictive Practices Commission, *Report on the Supply of Electric Lamps*, 1951.
10. This is quite apart from some extraordinary arguments employed by the E.L.M.A. in an effort to prove that what they were doing constituted competition. See Chapter 16 of the *Report on the Supply of Electric Lamps*, 1951.
11. *Report on the Supply and Export of Matches and the Supply of Match-Making Machinery*. The Monopolies and Restrictive Practices Commission, 1953.
12. In particular J. A. Schumpeter, *Capitalism, Socialism and Democracy*, Chap. VIII, and *Business Cycles*, Vol. I, Chap. III; J. K. Galbraith, *American Capitalism*, chap. VII; Sir Henry Clay, 'The Campaign Against Monopoly and Restrictive Practices', *Lloyds Bank Review*, April 1952; Dame Alix Kilroy, *The Task and Methods of the Monopolies Commission*, Manchester Statistical Society, March 1953. None of these writers, it is fair to state, could be considered as 'defending monopoly'; each one seems to favour certain forms of monopoly regulation.
13. U.S. v. Aluminium Co. of America, 1948, Fed. 2d., 416 (1945).
14. In the middle of the nineteenth century many eminent economists argued in favour of the abolition of the patents system. In recent years only Sir Arnold Plant 'Economic Theory Concerning Patents for Invention', *Economica*, 1934, and Professor Polanyi, 'Patent Reform', *Review of Economic Studies*, 1944, have raised fundamental questions about it.
15. At some points, however, Schumpeter brings in other apparently secondary lines of defence of monopoly. For example, he states that 'there are superior methods available to the monopolist which either are not available at all to

a crowd of competitors or are not available to them so readily,' claiming that 'monopolization may increase the sphere of influence of the . . . better brains'. He returns to the point later: 'in the last resort American agriculture, English coalmining, the English textile industry . . . are affecting *total* output much more injuriously than they would if controlled, each of them by a dozen good brains'. These claims for the virtually unlimited economies of scale are rasher statements than Schumpeter was accustomed to make. Did he really believe that American agriculture would be most efficiently operated if there were only twelve large farms? As for the Lancashire textile industry there is no evidence that the very large combines are more efficiently operated than the smaller firms. And the experience of the National Coal Board does not support his contention of the gains to be achieved by massive administration.

16. Scattered throughout the writings of Schumpeter are vivid phrases of the power of the innovator to break down vested interests. 'In manufacturing industry, a monopoly position is in general no cushion to sleep on. As it can be gained, so it can be retained only by alertness and energy.' 'Even in the world of giant firms, new ones arise and others fall into the background. Innovations still emerge primarily with the "young" ones'. 'The process of incessant rise and decay of firms and industries which is the central – though much neglected – fact about capitalism'.

17. Professor Galbraith seems to resurrect the idea of a 'hidden hand' at work in economic society. 'A benign providence . . . has made the modern industry of a few large firms an almost perfect instrument for inducing technical changes.'

18. G. Unwin, *Studies in Economic History*, p. 324, 'When one contemplates the widespread activity (in the Elizabethan period) one is tempted to ask why so little is heard of it in the annals of the time, and why the Industrial Revolution did not happen a century earlier. The answer to both questions is the same. The triumph of honest enterprise was overshadowed by the feverish delusions of speculation and the selfish greed of monopoly.' G. N. Clark, *Science and Social Welfare in the Age of Newton*, p. 111, 'Such was the experience of the industrial countries of Europe from the half abortive industrial revolution of Elizabeth's time to the half abortive revolution which began in Charles II's time. The new industrial organisation, like the old, constantly tended towards monopoly; the new forms of monopoly, like the old, constantly tended to stifle enterprise.'

19. T. S. Ashton, *The Industrial Revolution*, p. 12.

20. See in particular H. G. Fox, *Monopolies and Patents*, Chap. XIV. But although the author concludes that 'the monopoly of the 16th and 17th centuries was based on sound and legitimate economic principles and was a sincere effort to further new industries and arts' he yet admits that 'the patents issued in pursuance of that policy . . . were perverted in operation'.

21. Of the 58 Reports by the Anglo-American Productivity Teams, 33 gave 'the spirit of competition' as the most important general factor responsible for the high level of productivity in the United States.

22. In point of fact this statement is not true of the 58 Anglo-American Productivity Teams which visited the United States. They visited many of the small-scale industries, including textiles and coal. They did not visit the oil or the motor vehicle industries.

23. Professor Galbraith points out that 'in a community which sets great store by progress, technical progress is an important source of business prestige. An American business concern simply cannot afford the reputation of being unprogressive. If it has no laboratories it must imagine some; an annual report that makes no reference to research is unthinkable.' In such an atmosphere it is not difficult to imagine that a good deal of technical research is misdirected effort.
24. R. N. Anthony, *Management Controls in Industrial Research Organisations*, p. 85.
25. One acute observer, H. S. Hatfield, *The Inventor and His World*, has concluded, largely for such reasons, that 'So far, the great laboratories have been singularly unproductive of really new departures, which have mostly been the work of individuals in conception and inception'.
26. J. A. Schumpeter, *Business Cycles*, Vol. I, p. 369.
27. E. E. Morison, *A Case Study of Innovation*, Massachusetts Institute of Technology, Publications in Social Sciences Series, 3, No. 10.
28. G. G. Smith, *Gas Turbines and Jet Propulsion*, p. 135.
29. *Letters of T. E. Lawrence*, p. 852.
30. See in particular W. I. B. Beveridge, *The Art of Scientific Investigation*, Chap. IX. The comment of Rommel on military strategy is pertinent: 'Prejudice against innovation is a typical characteristic of an Officer Corps which has grown up in a well-tried and proven system. Thus it was that the Prussian Army was defeated by Napoleon. This attitude was also evident during this war, in German as well as British officer circles where, with their minds fixed on complicated theories, people lost the ability to come to terms with reality. A military doctrine had been worked out to the last detail and it was now regarded as the summit of all military wisdom. The only military thinking which was acceptable was that which followed their standardised rules. Everything outside the rules was regarded as a gamble; if it succeeded then it was the result of luck and accident. This attitude of mind creates fixed preconceived ideas, the consequences of which are incalculable'. *The Rommel Papers*, pp. 203–4.
31. F. Redlich, 'Rôle of Theory in the Study of Business History', *Explorations in Entrepreneurial History*, Vol. IV, 1951–52.
32. A. A. Bright, *The Electric Lamp Industry*, p. 456.
33. The Monopolies and Restrictive Practices Commission, *Report on the Supply of Electric Lamps*, 1951, p. 39.
34. The whole of the foregoing and much of the following paragraph is based upon Professor Maclaurin's *Invention and Innovation in the Radio Industry*. Professor Maclaurin, himself a pioneer in this type of social research, has placed all students of the dynamics of industry deeply in his debt.
35. M. Gorham, *Broadcasting and Television since 1900*, p. 120.
36. Sydney Moseley, *John Baird*, pp. 71, 74, 81, 110, 113, 119. Mosley's conclusion is that 'the attitude of the B.B.C. in regard to John's invention was precisely what might have been expected from a great monopoly suddenly confronted with an innovation which might conceivably force it to modify its entire programme and even to change its basic policy'. See also M. Gorham, *Ibid.*, p. 117.
37. Maclaurin, *ibid.*, p. 52.
38. Moseley, *ibid.*, p. 210.
39. R. H. Coase, *British Broadcasting*, pp. 3, 4.

40. Maclaurin, *ibid.*, p. 36.

41. Gorham, *ibid.*, p. 24; Coase, *ibid.*, p. 5.

42. Coase, *ibid.*, p. 23; Gorham, *ibid.*, p. 26.

43. Thus Lord Reith, the first Director-General, believed that the success of the B.B.C. derived mainly from what he called 'brute monopoly' power. (*Into the Wind*, p. 99). The second Director-General, Sir Frederick Ogilvie, declared that 'my chief impressions (of the B.B.C.) were two: the evils of the monopoly system and the gallant work of a very able and delightful executive staff in trying to overcome them' (Coase, *ibid.*, p. 155). Contemporary opinions of the B.B.C. range from the passionate belief that it is 'the best in the world' to the view that, although on special occasions the B.B.C. is highly competent, for at least two-thirds of the listening time when entertainment is provided, the programmes are costive and unimaginative.

44. J. C. W. Reith, *Into the Wind*, p. 100.

45. *Report of the Broadcasting Committee, 1949*, p. 56.

46. *Idem*, p. 42. Oddly enough the B.B.C. sought to prove its case by a misplaced appeal to Gresham's Law. The Law states that bad money will drive out good because, when both are in circulation, people will hold on to the good and reject the bad. This, however, is exactly the opposite of the B.B.C.'s argument that, when confronted by 'good' and 'bad' programmes, listeners will embrace the bad and spurn the good.

47. Gorham, *ibid.*, p. 113.

48. *Ibid.*, p. 109.

49. Coase, *ibid.*, p. 112.

50. *Ibid.*, Appendix H, Paper 118.

51. Coase, *ibid'*, p. 94.

52. *Ibid.*, pp. 110–115.

53. Gorham, *ibid.*, p. 243.

54. *Report of the Broadcasting Committee, 1949*, p. 88.

55. *Report of the Broadcasting Committee, 1949*, p. 92.

56. *Idem*, pp. 76–79.

57. *Idem*, Appendix H, Paper 122. Memorandum of Evidence by Messrs Pye Ltd.

10 THE POPULATION SCARE*

In the past, political arithmeticians and economists who have been courageous enough to embark upon long-distance forecasts of changes in population and of their economic consequences have been notoriously unfortunate. Gregory King[1] estimated that the population of England would slowly grow to eleven millions by 2300 A.D. Malthus,[2] writing at a time when the population of England and Wales was around nine millions was palpably in error as to the limits of growth possible without a fall in the standard of living.

On the possibility of increasing very considerably the effective population of this country, I have expressed myself in some parts of my work more sanguinely perhaps than experience would warrant. I have said that, in the course of some centuries, it might contain two or three times as many inhabitants as at present and yet every person be both better fed and better clothed.

In the latter part of the nineteenth century the fear of 'a devastating torrent of babies' was stilled, partly by contemporary facts, partly by the growing realisation that if there was a 'law' of diminishing returns there was also a 'law' of progressive inventiveness on the part of man.[3] But the Malthusian devil was loosed for a time after the war. Mr Keynes, perhaps underestimating the regenerative economic power of the post-war world and apparently misinterpreting the available statistics bearing upon diminishing returns,[4] believed that we were confronted, in Europe at least, with a long period of population pressure. The Old World could not expect to continue to draw upon the fertility of the New and the post-war breakdown of economic relations would, apparently, hurry on tendencies well established even before the war.

Before the eighteenth century mankind entertained no false hopes. To lay the illusions which grew popular at that age's latter end, Malthus disclosed a Devil. For half-a-century all serious economical writings held that Devil in clear prospect. For the next half-century he was chained up and out of sight. Now perhaps we have loosed him again.[5]

*The Manchester School, October 1939.

Mr Keynes had his followers. Wright, quoting Mr Keynes and Dean Inge with approval in 1925, explains that these writers

> tell us in effect, that we are living, and that our parents have been living, for fifty years, in a fool's paradise, believing that they were building up our economic life upon solid foundations, and preparing the way for a happier posterity, whereas, in reality, they were squandering our family estates and wasting the gains of civilization on a mere increase in numbers.[6]

The resurrection of the Malthusian devil turned out, however, to be merely an exhumation, and since 1930 increasing emphasis has been placed upon imminent underpopulation, if not of actual race suicide. The subject has become a popular one. Estimates of future population have been courageously projected forward for a century with the most startling results. The quaintest explanations have been advanced for decreases in the birth-rate and for differences in experiences in different countries.[7] It would perhaps be unfair and futile to quote some of the more extreme forms in which the danger of underpopulation has been expressed.[8] But eminent economists have recently added their authority to the case for public alarm and remedial action. Mr Harrod, for instance,[9] has written: 'so that it may be that in these present and immediately coming years, we are at the very crisis and climax of human history, that this is the tide in the affairs of men, and that if we do not take it at the flood, albeit a flood which is beginning to ebb fast, the human experiment on this planet will peter out.'

The wheel, then, has come full circle. But, in view of their regrettable record in thinking of long-distance population problems, it seems important that, in this case at least, economists should avoid spectacular interpretations of available estimates; they should regard with the gravest suspicion any estimates made over more than a relatively short period and should give full weight to the possible appearance of new and unsuspected economic or social forces or events which might invalidate estimates projected into an unknown future.[10]

I

What is the substance of the alarm now being so authoritatively expressed? The net reproduction rate in Great Britain is below 1, so that the population is inevitably destined to fall in the absolute unless the rate is increased. But the likelihood is that the actual decline by 1971 will be relatively insignificant. We know that it is virtually certain that mortality rates will continue to fall in the future. The really uncertain elements are future fertility rates and, although this is a less important item, migration rates. But it does not appear to be without significance that the birth-rate in this country was, for the first time since 1870, constant between 1933 and 1938. And it would appear reasonable to assume that, at least for a number of years, migration to this country would be on the increase. If we take the estimate made by Enid Charles,[11] which ignores migration and assumes that mortality continues to fall whilst fertility remains at the 1931 level, the population of England and Wales is as follows: (in thousands) 1935, 40,563; 1945, 42,338; 1955, 43,651; 1965, 43,744; 1975, 43,021; and in 2035, 33,585.

That estimate has at least as strong a sanction as any other. Its probability value is as high as that of any other. Even if rather more pessimistic assumptions are accepted it is still reasonable to anticipate that any absolute decline in the population by 1971 will be relatively small.

Why then the scarifying urgency of contemporaneous population discussions? The answer usually given seems very unsatisfactory. It is commonly argued that we must now make a final and irrevocable decision as to what is to be done about population; that if the net reproduction rate is not raised *now*, then we do inevitably embark on a slippery slope from which there can be no recovery and which inexorably ends in national extermination. This surely is the point that Mr Harrod seeks to stress where he talks of 'this . . . tide in the affairs of men' which 'if we do not take it at the flood . . . the human experiment on this planet will peter out'. But it is a point which is far from being obvious.

If a community of 100 people has a net reproduction rate of 0.75 we can roughly assume that, at the end of one generation it will total 75 and at the end of two generations 55. Why should it not, having reached 55, now decide that any further fall is undesirable and take steps to raise the net reproduction rate to 1? Why would it necessarily be more difficult to do this at the end of the second generation than earlier? Curiously enough, although the 'slippery slope' argument is most vital for the really alarmist view of the population problem, no very convincing reasons appear to have been advanced to support it. Mr Carr-Saunders has argued[12] that if for long periods families are kept small 'all the habits connected with the small family system will harden into customs'. But I cannot see that present-day habits would be any easier to break down than customs in the future. He has also suggested that housing conditions would adjust themselves to the small family. But a declining population will surely safeguard us against a housing shortage. More recently[13] he has suggested that, if in the future a rather sudden increase in the size of the family took place, it would constitute a heavy burden in addition to that created by the more than proportionate increase in the number of older people in the community. Reference will be made to this argument later. But it should be clear that if there are serious drawbacks to a declining or a smaller population it would be much easier to raise the community to take action in the future when these consequences would be before our eyes than to do so now when the vast majority of people believe, and I think correctly, that we are becoming unduly pessimistic about them. I can see no reason why a community, if it consciously embarks upon the experiment of allowing the population to fall, does substantially weaken its power to call a halt and to stabilise at a lower level.

In most present-day discussions of population, no distinction is made between the alleged drawbacks of the actual process of a fall in population and the alleged drawbacks of a smaller, as against a larger, population. There may be economic aches and pains associated with the transition from one size of population to another. But that is quite distinct from the relative social and economic efficiency of two populations of different sizes.[14] Yet the arguments regarding the two are bundled together and, in particular, it is frequently implied that no community could ever experiment with a reduction of population because, in the transitional period, the forces making for a decline accumulate an impetus which cannot be controlled and which, in effect, will prevent any stability being reached save at zero population. If that view is correct it ought to be substantiated. It implies that public policy regarding population can only work in one of two directions, either increasing or maintaining the population. Conscious control working for a fall is out of the question. It is just at this point that the sceptics, who have been so often right, join issue with the population experts, who have been so often wrong. The doubters are not convinced that a smaller population will have any very serious drawbacks; they are frequently of the opinion that the opposite would be true. Why not, therefore, let the population fall? If the transitional problems prove to be serious then would be the time to take steps to raise the net reproduction rate to 1.

II

Mr Harrod, in his recent article, presents a gloomy picture of the economic effects of a fall in population. They appear to me to constitute an insecure basis upon which to erect the social policy which he advocates. Certain of these economic effects are transitional aches and pains; if we assume that the population could be stabilised at a lower level, they are, therefore, temporary in character.

Mr Harrod argues that 'in the coming decades we shall have a rapidly ageing population and the maintenance of the older members will be an increasing burden on those actively employed'. On the other hand, he omits to point out that there will be a smaller number of children to be maintained by the actively employed. Enid Charles, even on the basis of a forecast that the population of England and Wales will fall to 19 millions by 2035, also estimates that the number of persons aged 15–59 years, which was 64.3 per cent of the total population in 1935, will be

62.3 per cent in 1970 and 60.1 per cent in 2035.[15] This is a decline of insignificant magnitude. Other estimates give more optimistic conclusions. Thus Colin Clark argues[16] that 'owing to changing age composition, the economic productivity of the population is going to rise during the next generation' and that, even after 1975, the decline in the proportion of occupied males will be comparatively small. Two other important possible reactions must, however, be taken into account here. First, if the average size of family falls, it is not unlikely that there will be an increase in the proportion of females who are not unduly embarrassed by heavy family responsibilities and who, therefore, will be able to increase the total occupied population. Second, the increasing length of life means not only that people live longer but that they are capable of carrying on effective work to a later age. A great deal of play has been made with the idea of a 'nation in carpet slippers' but in fact, in the future, we can confidently expect that the average person will be able to delay the donning of his carpet slippers. The proportion of the occupied to the total population would then tend to increase. The presumption, therefore, is that the nation will gain, and not lose, within the next 30 years, from the changing proportion of occupied to nonoccupied persons.

There is, secondly, the argument that, where the population is declining, secular changes in the relative importance of industries will create greater dislocation of the labour market and make for increasing labour immobility and unemployment.[17] The validity of this argument, of course, is not to be doubted. It really constitutes a case for a rapidly increasing population, since a stationary population is also at some disadvantage here. But this surely is a factor of minor importance, certainly not one which should count heavily in reaching fundamental decisions relating to population policy. The upward pressure of population, even in Great Britain in the nineteenth century, scarcely exceeded 1 per cent per annum. Population in Great Britain in the next 30 years will probably decline by less than 0.25 per cent per annum. Normal retirement of personnel from an industry through old age or death is about 2 per cent per annum. And it must not be overlooked that a rapid increase in population leading to a swift growth of certain industries may, under free enterprise, produce dislocation in the labour market because of the faulty or short-sighted judgement of individual workers. The nineteenth century was not free from periods of severe maladjustment in the labour market, ranging from the plight of the hand-loom weavers down to the periodic gluts of labour in the building trades. In any case a policy of encouraging a large domestic population can bring little relief to industries mainly concerned with export. Cannan's balanced perspective is surely the correct one: '(the approach of a declining population) will provide more rather than less reason for promoting mobility of labour . . . we shall have to take more, rather than less care, than at present to

secure that arrangements which seem superficially desirable do not
hinder that mobility.' But when Mr Harrod seeks to magnify this point
and assert that mobility of labour is likely to decrease in the future, and
hence increase unemployment, it appears that he embarks upon
extremely dangerous surmise. It may be true, as he suggests, that the
growing importance of semi-luxury trades will increase the instability of
demand and hence the need for greater mobility. It is probably true that
the Unemployment Insurance Scheme has reduced mobility. And there
are many other points that might have been added. For instance, since
female labour is particularly immobile, any increase in its relative importance will increase general labour immobility. On the other hand,
there are many factors which might normally be expected in the future
to increase mobility. A higher proportion of workers are being trained
in more general forms of industrial skill, particularly in machine-
tending. In the future, we shall probably never have again the problem
of a dislocated labour market in the degree to which we suffered from it
after 1920; our export trades are relatively smaller; our industries less
intensely localised. It is only to be expected that, with increasing
experience, the placing work of the Employment Exchanges will become
more efficient: certainly their recently enlarged experiments in the
retraining of unemployed workers hold out enormous possibilities. I
am not suggesting, of course, that mobility of labour in the future will
be greater. In the midst of these, and many other counteracting and im-
ponderable factors, my answer would be that I don't know. But then, I
submit, neither does anyone else.

I turn now to the economic reasons for deploring a return to a
smaller population. Mr Harrod believes that a small population will
result in 'a net loss of production per head. The economies of large scale
have not yet reached their limit in this country and a contraction of the
market would lead to diminished efficiency in many fields'. This, of
course, is a crucial decision and Mr Harrod, presumably, has evidence,
which could not be given in one short paper, to back this decision. My
own impression would be exactly the contrary. Most industries in this
country consist of a relatively large number of independent firms and of
an even larger number of independent technical units. Moreover, these
units are of varying efficiency. I cannot think that the output per head
would decrease in coal mining, in iron and steel, in cotton, in clothing,
in engineering, in food or in building, if (say) the 20 per cent least
efficient firms were closed down. It is difficult to think of any one important industry or public service which could not seize upon the full
economies of large-scale production with (say) a market of 20 million
persons in an area as small as that of Great Britain. On the other side
the cost of congestion in our main centres of population in the way of
traffic delay and the time spent in reaching and returning from work
must be considerable. Clearly, innumerable and most intricate

problems involving economic, social and administrative issues would have to be settled here before any judgement, having any claim to scientific responsibility, could be arrived at. I suggest that we are not yet in a position to exercise that judgement.

Mr Harrod seeks, even, to snatch away from us the consolation that at least a diminished population will, by forcing the less efficient lands out of cultivation, increase agricultural productivity. He believes that 'the application of science to agriculture throws some doubt on whether the law of diminishing return works very strongly in the backward direction'. It may be true, although I am not aware of the evidence, that increasingly scientific methods in agriculture will somewhat lessen the consequences of inherent differentials in productivity between one piece of land and another. But those differences still remain substantial. Even in a country as small as our own, Mr Kendall has shown recently[18] what substantial variations there are in fertility, and the decline in arable area in the past ten years, county by county, confirms what most people up to now have regarded as a truism, that the least fertile land goes out of cultivation first. In the United States the yield per acre varies greatly for the same crop from one State to another. Certainly the decline in arable acreage in the United States since the war has taken place in the naturally less fertile lands.[19] It is just as dangerous now to underemphasise the importance of the law of diminishing returns as it was, in the time of Malthus, to overemphasise it.

Mr Harrod is particularly alarmed lest a decline in population, by leading to a deficient demand for new saving, will increase unemployment. This, again, is partly a problem of transition, although it is not wholly unrelated to the question of the size of the population. His conclusions are based upon a number of forecasts of probable secular changes in habits of saving and outlets for investment.

(a) 'The channels of overseas investment are closed and are not likely soon to be re-opened.' If by 'soon' is meant a decade the statement may have some probability value. But if 50 or 75 years is meant, and that is the period of which Mr Harrod must think in terms of his population policy, it would seem to have none. Who is to say that, within the next quarter of a century, there may not be enormous international investment in China, in South America, in Africa?

(b) 'The new technical inventions are not notably of a capital requiring kind.' Here again forecasting seems to be dangerous. But many will be surprised that the statement should be made even of the last decade.[20] It is true that there are, at present, no spectacular openings for investment such as that provided in this country in the nineteenth century by the construction of railways, but, after all, there has been practically no railway building for the past half-century. On the other hand, we have had enormous growth of investment in road transport and in the generation and distribution of electricity. Moreover a considerable number of industries provide illustrations of extremely heavy investment: branches of the chemical industry; the hydrogenation of coal; mechanisation in bottle-making and flour-milling. But it is not so much the general rule as the average case that is important. There is a universal tendency towards mechanisation at present which there is no reason to believe will slacken off in the future.[21] Estimates of the rate at which capital equipment is accumulating must inevitably be hazardous, but Douglas,[22] in the only elaborate calculation that has been made, indicates that, in the United States, between 1899 and 1922 there was certainly no tendency for the annual percentage rate of increase of capital equipment to slow down. And the fact that, in the United States, between 1922 and 1929 the output of durable goods and capital equipment was increasing much more rapidly than that of non-durable and consumption goods[23] should at least lead us into caution when forecasting future technical changes.

(c) A decline in population, *of itself*, might be expected to create a tendency towards long-period unemployment. When population is increasing the multiplication of capital goods of the existing types is a task which the entrepreneur confidently foresees; he has a fairly definitely pre-ordained function.[24] If the populaion is falling, the supply of capital goods will be maintained only if different kinds of capital goods are being brought forward. Recognising Mr Harrod's eminence in this field of economics I express doubt on his conclusions on this point only with the greatest reluctance. But I am not convinced that, in fact, the tendency mentioned above is particularly likely to become actual since possible counteracting forces cannot be ruled out.

There is the whole question of the rate of industrial invention. For many reasons this might be expected to increase rather than decrease in the future. Improvements in the general standard of education enlarge the field of the intellectually trained from whom new ideas may spring. The increase of mechanical mindedness which normal life demands of us all may be the forcing ground for further mechanical developments. The increasing proportion of the national income devoted to industrial and scientific research might have the same effect. Moreover, once a general body of scientific knowledge exists, each new invention is not only of value in itself; it becomes possible, very often, to link it with earlier techniques and apply it almost universally. Thus the internal combustion engine makes possible, for the first time, controlled flight in the air but the engine can also be harnessed to the boat, the road vehicle, the stationary machine. The conveyance of impressions by waves makes possible the transmission of sound and of form and colour but also opens up the possibility of more complete use of existing wire telephony. Each new invention is not merely the establishment of a new plant; it is a fertiliser which leads all the existing trees to push out all their boughs and branches a little further. It is at least tenable that, in the future, the consequences of a declining population upon possible avenues for investment might well be offset by the force of invention alone.

There is, too, the question of the increasing use of durable consumption goods. It may well be that an increasing proportion of the capital equipment of the community is now taking this form and will continue to do so. The equipment of homes with labour-saving devices; the association of leisure pursuits with the use of machines, such as television or motor cars; the replacement of hand-work by the typewriter and the dictaphone; the more complete control of temperature and air condition within buildings, including the domestic house; the replacement of the mass-provided public services, such as the public service vehicle, and cinema by the more convenient (but probably more expensive from the capital point of view) private motor car or home cinema: here are enormous potentialities over a long period in the case of which the consumer will be clamouring for the new technique. A rapid increase in the capital intensity of private possessions is certainly not out of the question. The possibilities are the greater here since the existing inequality in the distribution of wealth means that there are numerous forms of private capital equipment now in possession of the rich which, as it were, are on show to the rest of the community who may frequently seek, by economy on consumer goods, to take advantage of that kind of equipment. So the dinner parties disappear and the eight-cylinder car is bought, or the consumption of beer declines and the motor cycle replaces it.

As a population declines it acquires, almost as a legacy, an increasing quantity of equipment per head such as more factories, more roads. Some of that equipment will almost certainly not be found worth while to maintain. But other equipment, notably roads, would almost certainly be maintained. The cost of depreciation per head of the population would rise. An increased part of national savings would, therefore, be directed into these channels; an increased proportion of the populaton would find employment in these fields.

Finally, it must be borne in mind that, over the next 30 years in Great Britain the decline in population will be small; that the decline in the number of adults (who exercise the important demand for capital equipment) will go on more slowly than in the case of the population as a whole and that this decline will be foreseen with some confidence and will therefore not be so serious, from the angle from which we are at present discussing it, as might otherwise be the case.

(*d*) If Mr Harrod is thinking over a long period of the relation between the demand for new capital and the savings accruing, he must not leave out of account the possibility of secular changes in habits of saving. Mr Clark, indeed, has recently startled us all by the statement that 'net private saving has ceased or become negative'.[25] Whether that statement is true or not, it appears that changes in habits of saving are not impossible and it is possible that they would be in a direction which would lessen the evils feared.

Finally, Mr Harrod feels that 'our country will present the mournful aspect of a deserted and derelict area, its houses uninhabited and its equipment unused'. That is a value-judgement which many would not be prepared to accept. Others might be more prepared to mourn the fantastic pushing and jostling of our larger centres of population and the de-humanising influence of constantly living in a crowd which many of our citities enforce upon a large section of the population.

III

There are certain social and economic advantages associated with a smaller population which are generally understood, or, at least, used to be understood, which are perhaps worth repetition.

(1) The smaller family has in the past half-century been one of the important devices by which the more brutalising forms of poverty have been reduced. Bowley and Hogg[26] have shown that, excluding the effect of unemployment, the proportion of families, in five representative towns, below the poverty line had fallen, by 1924, to one-fifth of its pre-war level. Of this improvement, they argued, one-third could be attributed to the fall in the number of dependents per family. Recent social surveys have shown that 11 per cent of the families in London below the poverty line (in Southampton, 17 per cent; Northampton, 9 per cent; Warrington, 28 per cent; Reading, 23 per cent; Bolton 9 per cent; Bristol, 20 per cent and Stanley, 32 per cent), were cases where the natural head of the family was in full work but his income was insufficient to provide even the barest necessities of life.[27] I cannot help but feel that, in these cases, it would be better for everybody concerned if the number of dependents had been smaller.

(2) There are, at the moment, certain forms of our social equipment which are, by the general admission of enlightened folk, inadequate but in the case of which improvement is hampered by public ignorance, indifference or selfishness. Outstanding illustrations are houses, schools, hospitals, pre-natal clinics, playing fields, parks and libraries. A fall in population will automatically tend to increase the services available to each individual.

(3) The same is true of other long-lived equipment, such as roads, where an increased supply per unit of population would generally be regarded as of both economic and social value.

(4) Stationary, or even declining populations, escape some of the wastes invariably associated with expanding economies. Periods of rapid economic expansion may lead to numerous industrial mistakes, ill-conceived or overoptimistic enterprise, the uneconomical exploitation

of raw materials and the maldistribution of labour. It must not be overlooked that rapidly growing communities, such as Great Britain in the nineteenth century and the United States after 1880, have suffered the most violent economic dislocations which virtually stationary populations, such as France after 1861, appear to have largely escaped.

(5) The experience of countries such as Sweden and Switzerland leads many people to the view that a smaller community can more easily maintain administrative efficiency and the whole atmosphere of democracy. In the smaller country the personal contact of the citizen with leaders is closer; the feeling of democratic responsibility is more immediate; the guiding political and intellectual spirits of the age are less submerged by the task of running the administrative machine.

(6) The smaller family has brought inestimable non-economic gains. The release of women from the burden of unwanted and excessive childbirth constitutes perhaps the greatest step forward in human liberty that history has to record. The spacing of births may well have had as great an influence on the health of individuals as any great medical discovery of the past century. And the restraint that can now be exercised over births has given to the institution of marriage potentialities in the way of a long, free, full and equal companionship in most phases of life between men and women out of which may well arise the supreme achievement of the art of living and feeling.

IV

Mr Harrod's anxiety to prevent any fall in the population leads him to put forward a scheme of family allowances of a novel kind. The parental instinct, it is argued, may be relied upon to lead most parents to have one or two children; the allowances would apply only to the third and subsequent children. And the allowances must be generous enough to more than meet the full costs of nurture and education of the additional child so that, in effect, the conditions made possible for the existing children in the family would be improved. For each child over two, the parents would receive per annum a sum equal to one-quarter of their income. So that parents with an annual income of £160 would, when their family increased to three and then to four children, find their total income increased to £200 (i.e. £160 + £40) and then to £240. Similarly with parents with an annual income of £1600; their income would increase to £2000 (i.e. £1600 + £400) and then to £2400.

It is suggested that two alternative methods of financing such a scheme might be possible: the funds might be raised by taxation or loan or, alternatively, there might be a pool in each income class, the single and small family people, in effect, transferring a part of their income to the large families. The first method, whether the funds arise from general taxation or loans, seems to me both politically unthinkable and socially undesirable. The very heavy expenses that the middle-classes must meet in bringing up their children is largely due to the heavier costs of education in which they are incurred. A part of that cost is due, of course, to a real superiority in the education of middle-class children over that received by others. But a part of it is a payment which middle-class parents pay that their children may enjoy the privilege of passing through exceptionally expensive, although not necessarily exceptionally efficient, educational institutions, mere attendance at which confers a label of great value in their subsequent careers. The parents are, in fact, buying monopolies for their children. That, in a democracy, is not a pursuit which should be openly financed by the State. The inequality in educational opportunity is one of the most striking social anomalies of our times. To give it a further sanction by making special arrangements under which the parents in the higher income groups could be certain of providing a better education for their children than could those in the lower income group would be socially retrogressive. Quite apart from the real merits of the case, moreover, the fact that the rich man was obtaining £400 per year for doing something for which the poor man received only £40 a year would provide a weapon for political propaganda which no political party would dare to face.

Income pooling in each income class, if it were acceptable to the members of the classes, would not suffer from this defect. But even pooling might be expected to have its opponents. It would almost certainly produce a violent redistribution of income within each class. We have, of course, no information of how all those receiving (say) £800 a year are distributed as between single persons and married persons with one, two, three or more children. But let us assume the following percentage distribution of the population (which in fact assumes a net reproduction rate below 1).

Single	Married income receivers with children								Total
	0	1	2	3	4	5	6	7	
18	19	22	17	11	6	4	2	1	100

Let us further assume that Mr Harrod's scheme is completely under way,[28] that for each child over the second £200 is payable; that the funds necessary for this purpose are raised from the single and the married with no children or only one child, the single paying 50 per cent more than those who are married but are without children and three times as much as those who have one child. It is assumed that married persons with two children neither receive from nor subscribe to the pool. Then it can easily be calculated that the following annual deductions would have to be made from those with an income of £800 a year.

Single person	Married person	
	No children	One child
£252	£168	£84

When it is remembered that these deductions would be in addition to other taxation and that the pool deductions would be heavier if a distribution had been taken showing a net reproduction rate of about 1, it is clear that the scheme would involve an extraordinary redistribution, the economic consequences of which on personal initiative and habits of saving and consuming might be equally spectacular. It would constitute a plunge into the unknown.

Another rough way of calculating the total trasfer of income involved for all income classes can be made as follows. The annual number of births at present in Great Britain is about 700,000 and the net reproduction rate 0.75. About 230,000 extra births are necessary to raise the rate to 1. But all these extra births would not have to be paid for.[29] Assume that only 170,000 children are paid for and that the average allowance per child is only £80 and that allowances are paid for the first fifteen years of the child's life. Then the transfer in the first year would be £13½ millions and would rise to £204 millions a year at the end of fifteen years.

How far this scheme might affect the birth-rate it is not easy to say. The single young man with £800 a year who finds that, if he remains single, his income will be £550 but that if he can marry and accumulate three children his income will rise to £1000 might perhaps hurry on to this. Alternatively, faced with the prospect of having to live on less than £800 until he was married and had two children, and finding it difficult to save as a bachelor because of his contribution to the pool, he might give up the unequal struggle and decide to remain a bachelor. Some people who would normally on a salary of £800 have had one child and could or would not have more might decide that it was preferable not to have a child at all with an income of £632 than to have a child with an income of £716. On the whole, the scheme might, however, be expected to increase the birth-rate but simultaneously create a crop of economic and social dangers.

1 At the lower income levels the pool payments would throw very great hardship on the single man and the small family. If, as is certainly not unlikely, the single man with £160 had to pay £50, that would constitute an intolerable burden, even if it were only temporary.

2. In certain classes of society, where the birth-rate is even now very high, such as the very poorest quarters in a dock area, the scheme would probably increase the birth-rate very rapidly, consequently depress the standard of living of those in that income group who had small families,

and thus push the prudent section of the population below the poverty line in order to meet the allowances to be paid to the imprudent.

3. If the scheme were successful and the net reproduction rate were to rise higher than 1, presumably the allowances would be reduced. This would frustrate the legitimate expectations of those who had been led to increase the size of their family by the possibility of an allowance but had not yet qualified for allowance. And frequent changes of allowance would create several series of families being paid varying amounts for performing just the same services.

4. In so far as parents were influenced by the lure of the allowance they would seek to qualify in the minimum period. The relative disadvantage of having one or two children and the possibility that the allowances might suddenly be discontinued would lead people who did intend to have at least three children to have them as quickly as possible. This would destroy the wise spacing of births.

5. The administrative problems of such a scheme seem altogether formidable. At what age is it to be considered that financial pressure upon single men is no longer of value? Are single women to pay into the pool? If so, who is to decide whether they remain unmarried because they choose not to marry or because they can't find a husband? Are the allowances in each income group to be operated independently so that, if the net reproduction rate rises to 1, the allowance will be discontinued in one group whilst continuing to operate elsewhere? What is to happen if parents move from one income group to another? Would exemptions be given to parents where the small family was prudent on medical grounds?

6. Important repercussions on the family institution itself might be expected. The financial would be one of the elements which would now intrude into every decision about marriage. Or the inducements to further child-bearing offered by the lavish family allowances might well appear stronger to a father than to a mother and thus create family discord.

V

I arrive at a single and negative conclusion: that scientific knowledge of the economic and social consequences of changes in the size of a population is still too fragmentary to justify our framing of any population policy, much less one which constitutes a drastic revolution in the distribution of income. It is true that more, much more, is known concerning population movements now than half-a-century ago. But it is equally clear that other questions can be formulated to which answers cannot be provided with confidence. And beyond this there are factors, which we cannot even yet formulate precisely, but which we are dimly and obscurely aware might in the long run be of overwhelming significance. It is necessary to give the benefit of the doubt to what we do not know. At the present time the need is for patient and unambitious research into population problems and not for large scale and precipitous experiment or even for Royal Commissions. Another big mistake by economists on this subject would certainly put them out of court for the rest of this century.

NOTES

1. *Natural and Political Observations and Criticisms upon the State and Condition of England,* 1696.
2. *The Principle of Population,* 7th Edition, Appendix p. 489.
3. In a subject in which economists have always been a little inclined to lack restraint no one can fail to be impressed by the sturdy caution and common sense of Cannan in his writings on population. He was the most destructive critic of the Malthusian laws. He was one of the first to foresee the probable stationary population in this country. But his imagination as to its likely consequences was held rigidly in check by his knowledge of the dangers of forecasting and by his intuition that, over a long period, unforeseeable factors might intrude and that a scientist should not be prepared to leave these out of account.
4. The curious should read through the controversy between Mr Keynes and Sir William Beveridge, *Economic Journal,* 1923.
5. J. M. Keynes, *The Economic Consequences of the Peace,* Chapter II., p. 8.
6. H. Wright, *Population,* p. 59.
7. Enid Charles, (*The Twilight of Parenthood*) describes laissez-faire economics as 'biologically self-destructive' whilst in the U.S.S.R. there is to be found an ecology 'suitable for reproduction'. Unfortunately for the theory, the high birth-rate in the U.S.S.R. is due to high rates in the agricultural districts where the knowledge of and sympathy with the communist system have been weakest. In the large towns, where communism presumably is understood and accepted, the birth-rate appears to have been falling rapidly.
8. G. F. McCleary (*The Menace of British Depopulation*), for example, argues that there is a special duty on the part of mothers in Great Britain to seek to offset the tendency towards a decline in birth-rates in the Dominions. 'But unless fertility increases . . . we may not have enough young lives to spare for the peopling of the Overseas Dominions.' Another interesting consequence of the population discussions is that the law of Diminishing Returns is now being as grossly underestimated in importance as it was formerly grossly overestimated. See Enid Charles, *The Twilight of Parenthood,* Chapter I.
9. The *Manchester School,* Vol. X, No. 1.
10. The need for caution becomes all the more imperative when it is remembered that population forecasts made only four or five years ago have, mainly because of migration, already proved misleading. Thus, in 1935, Enid Charles made estimates of population in England and Wales

from 1935 to 2035. She gave three calculations based upon three sets of assumptions. Her estimates for the year 1939 were 40,654,000; 40,794,000; 41,271,000. Actually the population in 1939 was not less than 41,295,000. So that all three calculations, claiming some probability value over 100 years, underestimate the population after only four years.

11. Enid Charles, 'The Effect of Present Trends in Fertility and Mortality upon the Future Population of England and Wales and upon its Age Composition'. *London and Cambridge Economic Service*, Special Memorandum No. 40.

12. A. M. Carr-Saunders, *World Population*, p. 252.

13. *The Times*, 28 June 1939.

14. Suppose, for instance, it was held that a smaller population was preferable to a larger but that an expanding population was preferable to a declining. Wise public policy might still lead us to seek the smaller population. A decision could only be made by comparing the temporary disadvantages of decline with the permanent advantages of the smaller population. It is the conclusion of this paper that this balancing could not be scientifically worked out at the moment, because we do not know enough about the items to be balanced.

15. Enid Charles, *London and Cambridge Economic Service*, Special Memorandum No. 40.

16. Colin Clark, *National Income and Outlay*, p. 21.

17. Mr Harrod attributes this point to Mr H. D. Henderson. But, if academic priorities have to be established, the credit must go to Cannan, who often made the point in his writings (see *Economic Journal*, 1931, p. 531, and 1932, p. 361) and certainly had taught it for very many years before it was used by others. It is indeed one of the surprising features of the recent population campaign that well-known facts have been brought forward with an air of discovery and novelty. The consequence is that notable pioneers in this field, such as Cannan, Lotka and Bowley, sometimes remain unrecognised.

18. M. G. Kendall, *Journal of Royal Statistical Society, Part* I, 1939.

19. *Recent Social Trends*, Vol. I, p. 109.

20. Mr Harrod's view appears to run contrary to the school of thinkers who look upon increasing capital intensity as the most spectacular fact of our time and whose views as to the future social, political and economic structure of society are coloured by this supposed fact.

21. See, as indicative of conditions in the United States, H. Jerome, *Merchanisation in Industry*.

22. P. H. Douglas, *Real Wages in the United States*, p. 567.

23. F. C. Mills, *Recent Economic Tendencies*, p. 280.

24. See J. R. Hicks, 'Mr Keynes' Theory of Employment', *Economic Journal*, June 1936.

25. Colin Clark, *National Income and Outlay*, p. xv.

26. *Has Poverty Diminished?* p. 22.

27. *New Survey of London Life and Labour*, Vol. VI, p. 117; and *The Standard of Living in Bristol*, p. 46.

28. The scheme would take some time to reach its full cost since Mr Harrod would not pay for any existing children. This seems a little hard. It means that the parents who have felt it their duty to society to have three or more children in the past will receive nothing for these. Those who, apparently,

have been lacking in that sense of public responsibility are to be bribed at very substantial rates.

29. For example, a married couple might, without the family allowance scheme, have had no children. In order to qualify for the allowance they might have three children. But, of course, allowance would only be paid on one.

11 THE GROWTH OF WORLD INDUSTRY*

The question I am raising to-night is as old as economic thinking. It is that of industry against agriculture, of town against country as the source of opulence. I do not pretend, of course, to be able to answer this question but it may be worth while traversing the ground again, for in matters which impinge, as this does, upon contemporary economic policy it is the function of the economist, as I understand it, to state the dilemmas even when, as is nearly always the case, he does not know the answers.

I

There appear to be two distinct concepts of world economic progress, the one placing emphasis upon the proliferation of manufacturing industry, the other upon the advantages of international specialisation. The first, and the more widely held, can be summarised as follows. Manufacturing industry is still limited only because we are watching a continuing process, now in its early stages, which will see its end when industry has spread fairly evenly over the world and, indeed, over each country—much in the way that agricultural pursuits were universal 500 years ago. Progressive industrialisation is in the natural order of things. In the three-quarters of a century before 1938, the world output of manufactured goods increased seven or eight fold.[1] Despite the war it has probably increased further in the past ten years. 'World economic equilibrium has not yet been from obtained and indeed the world is still a very long distance from obtaining it.'[2] The forces making for widespread industrialisation are evident. As between countries, a high average real income is normally associated with a low proportion of workers in agriculture and other primary occupations.[3] History shows that in many countries industrialisation has been the direct means by which income per head has been raised or a larger population sustained at the same standard of living. Sometimes this view goes along with the

*Read before the Manchester Statistical Society, 11 January 1950.

belief that the spread of industry will reduce the volume of international trade, or cause it to expand less rapidly than production in general. It is, of course, this way of thinking which leads States to foster their own industries and which underlies the present-day efforts of the richer countries, either individually or through international organisations, to provide the means of industrialisation for the poorer. And it is upon this set of assumptions that academic writers, notably Clark in his brilliant 'Economics of 1960', have forecast rapid industrialisation in the next decade or two, even in the countries of the Far East.

The second view, less popular and leading to less spectacular conclusions, is that industrialisation, if it is to carry with it an enhanced standard of living, is only possible where certain conditions, not universally or even widely to be found, can be satisfied. The favourable circumstances, the forces which set the wheels turning to produce an industrial revolution – climate, the temperament and aptitude of the people, natural resources – will probably be rare. Manufactured goods, on this hypothesis, will continue to be produced mainly in a few areas of small dimensions. These areas will supply the world freely with cheap industrial goods and draw on other areas for food and raw materials and international trade will increase *pari passu* with production. The association of high industrialisation and high income is not cause and effect, the industry and the opulence are both to be ascribed to a common cause – the natural ability of the people and the occurrence of natural resources. Many countries, such as Canada, Australia, New Zealand, Eire and Denmark are rich though still much dependent upon agriculture and might be still richer but for ill-starred attempts to encourage industry which have lowered and not raised their income per head.

Some pretty effective statistics can also be woven into this case. The industrial areas of the world, with their factories, machines and workers, still remain tiny and few – ludicrously tiny in relation to the sweeping social and economic changes they have brought about. Before the last war the annual average value of finished factory products per head of world population was still only about $38.[4] The total number of industrial factory workers probably did not exceed 100 millions, perhaps 4 per cent of the total world population or 6 per cent of the population at working ages. In 1938, two-thirds of the world manufacturing output was still to be found in the United States, Germany and the United Kingdom; the proportion was much the same in 1870.[5] Even in countries normally regarded as highly industrialised, only a relatively small part of the total area of the country and of the working population was devoted to manufacture. In 1939 in the United States the 33 main industrial areas, comprising only 1.7 per cent of the total area and 35.4 per cent of the total population, accounted for 54.7 per cent of the total wage earners and 60.4 per cent of the value of manufacturing product in the whole country. A detailed study of industrial change in the United States has shown that 'the most pervasive locational forces have operated to diffuse manufactures among the 200 industrial counties rather than to scatter manufactures broadcast among the remaining 2,800 counties. ... The facts suggest that manufacturing industry is either affected by a very high degree of inertia or else on the whole it has been reasonably well located with respect to economic advantages'.[6] In Great Britain, in 1931, the 38 largest industrial towns, covering 1.5 per cent of the total area and 35.4 per cent of the population accounted for 44.2 per cent of the manufacturing population. And even a great war followed by four years of a vigorous 'balanced distribution of industry' policy has made little change in the broad distribution of industry. Facts such as these, it is argued, reveal manufacturing industry as a secondary way of making a living, still largely confined to a few countries and, within these countries, still highly concentrated within quite small areas. It was Marshall himself who wrote: 'So long as the main conditions of economic development remain nearly as they are now, the chief in-itiative seems likely to be with countries, whose great size, rich natural resources, and accumulated capital enable them to concentrate large and highly organised mental and material appliances on the translation into practice of the architectonic ideas of the scientific student and the inventor.'[7]

These are the two views. They seem to me to arise out of very different ways of speculating about economic organisation and the springs of economic change. The first is a more mechanistic approach. It simplifies industrial change by isolating the known and measurable factors associated with growth – such as the rate of investment – and assumes that quantitative relations which have occurred in one society, or at one time, will recur elsewhere. Those who adopt it underline the similarity between societies. They stress the disadvantages of an early start in the industrial race – what one has done another can surely do better later. And they are probably more ready to predict the future (with what I am bound to confess seems to me the supreme confidence born of in-variable failure) and to advocate policies based on prediction. The second is the organic approach; it attaches greater importance to the influence of institutions, the problems of organising resources even when they are present, the human stuff out of which a system is built. Those who follow it emphasise the value of accumulated industrial knowledge, skill and resource and they think in terms of differences between societies.

I do not wish to take sides in the kind of controversy I have outlined except perhaps to suggest that it is a waste of time for economists to make predictions as to where, and at what rate, industries will grow up in future. So many of the forces at work are non-economic: the great outbursts of practical energy in the past have invariably been released by movements which have had little or nothing to do with economic motive. And even where the factors are more narrowly economic they seem to me highly unpredictable. It is difficult enough to explain the spread and location of industry after the event; it is palpably impossible to do so before it. All I can do is to try to assemble a little of what is known, or surmised, about what makes or mars industrial revolutions.

II

We know that the early stages of industrialisation have always been painful, the pains perhaps being more social than economic. Agricultural communities differ from industrial not only in the things they make but in the way they live. Deeply engrained social habits cannot be disturbed without distress. Work in factories and life in towns are not in the first instance pleasurable.[8] In one way or another the human resistance to change must be overcome by inducement or broken down by force.

The most serious economic impediment is usually the lack of capital, for industrial growth seems to call both for more capital per worker[9] and more capital per unit of output.[10] The cost of factories and machines may be great,[11] but it is probably only a minor part of the bill that has to be met as a prelude to expansion. The other forms of the semi-permanent equipment of society – power, transport, credit and distribution facilities; towns with public services; governmental institutions – represent an inescapable preliminary cost of the growth of industry.[12] The accumulation of capital demands a present-day sacrifice. The restriction of consumption may be undertaken by the domestic population – if it has a sufficient margin to make that possible without starvation – or it may be undergone by outside lenders. In the absence of outside loans, it may be brought about by voluntary saving, by inflation or by authoritarian systems of rationing. But all large-scale and rapid industrial growth leads to capital shortage, even in regions which are part of an otherwise rich country.[13] In poor, undeveloped countries the shortage may be the decisive brake on change.

It is these obstacles which confront those who are anxious to engineer industrialisation in the backward areas. They must find some way of breaking vicious circles. One circle runs as follows: poor countries are poor because they are not industrialised; they are not industrialised because they have no capital; they have no capital because they cannot save; they cannot save because they are poor.[14] Another is: industry cannot develop until transport and other services are provided; such services will not be provided unless clearly there is a demand for them; the demand for them must wait on the growth of manufacture. And it is not always evident that the breaking of these circles will be easier or more

232   *A Return to Free Market Economics?*

fruitful than the pursuit of other lines of economic progress by non-industrialised countries.

III

Yet, we know that a number of countries have successfully made the crossing from agriculture to industry and reached a point where industrial progress seems to have become, as it were, automatically self-generating. What set the wheels going in these cases, how was the crucial transition affected, what costs were involved? Only economic historians (and I certainly am not such), could answer these questions but I have conned over much of their wisdom and I find it useful myself to do, what the historians would almost certainly disapprove of, and to think of the cases in terms of four groups:

First, 'spontaneous' transitions where State direction has been at a minimum and the necessary capital has been provided internally.

Second, 'engineered' transitions where the State has provided most of the driving force and has deliberately organised the sacrifices necessary for investment.

Third, 'assisted' transitions which fall between the first two in the sense that State intervention has been limited, either in extent or time, and where normally investment has been provided, at least in part, from outside.

Fourth, 'abortive' transitions where, despite State intervention, the system seems to fail to gather sufficient momentum to justify the use of the term industrial revolution.

There follows one case illustrative of each class, my references being limited to those thefts of ideas too gross to be ignored even in such a summary treatment as this.

Great Britain is my illustration of the spontaneous transition. It was given a powerful push in the later stages by a series of important inventions. But its outstanding feature was that the spectacular progress of the nineteenth century was preceded by a long period of preparation which saw the appearance of domestic manufacture, the emergence and organisation of a wage-earning class and the slow acquisition of industrial habits and skills – all long before the appearance of the factory. Britain had a long period of pre-capitalism. At every stage the merchant played a crucial role in providing transport, in distributing raw materials, in discovering markets, in acting as capitalist by carrying stocks and financing the manufacturer. The capital for the first industries came from internal savings. Capital flowed freely to break the bottlenecks inevitable in an expanding economy. The pains of the revolution, severe as they may have been, were minimised by a slow organic growth of the institutions required for our industrial society, by the grafting of a new system on an old stock, by the long maintenance of the link between industry and agriculture, by the creation of industry in relatively small units, by the frugality of the population and the mobility of capital.[15]

The recent industrial expansion of Russia is perhaps the outstanding case of an 'engineered' transition. We know little enough about it, despite the volume of writing on it, and it is still possible to doubt whether it has enjoyed, after the first pains of the transition, a momentum of its own or whether it continues to be forced along by the efforts of the State. Certainly, however, it has been a speedy and an enforced change. There was little on which to graft large-scale production; yet the emphasis throughout has been on large-scale operation, partly perhaps for administrative reasons, partly for doctrinal. Little capital has been available from abroad, most of it has been wrested from the citizens by the control of consumption and by inflation. The State, too, has been compelled to create the required industrial skills and to break down old habits by mass education and propaganda and to provide transport, distribution and housing as an integral part of the engineered economy. This has probably been the most painful industrial revolution to date.

An intermediate case, of assisted transition, has been that of Japan, where the State was apparently successful in giving an initial impulse to a system which subsequently developed its own motive power. In the early stages the Government helped by raising foreign loans, by erecting textile factories, by handling exports and purchasing imports, by buying and loaning machinery. 'During the latter decades of the nineteenth century there was scarcely any important Japanese industry of the western type which did not owe its establishment to State initiative.' But private industry built rapidly upon these foundations so that between the two wars the State played no predominant part in any industry save iron and steel in its primary stages. This is a striking example of assistance applied temporarily at the right points and then withdrawn. But, undoubtedly other factors contributed to the success. Labour was abundant, cheap, assiduous. Industrial expansion was first built up on native supplies, such as silk. Small-scale operation and widely scattered factories kept down the demands for manufacturing, transport and social capital to a minimum and foreign capital, much of it British, was available to supplement domestic sources.[16]

India seems to me a case where the transition has hardly got under way. Before the last war, income per head and the proportion of the working population in industry were among the lowest in the world. This retardation is, at first sight, surprising, for India would seem to have had many advantages of the kind which have often made for industrial growth: large-scale foreign investment – by 1910 British capital in India amounted to £439m;[17] a first-class railway system – by 1913

India had the third largest railway system in the world; domestic supplies of jute and cotton, coal and iron ore; the peace and order of British rule; a strong nationalist movement which now for nearly 50 years has called for industrialisation and self-sufficiency; an opportunity in two world wars to develop industry for military purposes. Yet, by 1900, apart from jute and cotton, no manufacturing industry employed as many as 20,000 persons and even now the authentic industrial impetus seems to be so lacking that some planners are prepared to bring about the desired results by coercion.[18] India, rich in industrial possibilities, has proved poor in manufacturing accomplishment.

Every country, of course, presents peculiarities about which it is easier to speculate than to reach firm conclusions. I suspect that the recent economic history of Eire, New Zealand, and perhaps Australia, represent instances of abortive industrial growth. I suppose that the expansion of the United States and, more recently, of Canada constitute the easiest transitions of which we have record. But in every case there have been pains, the sharpness of which have varied with the speed of the change, the degree to which outside help could be obtained, the power of the State to override individual rights and the disposition of the people themselves. At least it is clear that machine industry is not something which emerges from simply thinking and talking about it. It is not something spontaneously generated by the provision in prescribed amounts of the objective matter needed for industrialisation. In every case it has been the complicated issue of a tangle of social forces which, for lack of a better term, we call institutional.

IV

I turn now to the next logical question. What conditions must be satisfied if a country, having surmounted the first big hurdles, having become industrialised, is to maintain its position among the industrial countries? Can it normally be expected to carry a momentum which will make it difficult, or impossible, for other, agricultural, countries to get into this field? Or are there good reasons for supposing that, sooner or later, industrial expansion brings about its own retardation, thus providing opportunities for industrialisation elsewhere? How far does a country enjoy advantages or suffer from disadvantages just because it had an early start?

The inherent momentum of expansion is usually described thus. The increasing size of the system as a whole brings a double advantage: it renders possible bigger factories and bigger firms and it opens up the way to greater specialisation. Specialisation lowers cost, widens the market and creates scope for more specialisation. Expanding profits create an internal source of profits which can be ploughed back. The rising standard of living makes voluntary saving easier. Scientific interest branches out increasingly into technology and towards economic objects. Each new invention opens up a wider range of technical exploitation of the work of the scientist.[19] Checks are inevitable: crucial materials may be scarce, holding up the line as a whole; technical development may lag at one stage for a time; the trade cycle may apply a brake periodically. But, so long as men are free and goods, capital and labour are mobile, these checks will be temporary.

This is undoubtedly a reliable general record of the experience of many industrial countries at some stage in their growth. It represents, to take the most spectacular example, what has been occurring in the United States in the past 50 years by which that country has raised itself to what appears to be an almost impregnable position as *the* industrial producer of the world.

There is, however, the conflicting theory that every industrial country will ultimately suffer from retardation or even decline. The alleged disadvantage of the early start may be summarised in the form in which it is normally applied to Great Britain (though oddly enough not to the United States, which has now had almost a century's experience of industrial expansion).[20] Pioneer industrial countries, as all pioneers, will make costly mistakes which other countries, following on, will avoid. The pioneer country will find itself with obsolete equipment and badly located industries. Its business men will become old-fashioned and torpid. So its industrial supremacy will slip away. The analogy is the biological one of growth and decline in a mortal being.[21]

Now, no one can deny that this *may* happen. Business men, or even economic dictators, may suddenly change their character and hang on to industrial antiques much as older people cherish the domestic equipment of their youth.[22] But of course this theory goes further than that and makes the very odd suggestion that grandsons will be lethargic *because* their grandfathers were energetic.

Put in its crude form the theory of the disadvantages of the early start seems to me to make little sense. For if an early start is a disadvantage the happiest position for any country would be that in which no start had ever been made at all, or indeed no start ever would be made. I cannot believe that the future of the British textile industries would be brighter now than it actually is if no pound of yarn had ever yet been spun here. And I do not think that Japan and Germany, by having a lot of their machinery blown to bits in the last war, have benefited by being relieved of the disadvantages of an early start. Do these disadvantages last for ever or merely for a term? And is it a mistake to establish now new industries in Great Britain since, by definition, these will be early starters? Industrial progress consists of discarding old methods for new. There is no reason to think that this is inherently more difficult, or more likely to breed stifling inhibitions, than the installation of the new methods from scratch.

There are, however, other more solid grounds on which it may be suggested that industrial supremacy may contain the seeds of its own decay and that industrial activity may, thereby, be encouraged elsewhere.

The first is that an industrial revolution can never be carried out once for all: the whole of the industrial life of a nation is the same continuing process. The features of the early stages of an industrial revolution are not really unique. Every industrial country, if it is to avoid decline, must be prepared to meet the pains and cost of adjustment however invulnerable its position may momentarily appear to be. Burns[23] has established, from a study of American conditions from 1870, that most industries suffer, after a time, from an appreciable and continuous weakening of their speed of advance. This evidence is of special significance because it is drawn from an industrial system which was expanding rapidly and was probably not showing any general retardation in its rate of advance. From this he deduces that 'retardation in the growth of individual industries is one of the expressions of the progressiveness of American industry'. Stigler[24] has produced further evidence that the rate of growth of an industry group is associated with the heterogeneity of the rates of growth of the industries constituting the group. In brief, flexibility is a prerequisite for the maintenance of industrial supremacy. The decline, relative or absolute, of individual industries is the condition precedent to the maintenance of progress in the system as a whole. Progressive industrial systems are continually discarding types of employment and equipment in favour of other types which will yield a higher return.

Now flexibility means upset for individuals and the disturbance of expectations. Workers will be called on to change their jobs, entrepreneurs to scrap equipment, savers to provide new capital. This is the same problem in kind, if not in degree, as that confronting the backward countries undertaking industry for the first time. But an advanced industrial country will have created classes and institutions, vested interests each of which, it is arguable, will seek, in the last resort by political action, to maintain its own position. The entrepreneur may be powerful enough to force the State to give him protection, the trade union may seek to maintain the same earnings in the same industry for an undiminished number of workers. Of course the community as a whole cannot, by staking its claim, determine its economic standing (unless it can find some sucker in the international field). But the efforts of groups to do so may be successful and, by delaying necessary readjustments, undermine the position of an advanced industrial country. Some such cause, as it seems to me, lay at the root of the British industrial decline between the wars. Of course, industrial retardation of this kind is not inevitable. Even in a competitive society, where class interests do not always or fully coincide, it is conceivable that each group might recognise the degree to which its interests coincide with the interests of others and might be prepared to pay the price of restraint for the maintenance of some framework of society, commonly deemed desirable. This calls, however, for a high level of public intelligence and a well-developed sense of social responsibility.

A second possible retarding force lies in the steadily rising claims for consumption or leisure which may be made by an advanced industrial society. Before the war, it was often supposed that the stability of industrial countries was most likely to be disturbed by oversaving and the absence of profitable investment opportunities. All that has been changed by the destruction of equipment in the last war, by the movement towards more equal distribution of income and by heavy taxation destructive of saving – no one talks these days of the dangers of secular stagnation. Veblen[25] has sought to account for the rise of industrial Germany by contrasting the frugality of its hard-working population, content with a relatively parsimonious income, with that in Great Britain where wasteful consumption and leisure gradually came to be regarded as inalienable rights both by the rich (who had learned 'to consume large incomes with that unobtrusive efficiency that marks the gentleman of inherited wealth who has had the benefit of lifelong experience in a community of wasters') and by the working classes (with their high level of 'mandatory expenditure on decencies, physically superfluous and commonly aesthetically obnoxious' and their 'preoccupation with sportmanlike interests and value which has spread from the levels of gentility down through the body of the population, until this category of dissipations has become almost the sole ground of common interest on which working men meet or hold opinions').

Veblen assumed that increased consumption and a higher regard for leisure necessarily make for inefficiency. In that, of course, he was wrong. But there are at least four ways in which overanxiety to cash in on the fruits of industrial progress, in which 'a passion for worldly welfare', may defeat itself. First, by raising consumption to such a level that the necessary scale of new investment becomes impossible. Second, by forcing consumption into such channels as to reduce efficiency. (I always think it very odd, for example, that Great Britain has the most expensive medical service but one of the poorest dietaries among industrial countries; there is something to be said for a little less medicine and a little more food.) Third, by raising expectations concerning amenities to the point at which few or none are prepared to enter the stern and unpleasant occupations – the problem of manning the British coalmines is a case in point. Fourth, leisure may become so highly valued that leisure habits come to permeate the hours of work as well as of play. I pass no judgement on these aims and valuations, except to say that they may well be self-frustrating. Certainly if they normally take possession of advanced industrial countries, industrial supremacy is likely to be ephemeral.

A third possible major retarding factor is the increased scale on which a concentrated industrial region must provide tertiary industries – transport, distribution and the like – in order to integrate the more and more specialised industrial units into a co-ordinated working system. Clark[26] has shown that industrial expansion has almost universally been accompanied by a more than proportionate growth of these tertiary services. The proportion of the working population engaged in manufacturing proper appears to reach a peak and then decline. In the United States the peak was reached in 1920; in Great Britain and France in 1900; in Germany in 1925; in Japan in 1920. The peak is surprisingly low – in the United States about 30 per cent; in Great Britain a little higher. In most industrial countries the proportion of the working population in commerce, transport and other services has already far surpassed that in manufacturing proper. Now the growth of the tertiary services is sometimes spoken of as if it were the *cause* of increased production and a higher average income. (I fear I have myself written in that sense.) But the relation is really more complex than that because these services are in part producer services, in part consumer services, and it is difficult to disentangle the elements. Suppose, for instance, an industrial region expands to the point at which the density of population makes it necessary, if people are to get to their work at all, to build a costly underground railway. In so far as the Tube is essential for getting people to work, it is one of the costs of industry. In so far as it is used by people to go into the countryside on Sunday mornings, or in so far as people like riding in the Tube as a leisure occupation (if there are such), it is not a cost of that particular way of locating and organising industry. There is, I fancy, no way of measuring these tertiary costs, but the presumption is that they pile up rapidly in the older areas and they may ultimately constitute the opportunity of infant industrial areas, operating economically in smaller social units, to break into export markets or produce more economically for themselves.

There are, of course, many other forces which may finally impede the growth of established industrial areas. They are probably less important than those already mentioned. It is sometimes argued that more automatic machinery makes it easier for backward countries to industrialise by reducing the differential advantage possessed by the skilled workers of the older industrial area. But I suspect that the opposite is more usually true – that increased mechanisation puts a premium on advanced technical knowledge, skill and experience in the design, development and operation of the new machines. It is sometimes argued that the older industrial areas will finally succumb because of the depletion of their natural resources. But countries with high technical knowledge become extraordinarily skilful in discovering new sources and new ways round threatened material shortages. It is sometimes asserted that industrial skills can now be more easily transferred from one country to another than formerly. But when one thinks of the difficulty that one firm finds in employing the secrets of success of another firm in the same country; when one considers the lean results of the recent, much advertised, efforts to embody American industrial practice into British industry, both advanced industrial countries, there seem to be grounds for scepticism about the transferance of 'know how' from old to new industrial countries. For 'know how' involves two things: watching what the other does, which is easy, and then applying his methods with such modifications as are called for by the new environment in which they are to be applied, which is very difficult. It used to be argued before the war that the slowing down of the increase of population, held to be typical of mature countries, would inhibit further advance. But the old truth has now been rediscovered that a market can just as well be large with a few people at a high standard of living as with a lot of people with a low standard of living. And in any case, present population trends make the pre-war population estimates look silly.

I cannot hope to assess the relative importance of the points I have raised in this section. But one reasonable deduction would be that, from the technical and more narrowly economic angle, the established industrial countries have a big pull over future competitors, not so much in the actual possession of capital equipment – though that advantage may be considerable – as in the accumulation of their scientific knowledge and, above all, in their experience of the process of trial and error by which the innumerable bits of a complicated economy can be made to work together. There is nothing inherently impossible in a future in which the manufactured goods of the world would be largely made in a few places with the rest of the world, drawing on these sources, making a better living by supplying food and raw materials than would be possible for them in any other way of life.

V

In the long run, in so far as economic motives rule, people will try to make their living in the easiest way. Whether they move towards industry or towards agriculture will be determined by the yield of one hour's work and the rate at which one type of goods exchanges for the other. As for the future of the terms of trade between industrial and agricultural goods one may take one's choice between a number of violently differing estimates, each one supported by the highest authority. One may believe that the world is faced with starvation, due to the prodigal exploitation of the basic fertility of the earth; or that the problem of the future is a surplus of food and raw materials arising out of improved agricultural technique and the limited capacity of the human stomach. The pros and cons have been exhaustively listed in the recent Report of the Royal Commission on Population.[27] I believe that on this matter honesty is the best policy for the economist: he does not know what the future holds and his techniques provide him with no way of finding out. We do know that, generally speaking, in the past half century, the rate of exchange between industrial and agricultural goods has favoured industrialisation. Output per head has increased more rapidly in industry than in agriculture;[28] a unit of industrial goods has, apart perhaps from the period 1921-9, purchased an increased volume of agricultural products.[29] But he would be a bold, or a reckless, man, who would say this will be true of the future.

One conclusion is, however, less risky than others. The equilibrium between industry and agriculture must be a moving point. If for any reason industry extends through the world, each advance would make the next advance less likely. For the consequent diversion of resources away from agriculture, combined with the generally accepted inelasticity of demand for agricultural products, would tend to move the terms of trade sharply in favour of agriculture.[30]

VI

I have been at such pains to stress the futility of prediction that I must take care to observe my own injunctions. But what little I know of the past, taken with the principles of association for economic production as I understand them, leads me to the following views.

1. I see no scientific reason for assuming that world economic progress involves a movement towards an 'equilibrium' which calls for universal industrialisation. There is no more reason to suppose that the Indian farmer is likely to make himself better off by producing motor cars instead of growing food than that the Kansas farmer would make himself better off by making motor cars instead of growing food. If industry is to be fostered by international agency it might be best to foster it in the United States and then press for such freedom of trade that the bounties of American manufacturing genius can be rapidly dispersed over the globe.

2. If backward agricultural areas are to move towards industry, it would ease their transition if they could first devote their efforts to the improvement of their own agricultural systems. Whatever assistance may be available from outside, they will hardly be in a position to import the necessary machinery unless they can develop an export surplus. Increased agricultural productivity would release labour for industrial purposes and the methods of improving agriculture – in cultivation,

marketing, grading, inspection, storage, transport and financing – will themselves help to build up the systematic habits of trading and work which are prerequisites of industrial growth.

3. If mature countries are to assist immature with capital they must have a surplus. Anything which inhibits savings at home must reduce the help it is possible to afford abroad. In that sense, an overenergetic drive for equality of income within the mature countries may perpetuate the inequalities between the poor and the richer countries.

4. If there are to be schemes for fostering industrialisation on a large scale, in the backward areas, undertaken by state and international agencies, there may be big successes but we must also be prepared for large-scale failures. No one should be surprised or distressed or indig-nant over the African ground nuts scheme. Such events emerge naturally from the nature of that form of economic engineering. It may be indeed that even the gigantic blunders pay, in the long run. Buchanan, one of the shrewdest writers on this subject, has concluded:[31]

> Certainly, the attempt to push industrialization has a powerful drive from several sides. And since real capital investment has the character it does, much of the investment undertaken will remain beyond any population crises that may develop. In other words, the resulting capital goods and equipment will not be wiped out – even though several millions should die of starvation either through miscalcula-tion or too hurried a pace in the industrialisation programme. The next attempt will start from a higher plane. Consequently from a long-term point of view even an industrial programme that misfires is likely to have lasting benefits.

Maybe: but I do not think that economists can judge infallibly in such sombre social assessments. One's view would turn so much on whether one was destined to be one of the 'several millions'. I myself would be alarmed lest one or two such cases of planned starvation should com-pletely destroy the belief in economic rationality.

5. Industrial revolutions are painful processes, they are essentially periods of vast and sweeping austerity. If one had regard for the social costs they involved, one would, therefore, try to carry them out on the cheap. On the cheap means, if past experience is anything to go on, building up in small industrial and social units, improvising with in-adequate social equipment rather than planning from the green field, strengthening one's capacity in what one knows about instead of plunging into the vacuum of unknown problems. Much contemporary discussion seems to assume that these transitions can be painless or even pleasant. Welfare first and the means to pay for it afterwards. No one can fail to sympathise with the humanitarianism that demands im-proved living conditions in the backward areas. But that calls for inter-

national charity. It should not be confused with the process by which industry may make possible a higher standard of living.

NOTES

1. *Industrialization and Foreign Trade*, F. Hilgerdt, Chapter II.
2. C. Clark, *Conditions of Economic Progress*, p. 341.
3. C. Clark, *Conditions of Economic Progress*, p. 179.
4. *Industrialization and Foreign Trade*, F. Hilgerdt, p. 22.
5. *Industrialization and Foreign Trade*, F. Hilgerdt, p. 22.
6. *Migration and Economic Opportunity*, Goodrich and others, p. 344.
7. *Industry and Trade*, p. 159.
8. Indian labour at the beginning of the twentieth century has been described as 'not responding easily to any stimulus whether of competition, high wages, good conditions or professional pride in work – uniform material almost entirely without enterprise and initiative'. (L. Knowles, *Economic Development of Overseas Empires*.) But an early English master complained of his hands in much the same way. 'If you offer them work, they will tell you that they must go to lock up their sheep, cut furzes, get their cow out of the pound or perhaps say that they must take their horse to be shod that he may carry them to a cricket match.' (Lewis and Maude, *The English Middle Classes*, p. 53.)
9. J. Spengler, 'Aspects of the Economics of Population Growth', *Southern Economic Journal*, January 1948.
10. G. Terborgh, *Bogey of Economic Maturity*, p. 95.
11. In 1937, in the United States, each wage earner in manufacturing industry operated with $2474 of capital. (S. Fabricant, *Employment in Manufacturing, 1899–1939*, p. 257.)
12. Prest, *War Economies of Primary Producing Countries* provides a very interesting study of how the lack of such facilities impeded the attempts made during the last war to increase output in a number of agricultural countries.
13. The advocates of rapid industrialisation in the south-east States of America find the shortage of capital a serious impediment to their plans.
14. H. Singer, 'Economic Progress in Undeveloped Countries', *Social Research*, March 1949.
15. G. W. Daniels, *Early English Cotton Industry*; T. S. Ashton, *Industrial Revolution*.
16. G. C. Allen, *A Short Economic History of Modern Japan*.
17. G. Paish, 'Great Britain's Capital Investments', *Journal of Royal Statistical Society*, January 1911.
18. *A Plan of Economic Development for India*, p. 55 – 'Practically every aspect of economic life will have to be so rigorously controlled by government that individual liberty and freedom of enterprise will suffer a temporary eclipse.'
19. A. Young, 'Increasing Returns and Economic Progress', *Economic Journal*, 1928.
20. I understand, however, that there are some economists who, working more slowly than the ebb and flow of popular economic delusion, are still writing books under such titles as *Maturity and Stagnation in the American Economy*.

21. See a notable article on this subject by F. R. J. Jervis, 'The Handicap of Britain's Early Start', *Manchester School*, January 1947.

22. cf. Toynbee (abridgement by Somervell), *A Study of History*, p. 330. 'If one were to single out the point in which Great Britain has been most at fault, one would put his finger on the conservatism of our captains of industry who have idolized the obsolescent techniques which had made the fortunes of their grandfathers.'

23. Burns, *Production Trends in the United States since* 1870, Chapter IV.

24. Stigler, *Trends in Output and Employment.*

25. *Imperial Germany*, Chapters IV and VI.

26. C. Clark, *The Conditions of Economic Progress*, Chap. V. J. A. Hobson, *The Evolution of Modern Capitalism*, Chap XVI had seized upon the same point much earlier.

27. Chapter X.

28. G. J. Stigler, *Trends in Output and Employment.*

29. C. Clark, *Conditions of Economic Progress*, p. 453.

30. C. Clark, *Economics of 1960* assumes a 90 per cent improvement in the terms of trade in favour of agricultural products between 1925 and 1960.

31. 'The Industrialization of Backward Areas', *Economic Journal*, December 1946.

INDEX

References to numbered notes have generally been made only where the note has introduced new material or substantially complemented the text.

Wilson, Sir Harold, 165n1
Wincott, Harold, 119
Wood, John, 47, 51n25
Woolton, Lord, 41, 43

Wright, H., 212

Ziolkowsky, K. E., 108
Zworykin, Vladimir, 202